D1162177

AMERICAN AID TO FRANCE, 1938-1940

AMERICAN AID TO FRANCE, 1938-1940

John McVickar Haight, Jr.

ATHENEUM

New York

1970

John McVickar Haight, Jr.

John McVickar Haight, Jr., is Professor of History at Lehigh University, Bethlehem, Pennsylvania. He has contributed to such journals as *Foreign Affairs, Journal of Modern History* and *Revue d'Histoire de la Deuxième Guerre Mondiale*

Library of Congress catalog card number 70–108828
Published simultaneously in Canada by McClelland and Stewart Ltd.
Manufactured in the United States of America by
Kingsport Press, Inc., Kingsport, Tennessee
Designed by Kathleen Carey
First Edition

Preface

FRANCE BEGAN ITS SEARCH FOR American aid in the winter of 1938, and intensified its efforts after the Munich crisis the following September. Confronted with Germany's overwhelming aerial superiority, France desperately needed military planes. Though it found American aircraft deficient in both quantity and quality, France by January 1939 placed orders for 555 combat planes, all that could be delivered by the end of that year. After war broke out nine months later, a third French mission purchased an additional 1,000 fighters and bombers, with deliveries scheduled for the last six months of 1940. France at that time also took an important step to overcome the bottleneck of American plane production by investing ten million dollars to double assembly lines for aircraft engines. Finally in March 1940 France persuaded Britain to join in an order for some 4,500 war planes. Altogether these orders not only quadrupled production, but speeded the mass production of American war planes by some twelve to eighteen months. Obviously American aid for France had become a two-way street which promised to benefit both nations. However, with the fall of France in

June, 1940, Britain became the beneficiary of the French plane orders.

The story of American aid to France also provides new insights into the roles of both French and American leaders. For France three individuals led the way: Premier Edouard Daladier; his Air Minister, Guy La Chambre; and a Frenchman little known at the time, who later fathered Europe's Common Market, Jean Monnet. On the American side President Franklin D. Roosevelt courageously overcame isolationist opposition and serious domestic obstacles to the sale of planes to France. In this he was ably assisted by his Secretary of Treasury, Henry Morgenthau.

Together Daladier and La Chambre faced the inferiority of their nation's air power and recognized that their only source for planes outside of France was the United States. They met and overcame serious French obstacles to these purchases, not the least of which was the opposition of Paul Reynaud, who as Minister of Finance fought the expenditure of France's gold reserves for American aircraft. The Premier and his Air Minister also faced American obstacles, which included not only the deficiency in quality and quantity of American combat types but also the resistance of the U.S. Army Air Corps to the release of planes of latest design. The two French leaders found Jean Monnet ingenious in overcoming these obstacles. His persistent and indefatigable efforts helped open the American aircraft industry, for France first and then, in the winter of 1940, for France and Britain together. The techniques he perfected and the contacts he made in Washington before the fall of France were to serve him in good stead after June 1940 when he returned to the United States in the service of Great Britain and contributed significantly toward planning the Victory Program with its vast expansion of the American arsenal before December 7, 1941, and the Japanese attack upon Pearl Harbor.

On the side of the United States, President Roosevelt played the dominant role. From January 1938, when he was first faced with France's search for American planes, he showed himself interested, as one Frenchman reported, "in every measure which can reenforce French military power." Indeed, in that March he took direct action to overcome his Air Corps' opposition to the release of its latest fighter. He did so again in the winter of 1939 because he recognized, as he said first to Secretary Morgenthau and later to the Senate Military Affairs Committee, that the frontiers of the United States lay on the Rhine. Then in March 1940 when General H. H. Arnold, chief of the Air Corps, threatened to obstruct the Anglo-French order for 4,500 American planes, Roosevelt silenced him effectively with the threat of exile to the island of Guam.

Roosevelt's assistance to France in obtaining American planes reveals his determination to protect his nation's security by aiding those nations which opposed the Axis aggressors. He was indeed sensitive to isolationist opposition and moved as carefully as he could. However, after his efforts were discovered when one of the latest American bombers crashed with a French aviator on board, Roosevelt nevertheless continued to prove as cooperative as Jean Monnet had found him that winter of 1939.

The President had able support from Secretary Morgenthau in obtaining aid for France. Morgenthau's role, which has already been traced in his published diaries, is even more fully revealed from available French documents. Together Roosevelt and Morgenthau made a vital team in aiding France as well as Britain strengthen air defenses against Germany. In turn, France and Britain helped rebuild the American aircraft industry for the defense of their own nation.

For the French side of the story, I am particularly grateful to Guy La Chambre, who provided me with key documents from his private papers—letters, reports and memoranda which came to him as Minister for Air from January 1938 to his resignation in March 1940. Another rich hoard of private papers was opened by Jean Monnet. While his papers relative to his 1938 missions to the United States were destroyed during the Occupation, his documents provide a remarkable record of his work with the Anglo-French Economic Coordinating Committee. Both M. La Chambre and M. Monnet patiently endured long interviews which clarified many points for me. I am grateful to Baroness Amaury de La Grange, who permitted me to read her deceased husband's papers concerning his efforts in early 1938 to purchase American planes for France. The Baroness kindly extended secretarial assistance to me as well. Generals Paul Jacquin and Stéphane Thouvenot both turned over to me key papers on their missions to the States and gave a good deal of time in interviews. So, too, did Roger Hoppenot, who was Guy La Chambre's *chef de cabinet civil* and accompanied Monnet to Washington in December 1938. René Pleven took time from his busy political life to recall his mission in late 1939. Without the cooperation of these Frenchmen it would have been impossible to piece together this account of France's purchase of American military planes. The only official French records open to research were those held by the Service Historique de l'Armée de l'Air at Versailles. Commandant Parot extended every courtesy to me, while M. Veujos cooperated with deep interest in locating pertinent material.

For the British side of the Anglo-French plane purchase of March 1940, Sir Henry Self, who headed the mission, filled in details which were left out of the official histories. Air Force Marshal George B. A. Baker, who was Sir Henry's technical assistant, contributed important insights.

In the United States, Victor Gondos and his Army Air Corps Branch of the National Archives and especially John E. Taylor patiently, and always cheerfully, dug up the files on the French negotiations for American planes. Sherrod East's World War II Division of the Archives gave invaluable assistance. Like so many others who have used State Department records, I owe a special vote of thanks to Mrs. Patricia Dowling for her willing guidance. The late E. Taylor Parks of the Historical Division of the State Department proved a constant encouragement and advice. A special tribute must go to the staff of the Franklin D. Roosevelt Library and its former director, Elizabeth B. Dewery, for the warm welcome they always extended and for their friendly assistance.

I must also express my gratitude to the widows of General H. H. Arnold and Jay Pierrepont Moffat for permitting me to read their papers.

Lehigh University's Institute of Research generously supported my research in this country and in France. A grant from the Society for French-American Cultural Services and Educational Aid (FACSEA) made my first flight to France possible, and for this I give warmest thanks to Edouard Morot-Sir, France's Cultural Attaché. A second trip was financed by a grant from the Penrose Fund of the American Philosophical Society.

The encouragement, editorial assistance and patience of Laura Johnson has made working with Atheneum a pleasure. Finally, and of course most important, I give my deepest thanks to my wife, to whom I dedicate this book. I know she will share with me a sense of relief and accomplishment that it is at long last completed.

Contents

AMERICAN AID TO FRANCE, 1938-1940

CHAPTER

1

The First Hundred Planes

FRANCE TOOK ITS FIRST STEP toward prying open the American arsenal in the spring of 1938 when it ordered 100 fighter planes similar to Curtiss-Wright's P-36.[1] The order came as a result of the decline of France's air power in the face of the rapid expansion of Hitler's new Luftwaffe. In January 1938 the French Air Ministry sent a French Senator, Baron Amaury de La Grange, across the Atlantic in expectation that he could rapidly obtain 1,000 of the latest American aircraft and thus "harness American industry to the French war machine," but these expectations foundered upon one major obstacle, the lack of adequate American war planes.

Other French and American obstacles to France's purchase of American aircraft during the spring of 1938 were so extensive that only a major catastrophe could induce the Air Ministry to turn again to the United States. The

[1] This chapter condenses material first published in John McVickar Haight, Jr., "Les Négociations Françaises pour la Fourniture d'Avions Américains, lère partie—Avant Munich," *Forces Aériennes Françaises,* No. 198, December 1963, pp. 807–39.

Munich settlement of the Czechoslovakian crisis in late September 1938 provided this motivation. Three days after Premier Daladier returned to Paris from Munich, he proposed that a second mission cross the Atlantic to buy more planes for France's defense. Led by Jean Monnet, who a decade later would win fame as the father of the European Common Market, this mission proved more fruitful and pushed France further toward eliciting a commitment from American industry to build war planes for France.

The first air mission to the States had been proposed after France's Premier Camille Chautemps finally faced up to the deficiency of his nation's air power. During a conference in London in late November 1937, Britain's Prime Minister Neville Chamberlain had spoken to Chautemps about the "lamentable" condition of France's Air Force and added, "You have no modern planes and are not ready to produce any. . . . This is a great danger to your country." Chautemps returned to Paris determined to rectify the situation.[2]

France's air power had not always been in such a lamentable state. France had prided itself on the largest Air Force in Europe from 1918 to the mid-1930s, when a

[2] Chamberlain's remarks during the Anglo-French talks of November 29 and 30 are quoted in Georges Bonnet, *Défense de la Paix,* vol. I, *De Washington au Quai d'Orsay* (Geneva, 1946), pp. 49–50, and Keith Feiling, *The Life of Neville Chamberlain* (London, 1946), p. 334. For Chautemps' reactions, see Pierre Cot, *Triumph of Treason* (New York, 1944), p. 314, and testimony of Léon Blum in *Les Événements Survenus en France de 1933 à 1945, Témoignages et Documents Recueillis par la Commission d'Enquête Parlementaire* (Paris, 1947), vol. I, p. 227. (Hereafter cited as *Événements.*) See also Viscount Chilston, "The Rearmament of Great Britain, France and Germany Down to the Munich Agreement," in *Survey of International Affairs, 1938,* ed. V. M. Toynbee (London, 1953), vol. III, p. 482.

technological revolution in the construction of planes suddenly opened the way for Germany to establish a qualitative superiority. In 1935 Hitler ordered the rebuilding of German air power, which the Treaty of Versailles had prohibited, and Germany's aircraft industry rapidly adopted the new aluminum construction techniques that turned out planes able to carry heavier engines, fly faster, and bear more armament than France's canvas and wood models dating from the last war. As Senator La Grange reported in December 1937 from his position of advantage on the Senate's Air Commission, "German aviation can fly over our territory with impunity." He estimated that Germany already possessed 1,000 combat planes with speeds of more than 400 kilometers per hour (250 mph) of which 300 were Messerschmitt 109s, a fighter with speed of more than 450 kmh. In contrast, as La Grange stated, France "does not have a single plane to worry them." Indeed, France's fastest operational fighter flew at a top speed of 385 kmh and only 27 of these were available. All other planes were World War I types and thoroughly outclassed. French production of more advanced design would not begin until the spring of 1939, and then would produce only limited numbers of planes. "In short," the Senator added, "during 1938 Germany will produce in one month as many planes exceeding 400 kmh as France will produce during the whole year." [3] Such gloomy prognostications were fully recognized by a General in the French

[3] Letter from Senator Baron Amaury de La Grange to Premier Chautemps, December 23, 1937, as reprinted in Senator La Grange's manuscript, "The Campaign Led in the Senate Between 1937 and 1940," pp. 80–81. (Hereafter cited as "Senate Campaign.") Private Papers of Senator La Grange. These papers are held in France by his widow, who kindly opened them to the author during the summer of 1961.

Air Force, who wrote in mid-January 1938, just before he was appointed Chief of Staff for Air, "The situation is extremely grave. . . . I am convinced that if war comes this year, the French Air Force will be wiped out within a few days."[4]

During January 1938 Premier Chautemps, in an effort to overcome this deficiency, raised Edouard Daladier from Minister of War to Minister of Defense and brought in a new Air Minister, Guy La Chambre. Working at top speed with the leaders of the Air Force, La Chambre, by early March, had developed Plan V, which called for 2,617 first-line planes with some 1,000 fighters, 870 bombers, and 630 reconnaisance planes. The major problem was to manufacture new types, particularly as France lacked prototypes to which mass production techniques could be adapted. After Hitler had marched into Austria the Air Ministry canceled orders for all obsolete models and focused only on the new ones. It was expected that by April 1939, the end of the first phase of Plan V, France would have sufficient power to guarantee her defense. However, as Chautemps and his advisers realized in March 1938, for the following twelve months France would remain defenseless in the air and thus could not run the risk of war.[5]

In another phase of France's search for modern war planes, Premier Chautemps authorized Senator La Grange to proceed to Washington to explore his recommendation that France should purchase 1,000 planes "now in use in

[4] Letter from General Vuillemin, Commander 1st Aerial Corps, French Air Force, to Minister for Air, January 15, 1938, as cited by La Chambre in *Événements,* vol. II, pp. 300–02.

[5] The Minister for Air passed on this warning to the Senate Air Committee in February 1938, and La Chambre had gone on to win the committee's unanimous support for Plan V. See La Grange Papers, "Senate Campaign," p. 126. See also La Chambre's testimony in *Événements,* vol. II, p. 312.

the American Army." Taking advantage of a long personal friendship with President Franklin D. Roosevelt, La Grange spent a weekend during mid-January at the White House and in private conversation outlined France's dilemma. The Senator reported his talk "crowned with success":

> [Roosevelt] is well informed about what is going on in Germany and he appears to be very concerned about the effort being made by [France] in the field of aviation. . . . It is his conviction that more and more Japan will depend on Germany and Italy and that, in order to contain the ambitions of these three powers, England, France and America will be obliged to combine their efforts.
>
> The President is thus completely in favor of all measures that the French Government might believe necessary to reinforce its air formation in time of peace and in time of war.[6]

Although the Neutrality Act of August 1935 included an embargo of arms to all belligerents, La Grange commented in his final report that "as long as the White House is occupied by Mr. Roosevelt, who is Francophile and fears German expansion," France could expect either repeal or a favorable interpretation of the Neutrality Act. However, La Grange also reported that Roosevelt had advised him to exercise "caution and discretion" when he surveyed the American aircraft industry because "although

[6] Letter from La Grange to Joseph C. Caillux, President of the French Senate, January 21, 1938, La Grange Papers. For the President's other plans at this time to "contain the ambitions" of Japan, see John McVickar Haight, Jr., "Franklin D. Roosevelt and a Naval Quarantine of Japan," to be published in *Pacific Historical Review.*

the export of arms is free in peacetime, it is better to avoid alerting the press or Congress." [7]

There was no question that La Grange sought, as one State Department official reported, "to harness American industry to the French war machine." [8] However the French Senator's expectations of obtaining 1,000 planes for rapid delivery dimmed as he toured the American aircraft industry. He discovered that it lagged almost as much as French industry in the shift from canvas and wood construction to the new stressed skin aluminum frames of Germany's latest war models. American factory space was more than ample, but modern machine tools and up-to-date assembly lines were lacking. La Grange was forced to conclude in his final report of February 15 that "the American aircraft industry is not in a position to deliver utilizable material before 1939. . . . It is indeed regrettable that we cannot immediately obtain from the United States planes needed to reinforce our weak aviation." [9]

Even though France could not gain American aid immediately, Senator La Grange urged that orders be placed for planes and engines so as "to prepare mobilization in peacetime" and thus "give us the advantage of obtaining quickly in case of war, material from the United States." [10] La Grange reported that one American single-engine fighter, Curtiss-Wright's P-36, could approximate Euro-

[7] "Final Report on American Trip, February 15, 1938," La Grange Papers, "Senate Campaign," pp. 85–98.

[8] Memorandum by Joseph C. Green, Chief of Office of Arms and Munitions Control, of conversation with Senator La Grange, January 18, 1938, in *Foreign Relations of the United States, 1938* (Washington, 1955), vol. II, p. 298. (Hereafter cited as *FR, 1938*.)

[9] "Final Report on American Trip, February 15, 1938," La Grange Papers, "Senate Campaign," p. 96.

[10] *Ibid.*, p. 96.

pean combat standards. However, only 100 could be produced by April 1939, and France would be required to pay almost $1 million for the machine tools needed for a new production line.[11]

La Grange's report on the deficiency of American aircraft production came as an unpleasant surprise to the French Air Minister, for, as he admitted later, "We thought we would find everything on the American market. Now we found nearly nothing because American industry, though very developed in the production of commercial planes, was almost non-existent for war planes." [12] Nevertheless La Chambre realized France's need for planes and so determined to purchase the 100 P-36s which could be produced over the next twelve months. In this he had the backing of Defense Minister Daladier, who in mid-April also became Premier of France. Before the Air Minister could place this order, however, he had to overcome a series of domestic obstacles. The Minister of Finance, Georges Bonnet, opposed reducing France's limited gold reserves further by paying cash for those planes as required by the American Neutrality Act.[13] In turn, the Air Committee of the Chamber of Deputies jealously fought to protect the French aviation industry from imports of American planes.[14] French labor, fearing the loss

[11] *Ibid.*, p. 98.

[12] See La Chambre's testimony in *Événements,* vol. II, p. 307.

[13] La Chambre, during an interview with the author in June 1961, spoke of Bonnet's hesitancy to buy American planes. See also Cot, *Triumph of Treason,* p. 300.

[14] See La Chambre's testimony, *Événements,* vol. II, p. 308. Pierre Dignac, then Vice President of the Chamber of Deputies, opposed foreign purchases in January 1938: "There are no American planes that can meet German and Italian competition." See his *Malfaiteurs publics, documents d'histoire, 1924–1940* (Grenoble, 1944), pp. 147–56. During a secret debate within the Chamber of Deputies two years later, La Chambre described his appearance before the Air

of jobs and wages to foreign competition, for once joined management; together they campaigned against purchasing planes and their engines from the United States.[15] Opposition also came from within the Air Ministry, where technicians questioned the quality of American war planes and demanded extensive flight tests before purchase. The French press entered the debate with enthusiasm.[16]

The Air Minister proved with a survey that the French aviation industry could not produce sufficient planes for France's defense, but he bowed to the demand for a flight test of the Curtiss fighter. The test required the approval of the United States Army Air Corps, however, because it possessed the only three P-36s ready to fly and these were the first to be produced on the Air Corps' current order for 200. The Assistant Chief of the Air Corps, General H. H. Arnold, recognized certain advantages to the sale of American planes to France, but he balked at turning over the

---

Committee on February 16, 1938; see *Journal Officiel, Débat Parlementaire, Chambre de Députés, Comité Secret, Fevrier 9, 1940,* (Paris, 1940), p. 11. See also *The New York Times,* February 17, 1938, p. 2, col. 5, and February 24, p. 11, col. 2.

[15] La Chambre's testimony, *Événements,* vol. II, pp. 308–9.

[16] See two articles by Peyronnet de Torres, "Tomorrow in the Sky —Part III," *L'Intransigeant,* February 11, 1939, p. 1, and "Buying Planes in America," *Ibid.,* May 1, 1938, p. 1. For a summary of the debate, see Christian Jayle, "Should France Buy American Planes?" *L'Europe Nouvelle,* April 23, 1938, pp. 453–54. For voices of opposition, see "American Planes," *L'Air,* No. 444, May 1, 1938; "Our Aviation, How to Rebuild It," *Revue des Deux Mondes,* May 15, 1938, pp. 279–80; General Armengaud, "Spiritual Division of the French and the Air Deficiency of France," *L'Europe Nouvelle,* May 21, 1938, pp. 537–38; General Armengaud, "For a Stronger Air Force," *Revue Militaire Générale,* May 1938, pp. 531–38. The arguments in favor of American planes are summed up in "The Great Problem of French Aviation," *L'Europe Nouvelle,* May 7, 1938, pp. 457–58, and Henry Bouché, "For a Stronger Army of the Air," *L'Aéronautique,* May 1938, pp. 89–90. See also "Press Comments," *L'Air,* May 20 and June 1, 1938.

latest fighter just as it was becoming operational in American squadrons. Arnold was jealous of every secret built into the P-36 and he opposed giving permission for France's leading flyer, Michael Detroyat, to fly the plane:

> M. Detroyat is an engineer of unusual ability, a skilled test pilot and a skilled pilot of racing planes. He could learn more in twenty minutes alone on this plane than the average engineer could learn from a week's study of both the plane and its blueprints.[17]

Senator La Grange had stated in his final report that he had found President Roosevelt interested "in every measure which can reenforce French military power," and so on February 23 France asked the White House for clearance of Detroyat's flight, routing the appeal through the American Ambassador in Paris, William C. Bullitt.[18] The President lived up to expectations and issued directions to the Army Chief of Staff, General Malin Craig, for the Frenchman to fly one of the Army's P-36s in secret and just for twenty minutes.[19] As Arnold predicted, that was ample time for Detroyat. He reported that the Curtiss

[17] Memo by General Arnold for Army Chief of Staff Malin Craig, March 9, 1938, Adjutant General Office File 453 (3–9–38), National Archives, Record Group 94.

[18] La Grange's appeal to Roosevelt was relayed by the American Ambassador, William C. Bullitt, to the Secretary of State, February 23, 1938, *FR, 1938,* vol. II, pp. 303–4.

[19] On March 10, General Arnold noted in the "Daily Air Corps Record": "The President of the United States directed the Chief of Staff to permit Detroyat to fly the Curtiss P-36" with secret instruments removed and to make the flight "with the utmost secrecy." Arnold Papers, Box 56, Folder 529. (Arnold Papers are held by the Manuscript Division, Library of Congress.) For arrangements made for Detroyat's flight on March 20, see also memo by Joseph C. Green of conversation with Burdette Wright, of Curtiss-Wright Corporation, March 19, 1938, State Department unpublished documents (SD), 851.248/56, National Archives, Record Group 19.

plane was equal not only to France's latest fighter but also to Germany's Messerschmitt-109.[20]

Even after Detroyat's favorable report, France's Air Minister was delayed in placing orders for the 100 P-36s until mid-May. It took that long for La Chambre to overcome the opposition of the technicians within his ministry to the purchase of American planes.[21] One hundred was not a large order and it was surpassed a few weeks later when Britain ordered 400 planes from the United States. Britain split its order between trainers and a Lockheed transport, the latter being hastily converted into coastal patrol bomber. These orders contributed significantly to the American capacity to build aerial engines, but, unlike the French order, they did not develop the production of combat planes. France made a further contribution toward mobilizing the American aircraft industry when it financed for $940,000 a new production line for the P-36s. Premier Daladier's decision meant diverting capital funds from the construction of French factories, and this took political courage, for, as Guy La Chambre pointed out after the war, "at the time our decision was far from being received with approval." When the former Air Minister gave this testimony he justly added, "This policy of investment made an important favorable contribution towards overcoming the delay in the production of planes by the American war industry." [22] Both La Chambre and Daladier had been fully conscious of the significance of

[20] "Orders for Seversky and Curtiss 75A," no date, Private Papers of Guy La Chambre, "Commander Américaines," Document no. 2. (These papers are held in Paris by M. La Chambre, who kindly opened them to the author in the summer of 1961.)

[21] For this opposition, see procès-verbal de Comité de Matériel, May 20, 1938, Box B/104, Service Historique de l'Armée de l'Air, Versailles. See also the procès-verbal for April 15 and 28.

[22] *Événements,* vol. II, p. 307.

this contribution in the spring of 1938, for they had come to support Senator La Grange's goal to have American industry make a commitment to build war planes for France.

Premier Daladier and his Air Minister had to wait until after the Munich settlement of the Czechoslovakian crisis on September 30, 1938, before they could make further progress toward that goal. Three days after Daladier's return to Paris from Munich the Premier called in Ambassador Bullitt for a lunch together with Guy La Chambre and Jean Monnet. According to Bullitt, Daladier saw "the situation entirely, clearly and realizes fully that the meeting in Munich was an immense diplomatic defeat for France and England." As France's main reason for backing down before Hitler, the Premier gave the lack of defense against the German Luftwaffe. Bullitt was so impressed with Daladier's analysis of "the aviation position and ways and means of remedying it" that he sailed immediately for the United States to pave the way for France's second air mission under Jean Monnet.[23]

The inferiority of the French Air Force before Germany's Luftwaffe during the Czech crisis was much greater than the figures released by Daladier's government indicated. While France publicly claimed 600 front-line planes, its Air Force could count at the end of September, when the Munich crisis was blackest and war was expected momentarily, no more than seventeen modern planes. All of these were Potez 63s, which were two-seated fighter command planes.[24] The French Chief of Staff for Air,

[23] Bullitt, October 3, 1938, *FR, 1938,* vol. I, pp. 711–12.

[24] For this accounting, see procès-verbal de Comité de Matériel, September 29, 1938, File B/104, Service Historique de L'Armée de L'Air, Versailles.

General Vuillemin, had not hidden the tragic condition of his Air Force. In a letter of September 26 to the Air Minister he admitted all 600 front-line planes were "extremely inferior [to German front-line planes] in performance" and the General then stated, "The French Air Force can only with extreme difficulties and at a price of heavy losses fulfill the missions assigned to it." [25] La Chambre forwarded Vuillemin's report to Premier Daladier. Two days later the Air Minister also provided Ambassador Bullitt with the "actual figures on the aviation situation," and he added that in his opinion "German bomber planes would be able to bomb Paris at will. . . . There would be no planes for the defense of Paris. Antiaircraft artillery was also most inadequate in quantity." [26] Premier Daladier carried to Munich this knowledge of France's vulnerability to air attack.[27]

During the weeks before the Munich settlement President Roosevelt had also kept himself well informed concerning the imbalance of air power in Europe. In addition to information collected by the State Department and Armed Services from the usual sources, Roosevelt had called upon a number of American aircraft producers to

[25] For Vuillemin's letter, see testimony of La Chambre, *Événements,* vol. II, p. 312.

[26] Bullitt to F.D.R., September 28, 1938, President Secretary's File, Box 3, France, William C. Bullitt Folder, Roosevelt Library.

[27] While in Munich and just after Hitler's terms were accepted, Daladier talked of France's air power with Colonel Paul Stehlin, a member of the Intelligence Division of the French Air Force General Staff and air attaché in Berlin: "I have seen General Vuillemin, your chief. He was terribly worried. . . . Do you agree with Vuillemin we would have no more planes after a few days of combat?" When Stehlin declined to judge his superior officer's opinion, the Premier remarked, "Now it's done. Perhaps we had no other choice" (Stehlin, *Témoignage pour L'Histoire* [Paris, 1964], p. 104). Daladier, commenting thirty years later, repeated that there was no alternative. *The New York Times,* September 30, 1968, p. 20, col. 6.

tour the aviation industry of France, Britain, and Germany.[28] All reported the deficiencies of the European democracies, especially that of France.[29] The President also by September 22 had received another first-hand account. This came from the noted American aviator Colonel Charles A. Lindbergh, who had just completed a three-week tour which included a stopover in Poland, some two weeks in the Soviet Union, five days in Czechoslovakia, and two days in Germany. By September 9 he arrived in France for several days.[30] His findings further verified Hitler's enormous aerial superiority, and on September 22 he summarized his thinking for the American Ambassador in London, Joseph P. Kennedy:

> German military strength now makes [the Germans] inseparable from the welfare of every civilization, for they have the power either to preserve it or

[28] Joseph Alsop and Robert Kintner, *American White Paper* (New York, 1940), p. 29.

[29] For report by Glenn Martin, president of Glenn L. Martin Corporation, see memo to Assistant Secretary of War (ASW) from Colonel J. H. Burns, Executive Officer to ASW, June 23, 1938, President Secretary's File, War Department, Roosevelt Library; for comments of Burdett Wright, vice president of Curtiss-Wright Corporation, see "Daily Air Corps Record," by General Arnold, June 28, 1938, Arnold Papers, Box 56, No. 529. See also the memo on the conversation with J. H. Kindelberger, president of North American Aviation, by General Arnold, July 12, 1938, Army Air Force (AAF), File 452.1, Foreign Planes, National Archives, Record Group 18; for Lawrence D. Bell's report, see Marc A. Rose, "Hitler's Aerial Triumph," *Forum,* 101, March 1939, p. 126; the impressions of Charles A. Van Duzen, of Consolidated Aircraft, are noted in "Diplomatic Journals of Jay Pierrepont Moffat, 1919–1943," September 2, 1938 (manuscript at Houghton Library, Harvard University).

[30] For details of Lindbergh's meeting with Bullitt and La Chambre in Paris, see John W. Wheeler-Bennett, *Munich: Prologue to Tragedy* (New York, 1948), p. 99.

> destroy it. For the first time in history a nation has the power either to save or ruin the great cities of Europe. Germany has such a preponderance of war planes that she can bomb any city in Europe with comparatively little resistance. England and France are far too weak in the air to protect themselves.[31]

That evening Lindbergh stated his final conclusion to a British flying officer: "Our only sound policy is to avoid war now at almost any cost." [32]

By the time Lindbergh's report officially arrived in Washington, President Roosevelt had already taken steps by which he could further extend American aid to the European democracies in building their air defenses. In mid-September, after an Air Corps survey of September 11 reported that the nation's aircraft industry possessed little excess capacity for foreign orders,[33] he began exploring ways in which American aircraft production could be expanded. When the President listened to a broadcast of Hitler's Nuremberg speech on September 12, he was so disturbed by the dictator's bombast that he asked Harry Hopkins, who headed the Works Projects Administration, to verify the Air Corps' findings by making a personal survey of the aircraft industry on the West Coast. Hopkins was to determine how many new plants should be constructed and to find the means by which funds from the

[31] Kennedy to Secretary of State, September 22, 1938, *FR, 1938*, vol. I, pp. 72–73.

[32] Lindbergh reported this to Squadron Leader John Slessor, Chief of the Plans Branch of the British Air Staff, on September 22, 1938; see Sir John Slessor, Marshal of the Royal Air Force, *The Central Blue: Recollections and Reflections* (London, 1956), p. 219.

[33] See memo for Secretary, Army-Navy Munitions Board, September 11, 1938, AAF File 452.1–3295, Sale of Planes Abroad.

WPA could be diverted to the project on the grounds of reducing unemployment.[34]

The President indicated in a number of other ways his concern for aiding the aerial rearmament of the European democracies. One came when, as the Munich crisis reached its climax, four representatives from the French Ministry of Marine arrived in America September 26 and asked to test fly several planes to determine whether they were suitable to land on French aircraft carriers.[35] The Chief of Naval Operations, Admiral William D. Leahy, officially had to oppose these flights on the grounds of a new Army-Navy policy on foreign negotiations for purchase of planes.[36] Nevertheless, with the approval of the Secretary of State, Cordell Hull, the President requested the Navy to permit the trial flights "as all of the planes have been or will be released for export in the near future," and Leahy willingly arranged the flights on an informal basis, thus avoiding the establishment of an official precedent. The White House accepted the Navy's proposal for secret flights.[37]

[34] Robert E. Sherwood, *Roosevelt and Hopkins: An Intimate History* (New York, 1948), pp. 99–100.

[35] For arrangements for the French naval air mission, see memorandum by Joseph C. Green, Chief of Office of Arms and Munitions Control, of conversation with the French Ambassador, September 14, 1938, SD 851.248/101. See also French Ambassador to Secretary of State, September 13, *FR, 1938,* vol. II, pp. 312–13, and Bullitt, September 23, SD 851.248/109.

[36] Admiral W. D. Leahy, Acting Secretary of the Navy, to Secretary of State, September 27, SD 851.248/112. For the basis of the Navy's initial opposition, see Chief Bureau of Aeronautics to Chief of Naval Operations, August 27, and to Director of Naval Intelligence, September 20, 1938, Navy Department Files, Bureau of Aeronautics General Correspondence, 1922–1944, France, EF 28/vv, National Archives, Record Group 72.

[37] Secretary of State to President, September 27, 1938, SD 851.248/109; Leahy to the President, September 29, 1938, SD

Another indication of President Roosevelt's personal thoughts during the height of the Munich crisis comes from a report sent back to London by the British air attaché in Washington. On September 27 he had been requested to estimate the types and numbers of American aircraft which Britain could buy within a month's time. Two days later the attaché listed only the two planes which Britain had first ordered during the past May, the Lockheed Hudson and North America's Harvard trainer. Delivery of these planes would be a gamble, however, because "in event of war the United Kingdom could not count on the Neutrality Act being amended in its favor before the end of the year at the earliest, if even then." The attaché went on to provide a remarkable summary of the American President's current thinking. Roosevelt, as the attaché cabled, regarded the Munich Agreement as being forced on the European democracies because of their inferiority in the air, and he was determined that his nation should never be put in such a position. The attaché noted that Roosevelt had ordered a survey of American plane production, for he believed that if Germany could turn out 30,000 aircraft, the United States should build 40,000. To avoid the arms embargo of the Neutrality Act, Roosevelt also considered supplying the democracies with partly finished basic material such as "fabricated aluminum, tubing, steel castings, magnetos and other accessories" with which the Allies could "build aircraft far in excess of German production." In addition, the President suggested the construction of a factory in Canada which

---

851.248/119. For the conclusion of these negotiations, see the memo by Green, October 8, 1938, and the record of Green's telephone call to the French Ambassador, October 11, 1938, *FR, 1938,* vol. II, pp. 313–14.

could assemble aircraft parts shipped from plants in the United States.[38]

During the last frantic days of the crisis over Czechoslovakia and its German-speaking Sudetenland, President Roosevelt sought some means by which his nation could help maintain Europe's peace.[39] In trying to develop a positive step he ran into resistance from the State Department, where Secretary Hull and, more particularly, Jay Pierrepont Moffat, the head of its European division, feared that

> if we emphasized peace as the essential we might be accused of endorsing Chamberlain's policy of "selling Czechoslovakia down the river." On the other hand, if we should emphasize the importance of a just settlement and England went to war, she might later say that we had given advice in that otherwise she would have sold the Czechs down the river and hence that we had assumed a moral responsibility.[40]

In contrast, Ambassador Bullitt in Paris urged action. On September 24, when Chamberlain left his Godesberg conference with Hitler and negotiations foundered on the

[38] H. Duncan Hall, *North American Supply: History of the Second World War, United Kingdom Civil Series* (London, 1955), p. 106. The original of the attaché's report cannot be located by the Air Historical Branch, Ministry of Defence, London. On September 24, Roosevelt had outlined for his cabinet methods of evading the arms embargo which closely paralleled the British attaché's account of sending semi-finished aircraft parts to Canada for assemblage. See *Secret Diaries of Harold L. Ickes* (New York, 1954), vol. II, p. 474.

[39] See John McVickar Haight, Jr., "France, the United States and the Munich Crisis," *Journal of Modern History,* vol. XXXII, December 1960, pp. 340–58.

[40] September 16, 1938, *Moffat Papers: Selections from the Diplomatic Journals of Jay Pierrepont Moffat, 1919–1934,* ed. Nancy Hooker (Cambridge, Mass., 1956), p. 205.

Führer's determination to march into the Sudetenland, Bullitt revived a proposal which he had first sent to the White House on May 20: if war seemed likely, the President should call a conference of Britain, France, Italy, Germany, and Poland, with the United States sending a representative.[41]

On September 25, as the democracies stiffened their resistance to Hitler, the President personally favored such a conference, but the State Department still hesitated.[42] It did, however, agree to a Presidential message to Hitler, Beneš of Czechoslovakia, Daladier, and Chamberlain. In a cable sent off early on September 26, Roosevelt spoke out against the horrors of war and urged that "reason and the spirit of equity" prevail so that "the world may thereby escape the madness of a new resort to war." He concluded,

> On behalf of the 130 millions of people of the United States of America and for the sake of humanity everywhere, I most earnestly appeal to you not to break off negotiations looking to a peaceful, fair and constructive settlement of the questions at issue.[43]

Bullitt was so infuriated by the vagueness of this message that he telephoned Moffat at 5:15 a.m. to insist that American arbitration should be offered "if we would save the situation." [44] But Roosevelt made no further move until September 27, when "information of unquestioned authenticity arrived warning that Hitler's troops would

[41] Bullitt, September 24, 1938, *FR, 1938,* vol. I, pp. 641–42. See also Bullitt, May 20, *Ibid.,* vol. I, pp. 509–12.

[42] *Moffat Papers,* pp. 211–12, and Alsop and Kintner, *American White Paper,* p. 9. See also *Memoirs of Cordell Hull* (New York, 1948), vol. I, pp. 590–92.

[43] For text, see *FR, 1938,* vol. I, pp. 657–58.

[44] *Moffat Papers,* pp. 212–13.

march into Czechoslovakia at 2:00 p.m. the next day unless the Godesberg terms were met."[45]

To help hold off an invasion, the State Department agreed to two steps: first, an appeal to Mussolini to use his influence on Hitler for peace, and, second, a message urging other nations throughout the world to join with the United States to plead for maintaining peace. A third step, Bullitt's plan for a conference, ran into renewed opposition from the Secretary of State.[46] The Under Secretary of State, Sumner Welles, who had just visited Ambassador Bullitt in Paris, refused to let the idea for the conference die, however. He took it to the White House and received the President's approval for sounding out Britain and France about a direct plea to Hitler to join a conference. Chamberlain gave cautious approval, believing that time for admonitions had passed and fearing that Hitler might be antagonized by a direct appeal to him and to no one else. In contrast, Daladier expressed "the greatest gratitude for the President's continued efforts to preserve the peace," and he approved of inviting Hitler to a conference which could "work out the transfer of Czech territory to Germany in peace."[47]

In his second message, addressed this time only to the German Chancellor, Roosevelt denounced force "as unnecessary as it is unjustifiable." He added that current negotiations stood open and "they can be continued if you give the word." He suggested that "a conference of all the

[45] Sumner Welles revealed the receipt of this message in his speech of October 3, 1938, reviewing American actions during the Munich crisis. See Department of State, *Press Releases,* 1938, p. 238.

[46] *Moffat Papers,* pp. 215–16, and Alsop and Kintner, *American White Paper,* p. 10.

[47] See memos of two telephone conversations between Welles and Bullitt on September 27, 1938, in *FR, 1938,* vol. I, pp. 675–76, and SD 760 F 62/117A.

nations directly interested" be held immediately.[48] Although Roosevelt's message announced that "the United States has no political involvements in Europe," undoubtedly the President forwarded this second message with a determination to swing his nation into the scales of European politics. Rather than backing the appeaser's goal of "peace at any price" Roosevelt was supporting the plan of Bullitt, Welles, and Daladier to negotiate with justice and fair dealing rather than capitulate before the threat of arms. The President realized that the terms of the Versailles Treaty should not be held inviolate and that revisions, such as the transfer of the Sudeten territories, were necessary, but he was against making a transfer under the threat of force. On September 28, when Roosevelt learned that Chamberlain had accepted the invitation to the Munich conference, he cabled, "Good Man." [49] The President did so not because he approved of surrender before the threat of force but because he recognized that the door of peace was being kept open.

The Munich settlement distressed President Roosevelt, who recognized that France and Britain had capitulated before Hitler's threats. Roosevelt regretted that he too lacked the force to make his voice heard, and so in the fall of 1938 he determined to build the one type of armed force with which he could henceforth influence European affairs: air power.[50] He thus welcomed the second French effort to "harness American industry to the French war machine," and through his direct actions he proved that he was ready to aid and assist France. The catastrophe of the Munich settlement in turn prompted Premier Daladier and his Air Minister to face again the obstacles to American plane purchases.

[48] For the text, see *FR, 1938,* vol. I, pp. 684–85.
[49] *Ibid.,* vol. I, p. 688. [50] See Chapter 3.

CHAPTER

2

American Planes to Deter Hitler

WITH THE CZECHOSLOVAKIAN CRISIS settled at Munich, France initiated the second and more significant phase of negotiations for American planes.[1] Three days after returning from Munich to Paris, Premier Daladier appealed through Ambassador Bullitt for aid in building France's aerial defenses. When Daladier's official representative, Jean Monnet, arrived in Washington, he discovered that President Roosevelt and his advisers were prepared to cooperate and speed the production of planes for France. Monnet also found that to meet the costs of these aircraft the Secretary of the Treasury, Henry Morgenthau, was ready to assist in recovering the gold which had been leaving France since

[1] This chapter amplifies material first published in John McVickar Haight, Jr., "Les Négociations Relatives aux Achats d'Avions Américains par la France pendant la Période qui Précéda Immédiament la Guerre," *Revue d'Histoire de la Deuxième Guerre Mondiale,* No. 58, April 1965, pp. 1–34. A garbled account of Monnet's air mission to the States in the fall of 1938 is found in Mary and Serge Bromberger, *Jean Monnet and the United States of Europe,* trans. E. P. Halperin (New York, 1969), pp. 23–26.

1934. Though this effort ran into the opposition of the new Finance Minister, Paul Reynaud, Premier Daladier was determined to overcome his nation's tragic "aerial inferiority," and by early December 1938 he had authorized the purchase of 1,000 American planes.

On October 3, 1938, Premier Daladier lunched with Ambassador Bullitt in Paris and spelled out a plan for France to obtain a large number of American planes. Bullitt immediately cabled Washington that Daladier saw Munich as "an immense diplomatic defeat for France and England." France's main reason for backing down before Hitler had been her lack of defense against the German Luftwaffe. Unless this deficiency could be corrected within the next twelve months, the Premier feared France would not be in a position to expect further diplomatic "give and take" ultimatums. Bullitt was so deeply impressed with Daladier's analysis of "the aviation position and ways and means of remedying it" that he cabled, "I believe that it is more discreet for me to report this portion of our conversation by word of mouth when I reach Washington at the end of this week rather than by cable." [2]

Bullitt, however, had already outlined this "means of remedying" France's lack of planes in his cable to the President on September 28. He reported not only the French Air Minister's evaluation of France's desperate aerial inferiority, but also a procedure of obtaining American planes beyond the limits of the Neutrality Act's arms embargo: France would "build huge factories for planes in Canada, possibly just opposite Detroit and Buffalo, so that American workmen living at home can be utilized readily." These Canadian assembly plants would depend upon the shipment of machine tools, plane parts, and instruments from the United States. In Guy La Chambre's opin-

[2] Bullitt, October 3, *FR, 1938,* vol. I, pp. 711–12.

ion, the outcome of the war would depend upon whether these plants could provide a vital supplement for France's Air Force. One question disturbed La Chambre, however: could such exports be made to a belligerent France without violating the Neutrality Act? Bullitt's cable also reported that the man best qualified to study this question was Jean Monnet, "an intimate friend of mine for many years, whom I trust as a brother." [3]

Apparently La Chambre approved of the Ambassador's recommendation, because Monnet was at that luncheon with the French Premier on October 3. Monnet later recalled that during that meeting he realized "Munich had not fooled Daladier," and the Premier knew that France must arm herself properly, because as Daladier admitted, "If I had 3,000 or 4,000 planes, there would have been no Munich." [4]

The air mission to the United States, which Monnet agreed to undertake, had three "purposes" which he summarized in the final report for the Air Minister in mid-November:

> A. To outline the possibility for manufacture in the United States of a maximum number of military planes, one half bombers of high performance, and half pursuit, so as not to interfere with the requirements of the military needs of the country: program to continue for one year from its inception.
>
> B. Possibility of creating in Canada assembly plants in case war prevents delivery of finished planes from

[3] Bullitt to F.D.R., September 28, 1938, President Secretary's File, Box 3, France, William C. Bullitt Folder, Roosevelt Library.

[4] Monnet recalled Daladier's comments during an interview in late December 1940 with Charles T. Lucey. See *New York World-Telegram,* December 30, 1940, p. 4.

the United States, their production based on the supply of parts manufactured in the United States.

C. Possibility of introducing United States technical and quantity methods of production into the aircraft industry of France (motors and frames) in that new part of the nation's industry that it proposes to create in the immediate future through American cooperation.[5]

These "purposes" had been under consideration for several months, and they had appeared earlier in "Notes on the Subject of Creating a Foreign Manufacturing Potential" which had been given to the Air Minister in the spring of 1938. These "Notes" also addressed themselves to "the problem of supplementing French production of war planes by the immediate creation of new foreign manufacturing centers capable of rapid production with the potential of immediate and extensive expansion once war broke out." The solution was frankly stated: "Outside of Europe only American industry possesses the necessary technique and is adaptable to rapid expansion." In conclusion, the "Notes" pointed out the long-run purpose of developing North American production: "France will possess an extensive rapid assembly plant sheltered from enemy attacks while the military builds up its forces." [6]

The ground work for Monnet's mission was laid by

[5] "Memorandum," signed Jean Monnet, dated November 14, 1938, La Chambre Papers, "Commandes Américaines," Doc. no. 6.

[6] The "Notes" are unsigned and undated but identified by M. La Chambre as having been received in the spring of 1938. They are filed as Doc. no. 1 bis in La Chambre Papers, "Commandes Américaines." Possibly Ambassador Bullitt helped prepare the "Notes" upon his return to France in early May. He had been in the U.S. since March 1938, when he saw the President about clearing Detroyat for a trial flight.

Ambassador Bullitt after he arrived in Washington on October 13 and reported to the White House.[7] Over the next several days President Roosevelt launched several steps toward building up his own nation's Air Force as well as aiding France to build up hers. On October 14 the President called for the rearmament of the United States and spoke of asking Congress for a $500 million supplementary budget to finance new arms.[8] Bernard Baruch's report on October 12 dealt with the rearmament problems of the European democracies and the need for the United States to build its defenses in the face of Germany's call for rearmament.[9] Bullitt's appeal for planes for France also helped persuade Roosevelt to take the second step: a request to the Air Corps to prepare plans for extensive expansion.[10] Roosevelt's third move was to ask the State Department to study the removal of the arms embargo from the Neutrality Act.[11] Finally, Roosevelt approved Bullitt's proposal that Premier Daladier send Jean Monnet to study how the American aircraft industry could best serve France's need.

[7] For a summary of this conversation, see William L. Langer and S. Everett Gleason, *Challenge to Isolation, 1937–1940* (New York, 1952), pp. 37–38.

[8] *The New York Times,* October 15, 1938. See also *Press Conferences of Franklin D. Roosevelt, 1938,* vol. 12, microfilm roll 6, no. 491, October 14, 1938.

[9] Margaret L. Cort, *Mr. Baruch* (Boston, 1957), pp. 467–68.

[10] See Assistant Secretary of War (ASW) Louis Johnson, to Chief of Staff (CS) Malin Craig, October 14, 1938, Adjutant General File 580 (10–19–38), National Archives, Record Group 94. See also Arnold's circular letter to Aircraft Manufacturers, October 14, 1938, Arnold Papers Box 222, Subject File, Aircraft Production, 1938 October.

[11] State Department officials held their first major conference on this issue on October 18. See *Moffat Papers,* p. 228, note 70. See also Robert A. Divine, *The Illusion of Neutrality* (Chicago, 1962), pp. 231–33.

Having launched these steps, Roosevelt left on October 16 for an eight-day visit to his country estate at Hyde Park. Through talks with Secretary Morgenthau, Harry Hopkins, Ambassador Bullitt, Jean Monnet, and even a British houseguest, the President further developed plans to aid the European democracies.

Morgenthau spent the evening of Tuesday, October 18, with the President, and showed him a memorandum written in the Department of the Treasury which proposed that the United States take positive action in world affairs:

> We should learn the lesson which the history of the last seven years has to teach us. Let us not repeat the shortsighted mistakes of Britain and France. . . . Let us while we can peacefully do so, try to check the aggressors. Let us not be placed in a position of having to compound with them.

Morgenthau recommended extending credit to China and the Latin American countries to help them ward off Japan in the Far East and Nazi Germany in the Western Hemisphere. Morgenthau also advised raising countervailing duties against Germany's trade dumping. Both of these proposals indicated the Secretary's personal desire to resist the fascist states.[12]

The Secretary found the President much more interested in ways to expand American aircraft production. Morgenthau reported to his staff that the President had talked about "our producing 15,000 airplanes a year in

[12] See drafts of a letter from Morgenthau to Roosevelt prepared October 11–17, 1938, by H. Dexter White of the Treasury Department; and memo on German Trade Discrimination, also by White, October 6, 1938, Morgenthau Diary, Bk. 145, pp. 259–93; Bk. 146, pp. 108–49. (Unpublished manuscript in Roosevelt Library, Hyde Park, New York).

this country, giving private industry 3,000 and we [the Government] will produce 12,000." Production would have to be raised from 10 planes a day to 50. Morgenthau also reported that Harry Hopkins had just proposed to meet this production goal by building eight government plants throughout the United States.

Morgenthau also learned from the President that France planned to construct two Canadian assembly plants "in Montreal across from Niagara Falls, across from Detroit." The Secretary was against setting up Canadian plants, even though these plants would be able to produce 1,000 planes a month: "How long do we know that Canada and England are going to be our allies?"; the plants "would be a target for German bombers; they'll take our mechanics when we are short good mechanics."

Morgenthau talked with Ambassador Bullitt, another visitor at Hyde Park, about the French plans to purchase planes directly from the United States, and the Secretary reacted negatively. Morgenthau did not want, as he told his staff later, to have Roosevelt make a mistake and he felt "somebody has given the President a lot of misinformation." The Secretary supported his point by giving Roosevelt a three-page memo, prepared by the Treasury Department, which argued against both the Canadian assembly plants and the French purchase of large numbers of American planes. The memo's basic argument ran, "For every million dollars you take out of France—it just makes their foreign exchange that much worse."

Morgenthau reacted favorably toward Roosevelt's and Hopkins' plan to expand American aircraft production. He was "all bucked up over this thing. . . . I'm tickled to death the President is thinking of making the country so strong that nobody can attack us . . . we want enough planes to take care of the whole of the South American continent too." He was troubled only by France's plans to buy American planes: "they 'll have to do it the way the Germans do it, inside of France, help their own unemployment situation." [13]

President Roosevelt, however, was apparently little affected by Secretary Morgenthau's reaction against aiding the European democracies. In two conversations with Arthur C. Murray (later Lord Elibank), also a visitor to Hyde Park,[14] the President discussed the possibility of further British purchases of American planes. In their first discussion on October 21, Roosevelt talked about Germany having the capacity to produce 40,000 planes, while Britain together with Canada could turn out only 25,000 and France only 15,000. He then remarked that "the extra 20 to 30,000 planes to give the necessary overwhelming superiority over Germany and Italy" could only be found in the United States. According to Murray's notes, the President also referred to Canadian assembly plants:

> So far as [Roosevelt] was concerned, his object would be—in the event of Great Britain being at war with the dictatorships, and the United States not being engaged—to do his best to provide partly finished basic materials, which did not come within the Neutrality Law.[15]

[13] For Morgenthau's reactions, see notes on his staff conference, October 20, 1938, *Ibid.*, Bk. 146, pp. 279–94. See also the memo by White on French plants in Canada, October 18, 1938, *Ibid.*, Bk. 146, pp. 166–69.

[14] A snapshot dated October 19, 1938, in the Elibank Papers shows the British houseguest with Ambassador Bullitt at a picnic near the President's unfinished cottage hideaway.

[15] Lord Elibank, formerly Arthur C. Murray, "Franklin Roosevelt: Friend of Britain," *Contemporary Review*, CLXXXVII, June 1955, pp. 364–67.

During a second talk on October 23 Roosevelt requested Murray to discuss these plans with their friend Lord Tweedsmuir, Governor General of Canada, and advise him to suggest to the Canadian Prime Minister, Mackenzie King, that liaison officers be appointed both to facilitate plans between the United States and Canada and "to obviate any undue rise in contract prices." Roosevelt believed that

> through the liaison thus established, it would be possible for information as regards design, engines and other aspects of aeroplane manufacture, to pass confidentially between United States, Canadian and British Governments to the extent that each thought fit.

As his comments were "entirely sub-rosa," the President warned, "Existing official channels . . . should not for various reasons be used for this purpose." [16]

In addition, the President asked Murray to inform Prime Minister Chamberlain of their talks and to relay the President's assurance that "I will help all I can." [17] He told Murray that, if necessary, Chamberlain could announce publicly that "Great Britain in the event of war, could rely upon obtaining raw materials from the democracies of the world." [18]

[16] *Ibid.*, pp. 364–65. See also the letter from Murray to Roosevelt, October 30, 1938, reporting on conversation with Lord Tweedsmuir, who was "highly gratified," located in Lord Elibank's private papers in folder "F.D.R. Letters." (These papers are held in London and were kindly opened to the author by the late Lord Elibank during August 1961.)

[17] Elibank, "Franklin Roosevelt," *Contemporary Review,* June 1955, p. 365.

[18] Lord Elibank did not publish this statement in *Contemporary Review.* It is to be found in his original copy of "Note of certain conversation between President F.D.R. and Col. Hon. Arthur Murray during Col. and Mrs. Murray's stay with the President at Hyde Park

Although Roosevelt feared he would arouse isolationist opposition if he publicly stood for a policy of industrial aid for the European democracies, he hoped that he could persuade the majority of Americans to approve of his policy and was willing to wait until the proper time to announce the policy to the public. Arthur Murray communicated Roosevelt's position to the leaders of Britain, but Prime Minister Chamberlain made no reply to Roosevelt's proposals until mid-December.

In contrast, Premier Daladier and his Air Minister welcomed the offer of aid which Roosevelt relayed through their official representative, Jean Monnet. Monnet had arrived in New York October 18 and the next day he secretly met with President Roosevelt at Hyde Park. His recollections of that meeting closely parallel Murray's account of Roosevelt's thoughts and plans. The Frenchman remembered that, not quite a month after the Munich settlement, the President, like Premier Daladier, foresaw that Hitler would probably turn to war to take the territory he wanted. Roosevelt also talked with Monnet about developing aviation production by creating assembly plants in Canada. In comparing the relative strengths of the world's air forces, he gave Monnet the same figures which he gave Arthur Murray a few days later. The President jotted them down on a scratch pad and Monnet took the President's notes of these figures as a memento.[19] Ac-

---

on the Hudson, October 16th to 24th, 1938—Note handed to P.M., December 14, 1938," located in Elibank Papers.

[19] Monnet gave this account to the author in July 1961. He also stated that Roosevelt granted his request for the piece of scratch paper upon which the President had jotted down these production figures. This bit of documentary evidence, together with Monnet's other papers of this period, were destroyed during the German occupation of France.

cording to what Bullitt later told the Secretary of the Treasury, "the President had been most frank with Monnet; [and] . . . he had drawn a map and shown him just where outside of Montreal this plant should be located." He also talked of the plants to be built across from Detroit and across from Niagara Falls. Three plants, each on eight-hour shifts, could turn out 1,700 planes a year, and at this rate it would be possible to produce 5,000 planes a year by working three shifts.[20] Roosevelt arranged for Monnet and Bullitt to talk with Morgenthau in Washington about obtaining American planes, and on Saturday, October 22, the two men dined at the Secretary's home. Morgenthau again raised questions about France's gold reserves necessary for the purchase of planes from the United States. When Monnet estimated that an order of 1,700 planes would cost $85 million, the Secretary of the Treasury replied, "To my knowledge it is *impossible* for the French Treasury to find $85 million a year in foreign exchange." He pointed out that during the past four years "at least $4 billion of gold has left France" and that under such conditions "there isn't any use of talking about building airplanes or anything else."

The three men explored ways of getting around this formidable obstacle. Finally Morgenthau outlined an answer:

> If the French Government had the courage to put through decrees whereby they would make their citizens bring back their money or put them in jail, I say that overnight you would have such a change in your domestic situation it would be hard to even realize it.

[20] Morgenthau notes of October 24, 1938, on his dinner with Monnet and Bullitt on October 22, 1938, Morgenthau Diary, Bk. 147, pp. 185–88.

> . . . I am sure the American Government would assist you locate this money. I am sure the British would do the same. . . . You might have to put 1,000 people in jail.

The Secretary then outlined "what Bullitt said was an absolute stroke of genius": Prime Minister Daladier, under the cloak of the Tripartite Financial Agreement between France, Britain, and the United States, should announce government supervision of foreign exchange and issue decrees which would "make it a jail offense not to bring your money back." Morgenthau noted, "Both Mr. Monnet and Mr. Bullitt were beside themselves with joy over this suggestion." As they parted that evening, the Secretary stated, "Mr. Monnet, if you don't do something like this, your country is through." [21]

The Franco-American search to recover foreign exchange to finance French purchase of American planes during the fall of 1938 is well documented in Morgenthau's diaries, and this information throws new light on the French effort to buy planes.

From the meeting on October 22 until Monnet departed for France at the end of the month, the French representative worked with the United States Treasury Department in seeking ways to distinguish between French flight capital and legitimate French investments abroad. The Treasury Department and Monnet concluded that during the past five years $1 billion "appears to have come to the United States directly from France" and at least half was identified as "hot money." Morgenthau stated that the United States, under its Trading with the Enemy Act, could require foreigners and their agents to

[21] *Ibid.*

disclose to France ownership of all property located in the United States and thus facilitate recovery of this "hot money." Monnet and the Treasury then drafted an agreement by which Britain and France, as members of the Tripartite Agreement, could further meet the threat of "the unrestricted movement of 'flight capital' [which] hangs at present like a Damoclean sword." [22]

Five days before Monnet sailed for France, Bullitt wrote out a brief report for France's Air Minister:

> As I said to you by telephone, Monnet has been received by President Roosevelt and Secretary Morgenthau, who offered complete and close cooperation in studying the program of which we spoke in Paris.
>
> In the course of long and frank conversations, which took place in my presence, certain questions have been raised which are of such importance and which open the way so constructively that Monnet will take the first boat to inform you and Premier Daladier.
>
> I have the greatest hope that the work you have initiated will not only end with the accomplishment of your program but will also greatly reinforce France and La Paix.
>
> I send this letter with Monnet so he can give it to you personally.[23]

[22] Memo from Hermann Oliphant to Morgenthau, October 27, 1938; memo prepared by White and original given to Monnet October 29, 1938; note drafted October 29, 1938, by Monnet and two Treasury officials, Bernstein and White; memo dated October 29, 1938, with note at top "Given to Monnet," Morgenthau Diary, Bk. 148, pp. 94–96, and 193–201.

[23] Bullitt to La Chambre, October 25, 1938, La Chambre Papers, "Commandes Américaines," Doc. no. 10.

The second paragraph gains substance in the light of Morgenthau's proposal to recover the capital which had fled France since 1934.

Monnet departed for France on October 30 carrying a letter of introduction from Morgenthau to Merle Cochran, the Treasury's representative in the American Embassy in Paris, who was instructed to extend to Monnet "every courtesy and furthermore I wish that you would cooperate with him fully." Cochran had already been requested in a cable on October 29, which the President had approved, to take an initial step: "Ask Daladier to see you alone at his home without letting any French or British official know. . . . Monnet has seen the President and myself and is carrying a very important and secret message relating to the French financial situation." [24]

Morgenthau's message found the French Premier in a cabinet crisis over France's troubled finances. The Finance Minister, Paul Marchandeau, argued for strict government action and his proposed methods for the recovery of flight capital paralleled Morgenthau's thinking, but on November 1 pressure within the cabinet forced Marchandeau to resign from the Finance Ministry. The Premier appointed Paul Reynaud in his place.[25]

When Monnet arrived in Paris on November 4, he found Daladier keenly interested in adopting Morgenthau's exchange-control plan. The Premier regretted that "he had not received [details] earlier. . . . Marchandeau would probably not have gone." Now it was expected that Reynaud would probably follow "an orthodox method."

[24] Letter from Morgenthau to Cochran, October 26, 1938, and telephone conversation between Morgenthau and Roosevelt, October 29, 1938, Morgenthau Diary, Bk. 148, pp. 22 and 183–84.

[25] Telephone conversation between Cochran and Morgenthau October 31, 1938, memo by Morgenthau on conversation with Roosevelt, October 31, 1938, *Ibid.*, Bk. 148, pp. 186–89 and 297–99.

The next few days proved the validity of that expectation, although "Monnet had the impression . . . Daladier would push the matter through even if Reynaud had to be thrown out and Daladier himself take over the portfolio of Minister of Finance." Despite Monnet's continual activities in support of a tripartite exchange control and Cochran's assurances of U.S. support, the die had already been cast when Marchandeau resigned. By November 9 Morgenthau had caught the drift of affairs in Paris. Reynaud's determination to "ride an entirely liberal horse" with his new financial decrees sabotaged Morgenthau's effort to help recover France's flight capital through French controls and Anglo-American cooperation. The chance of tapping this capital to finance extensive purchases of American planes was doomed.[26]

Monnet was, however, able to report on the availability of American planes. His formal report was dated November 14, but upon his arrival in France he gave Premier Daladier and La Chambre a verbal summary of the three purposes of his mission. His report was based on information provided him by the United States Navy's Bureau of Aeronautics. The Frenchman gained access to this source through Secretary Morgenthau, who had turned him over to the Treasury's Procurement Division on October 24. Since 1937 this division had acted as the chief purchasing agent for the government and, as Morgenthau later noted, the Procurement Division "had the special facilities and experience for supervising such sales [to France]." [27] The head of the division was Rear Admiral Christian Joy Peoples, a retired naval officer, and his assistant was Captain

[26] See Cochran's detailed report to Morgenthau of events from November 4–10, dated November 17, 1938, *Ibid.,* Bk. 151, pp. 134–99.

[27] Henry Morgenthau, "The Morgenthau Diaries, IV, The Story Behind Lend Lease," *Collier's,* October 18, 1947, p. 17.

Harry E. Collins. These officials turned to their fellow naval officers in the Bureau of Aeronautics, who had already cooperated several weeks earlier with the French Navy in arranging trial flights in American planes and were willing to aid Monnet's mission.[28]

Monnet outlined his purpose to Captain John H. Towers, the second in command of the Bureau of Aeronautics, and Captain Sydney M. Kraus, in charge of naval aircraft purchases: "The French and British Governments had been compelled to accept the terms of the Munich Agreement solely because of the preponderant strength of the German air force . . . both the French and British Government realized further demands could be expected from Germany." As a result both were determined to increase vastly their air strength. Because "the French aircraft industry was in a lamentable state, the French Government desired to establish a source of supply for aircraft on the North American continent" and in view of the Neutrality Act it was considering Canadian assembly plants. At Monnet's request, Towers and Kraus estimated costs and quantities of planes that France could purchase. At later meetings Captain Kraus furnished "more detailed but non-confidential information on existing types." [29]

[28] See memo for the Assistant Secretary of the Navy from Admiral Arthur B. Cook, Chief Bureau of Aeronautics, Subject: "French: Monnet's Mission," January 30, 1939, Navy Department File, Bureau of Aeronautics General Correspondence, 1922–1944, France, EF 28/A 21 confidential, National Archives, Record Group 72. See also the telephone conversation between Morgenthau and Admiral Peoples, October 24, 1938, Morgenthau Diary, Bk. 147, pp. 252–53; letters from Admiral Kraus to the author, January 19, 1962, and February 2, 1963; and Blum, *Morgenthau Diaries,* vol. II, pp. 46–47.

[29] Memo for the Assistant Secretary of Navy from Admiral Cook, Subject: "French: Monnet's Mission," January 30, 1939, Navy Department File, Bureau of Aeronautics . . . France, EF 28/A 21.

Monnet based his report of November 14 upon the figures which Captain Kraus had supplied. American aircraft capacity, Monnet wrote, would be able to produce planes at an annual rate of 500–750 bombers and 500–750 pursuits. "With certain but not extensive argumentation [this] can be raised to 1,000 to 1,200 bombers and 1,000 to 1,200 pursuits." If orders were placed before the end of 1938, deliveries could begin as follows:

April 1939	100
May–July	650, or 215 per month
August–October	750, or 250 per month
November–December	600, or 300 per month
January–February 1940	400

This would total 2,500 planes by early 1940, and make a sizable contribution to France's air power. Even more tempting was the final note: "Under special conditions, by July 1939, 700 bombers and 700 pursuits would be available." To accomplish this goal Monnet recommended that orders be placed only with those frame and engine companies which had their own designs already in production. Then, repeating a major proposal of the "Notes" filed with the Air Minister in the past spring, he stated that "only existing American models should be selected and limited to one or perhaps two for the bombers and the pursuits." Monnet urged that "this phase of the program must be expedited, not only because it offers the earliest source of additional high performance airplanes, but also because the production would be in a form most exposed to export restrictions" if the United States should be required to invoke the Neutrality Act against belligerent France.

As "an insurance against an eventual interruption of

deliveries" from the United States, Monnet proposed constructing Canadian facilities for future deliveries. With three labor shifts, these plants should produce 2,500 planes a year, but during peacetime they could operate on a provisional basis, producing only 6 planes a week, or 300 planes a year. The plants would receive from the United States "partially or fully fabricated individual parts, rough or semi-finished casting and forgings, wire tubing, etc." Two units for assembling frames were suggested and either one or two for engines and propellers. The costs of these Canadian assembly plants would run about $20 million to $25 million and they should be located across from Buffalo and across from Detroit to facilitate the hiring of trained American labor.

The final section of Monnet's report dealt with technical assistance from American firms in establishing plants in Canada and France. "American cooperation is particularly important for the manufacture of motors," and it was recommended that both Pratt and Whitney as well as Curtiss-Wright engines be produced in France. Because of the problem of shifting from inches to metric measurements, there would be a "need of considerable notice," and even if plants were rapidly constructed in France, there would still be a 12-to-14 month delay in production.[30]

Monnet's aviation report and Secretary Morgenthau's offer to cooperate with France in foreign exchange control must have been cheering for Daladier and La Chambre, since both men believed that France was unable to expand her aircraft production on her own. Monnet's evidence of American support must have been specially welcome considering the heavy attacks the French press had been mak-

[30] "Memorandum," signed by Jean Monnet, dated November 14, 1938, La Chambre Papers, "Commandes Américaines," Doc. no. 6.

ing upon their government's program for aerial rearmament.[31] Frances' editors agreed that the weakness of the French Air Force was largely responsible for their nation's backdown at Munich. One voice in the press, Pierre Cot, argued that if France had developed her military alliances with Britain and the Soviet Union, by now their combined aerial fleets would more than balance the Luftwaffe.[32] But Cot's opinion found little support, since editors from Left and Right called for domestic expansion of French aircraft production, although they differed in how to achieve it.

On the Right, F. O. Frossard of *L'Homme Libre* called for immediate production of 5,000 planes, or doubling Plan V's timetable.[33] Other Rightist editors expressed their opinions of the causes for France's weakness: (1) the lack of mass production facilities; (2) the confusion caused by the nationalization of airframe producers; (3) the administrative red tape which created the time lag between the planning stage and production stage; and (4) labor's refusal to make a patriotic contribution to the rearmament effort by forbidding slowdowns and giving up opposition to a work week of more than forty hours.[34] Leftists, led by the former Premier Léon Blum, joined the Right in discrediting Pierre Cot's opinion that France possessed sufficient planes. Blum called for an increase in the Air

[31] For La Chambre's reaction to these press attacks, see *Événements,* vol. II, p. 322.

[32] *L'Oeuvre,* Cot, "La Lutte Aérienne," October 7, 1938, p. 1.

[33] *L'Homme Libre,* October 13, 1938, p. 1. See also *L'Air,* Laurent-Eynac, "Vers le Plan des 5,000," November 1, 1938.

[34] *Le Figaro,* Philippe Roland, October 15, 17, and 20, 1938. Roland amplified this campaign with his pamphlet, *La Crise de matérial de l'aviation militaire française* (Paris, Societé d'études d'informations économiques, November 1938). See also *La République,* Emile Roche, October 18, 19, and 21, 1938; *Le Matin,* Stéphane Lauzane, October 21, 1938; *La Liberté,* Paul Marion, October 19, 1938.

Ministry's budget at the expense of the Navy, and an editor for communist-daily *L'Humanité* denied that labor had obstructed production by demanding the forty-hour week.[35]

Of all the voices speaking out, few urged turning to the United States for aid. One, Senator La Grange, who had taken the lead in proposing such action during the past winter, used *Le Journal,* on October 21, 1938, to reiterate his campaign. In turn, Henri de Kerillis of *L'Epoque* called for the purchase of 2,000 to 3,000 American planes. The aviation editor of *L'Intransigeant,* Peyronnet de Torres, limited his demand to American motors. In his estimation French airframes matched any produced by foreign industry, but France lacked engines of adequate horsepower.[36] In his series, "Des Avions, Des Avions," de Torres provided the most balanced analysis of the air situation in France. Critical of many aspects, he exhibited a definite respect for the work of the Air Minister, Guy La Chambre, who, in de Torres' estimation, was a "réalisateur." [37]

La Chambre, recognizing the support he had received from *L'Intran*'s editor, promised foreign purchases if the French motor industry could not meet the production of airframes.[38] In a conversation with *Le Petit Parisien,* France's most widely circulated daily, La Chambre reviewed the progress which had been made on Plan V

[35] *Le Populaire,* Léon Blum, October 19, 20, and 21, 1938; *L'Humanité,* P. L. Darnar, October 20, 1938; see also *Le Temps,* October 24, 1938, p. 3, for an account of the press conference held by the Metal Workers Union.

[36] *L'Epoque,* de Kerillis, October 20, 1938, p. 1; *L'Intransigeant,* de Torres, October 20, 1938, p. 3.

[37] *L'Intransigeant,* de Torres, "Des Avions, Des Avions," October 15, 16, 17, 18, 19, 20, 21, and 22, 1938.

[38] *Ibid.,* October 22, 1938.

between April 1 and September 1, 1938. He reported that 240 planes had been turned out, but he did not admit that only 17 were modern types. He stated that by the beginning of 1939, if sufficient credits were granted, the new techniques and methods would begin to pay off with a production raised to 200 a month. Production would be increased to 400 a month by July 1939.[39] After this interview, the journals relaxed their campaign.

The Air Minister knew that France's problems were not solved and even a production rate of 400 per month by mid-1939 would not balance the German planes. Thus Monnet's report that more than 1,000 war planes were obtainable from the United States by July 1939 must have cheered La Chambre.

Five days after Monnet's return to France, La Chambre convened a conference of his closest advisers within the Air Ministry "to determine what modern material will be available next spring—taking into account the President of the Council's desire for a better situation than last September." General Vuillemin responded. "If we have then the material planned for Plan V, this will be all that is necessary to equip the personnel available to the Army of the Air." A review of the production figures revealed that by the first of June France would have on hand 1,305 of the latest type of plane, of which 775 would be single-seat fighters, and 300 Potez 63s, the two-seated command fighters. The remainder were bombers, but of these some 150 were obsolete Bloch 131s. When the Minister asked Vuillemin, "Can the Air Army assure the defense of the country with these planes?" the General replied, "*Petitement.*" La Chambre then reported that Premier Dala-

[39] *La Petit Parisien,* Charles Morice, October 21, 1938. This daily had a circulation of some two million.

dier was thinking of buying planes in the United States and he asked Vuillemin what should be bought. The General advised bombers and reconnaissance planes.[40] Vuillemin's preferences reflected the difficulties which the Air Ministry faced in bringing into production these two types of planes. Despite the optimistic predictions for the Amiot 351, one of two light bombers, the company had run into production snags and no deliveries had been made. The other light bomber, the Breguet 690, was progressing on schedule, but no deliveries were expected before February 1939. In contrast, French assembly lines for fighters appeared to be developing satisfactorily toward meeting France's needs after March 1939.

Monnet's report that France could receive 700 bombers and 700 pursuits from the United States by the next July must have given the Air Minister and Premier Daladier more confidence in France's situation when they met with the British Prime Minister on November 24. Chamberlain was still concerned about France's air power and now the French Premier could project that his nation's aircraft production would be at 400 a month by the coming spring. He told Chamberlain that he hoped to purchase 1,000 American planes to strengthen France's defenses.[41]

At home Daladier and La Chambre still faced opposi-

[40] Minutes of a conference on November 9, 1938, between La Chambre, his Chef de Cabinet Militaire, General Bouscat, his Chef de Cabinet Civil, Roger Hoppenot, the Chief of Staff for Air, General Vuillemin, the Directour Technique et Industriel, Inspecteur General Joux, and Roger Caquot, president of the National Societies which controlled the nationalized section of the aircraft industry. These minutes are filed with those of Comité de Matériel, Box B-104, Service Historique de l'Armée de l'Air, Versailles.

[41] Record of Anglo-French conversation held at Quai d'Orsay on November 24, 1938, *Documents on British Foreign Policy, 1919–1939,* Third Series, 3 vols. (London, 1950), (*BD*) vol. III, pp. 289–90. See also *FR, 1938,* vol. I, pp. 104–105.

tion—mainly from the new Finance Minister, Paul Reynaud—to their plans for ordering American bombers and pursuits. Reynaud had called for resistance during the Munich crisis, and he had just been brought into the government as a symbol of strength. Long a proponent of rearmament and of armed warfare, Reynaud now was limited by his search for a balanced budget and his slogan, "To defend the franc is to defend France." In addition, he had turned down Morgenthau's plan for a tripartite recovery of flight capital, putting the damper on France's recovery of the "hot money" which would be sufficient to cover the entire $180 million which Monnet estimated as the cost of the 700 bombers and 700 pursuits.

Confronted with this opposition, Daladier on December 5 called a meeting of the Permanent Committee of National Defense. The Premier opened by stating,

> We presently have the possibility of receiving about 1,000 American planes of the latest model in use in the American army. The American Government has formally promised delivery but it must be kept absolutely secret. The cost of 2,500 million francs is not available in any budget. As delay is impossible, immediate action is necessary.[42]

Reynaud replied that it would be impossible to get that sum from new sources, and that 80 per cent of the nation's budget was already going to the Ministry of National Defense. He suggested that the sum needed for American purchases be deducted from the regular defense budget,

[42] For minutes of this meeting, see General Maurice Gamelin, *Servir,* vol. II, pp. 371–78. Daladier discussed this conference in his testimony on May 21, 1947, *Événements,* vol. I, pp. 19–20. For La Chambre's testimony, see *Événements,* vol. II, p. 334.

and that the number of planes ordered from French factories should be reduced by 1,000.

The Minister for Air argued that 1,000 American planes would permit France to have an air strength by the middle of 1939 which it otherwise could not possess before 1940. He argued against reducing French production of planes. As it was, France could turn out by the end of 1939 only 2,000 planes, while to defend herself adequately she required 3,000. He noted that "the nervous time will be between June and October" and this was when France would need to supplement its adequate fighter production with reconnaissance planes and bombers. Daladier concluded the meeting, "Our aerial inferiority is tragic. 1,000 American planes are necessary. We want to see a total of 2,000 planes in France by August 1939. Bombers are of the utmost importance as they are an element which acts for peace." [43]

Despite the strong support Daladier and La Chambre received from the other members of the Defense Committee, the Finance Minister would not change his position. Thus Daladier decided to take funds from other sections of his Ministry of National Defense, and at last Reynaud gave his consent.

On December 9 Daladier, in the presence of Monnet and the Ministers of Finance and Air, stated that France would order 1,000 U.S. planes for delivery before the end of July 1939. The Premier underscored two important conditions: "the types and characteristics of the planes . . . correspond to those required by the French Govern-

[43] During his talk with Chamberlain on November 24, Daladier had explained why he believed a strong French bomber force would act as a deterrent against Hitler leading Germany to war. *BD,* vol. III, pp. 292–93.

ment and that no delay in deliveries whatsoever will be permitted." Obviously the military technicians were still skeptical as to whether American industry could turn out planes which, when delivered some eight to twelve months hence, would meet the requirements of Europe's air battles. If the planes were delivered by the end of July they would ease France through what La Chambre had called "the nervous time." This deadline was set also because it coincided with the date at which French production of bombers and fighters was scheduled to meet the requirements of Plan V. Finally, Monnet was authorized to establish a Canadian corporation to assemble American planes.

Daladier ordered Monnet to return to the United States and to take with him three technicians of the Air Ministry. Together they were to determine the models and quantities available and inform the Air Minister as soon as possible.[44] Although the second phase of French negotiations for American planes was finally under way, details of expanding American aircraft production had to be dealt with before France's search for planes could bear results.

[44] "Conference of the President of the Council, Minister for Air, Minister for Finance, Paris, December, 1938," La Chambre Papers, "Commandes Américaines," Hoppenot Mission File. This memorandum and the official orders for Monnet and his assistants erroneously cite October 14 as the date of the Monnet report.

CHAPTER

3

10,000 Planes for the United States

PRESIDENT ROOSEVELT saw that he must expand American aircraft production if he was to satisfy Jean Monnet's request for 1,000 planes, which the Frenchman made during his second visit to the United States, which began on December 16, 1938. On October 14, the day after he had talked with Ambassador Bullitt, Roosevelt outlined to Louis Johnson, in charge of procurement of material, his plans to increase plane output. Johnson, as Assistant Secretary of War, called on the Army Chief of Staff and the Chief of the Air Corps for advice. From then until mid-December 1938 when Monnet arrived, Roosevelt fought a losing battle to focus his nation's rearmament upon aircraft. His opposition came primarily from the military, who demanded a balanced program, pro-rated between ground and air forces.

Initially, the Air Corps had offered little assistance to the President in his drive for large numbers of planes. According to the Baker plan of 1935 the Air Corps was limited to producing a total of 2,360 planes by the end of June 1940, and by October 1938 1,970 planes were on hand.[1] On October 19, 1938, the new Chief of the Air Corps, General H. H. Arnold, proposed a long-range goal of 6,360 by 1944, but this meant adding only 1,000 planes each year to the number specified in the original Baker plan.[2]

President Roosevelt had hoped that Arnold would be sympathetic to his goal of 10,000 planes a year. The President expected resistance from the Secretary of War, Harry Woodring, because he had always been against a large air force. But he counted on less resistance from the Army officers. On October 18, when Roosevelt first told Secretary Morgenthau of his wish to expand American aircraft production to 15,000 a year, the President gave no hint that he foresaw opposition from the Army Chief of Staff, General Malin Craig. Enthusiastic about expanding the American Air Force, Morgenthau called General Craig as soon as he returned to Washington. The Chief of Staff's response showed he was against expansion:

> What are we going to do with 15,000 planes? What are you going to fight, what are you going to do with them, with three thousand miles of ocean? . . . You're going to have a lot more wooden ships, the way we had in the Navy during the War and never used them.

[1] *Army Air Forces in World War II,* vol. VI, *Men and Planes,* eds. W. F. Craven and J. L. Cate (Chicago, 1955), pp. 171–73.

[2] Chief of Air Corps (CAC) to Secretary of War (S/W), Oct. 19, 1938, Army Air Force (AAF) File, Document Collection of Air Force Library. See also Arnold memo for S/W October 22, 1938, Arnold Papers, Box 222, Subject file, 1938 Aircraft Production, and Mark S. Watson, *Chief of Staff: Prewar Plans and Preparations* (Washington, 1950), p. 134.

This reaction prompted Morgenthau "to go to school" with the Chief of the Air Corps to find out whether, as General Craig believed, "what is being told the President is impossible." [3]

On October 24 General Craig presented a statement to the Bureau of the Budget. In the statement, which dealt with the President's proposal for a $500 million rearmament appropriation, General Craig expanded his position:

> The defense of this country and of any country, ultimately rests with the ground troops. . . . We need a further increase in air power . . . but the deplorable situation of our ground army, for the first year of war, demands more immediate attention. . . .
>
> A vast air force with a large reserve of planes is prohibitively expensive [because of] rapid obsolescence, costly storage requirements and costly maintenance even for reserve planes. . . .
>
> . . . If we correct our Ordinance deficiencies we procure material of a relatively enduring nature involving a minimum of maintenance and storage costs and subject to practically no obsolescence under twenty-five years. . . .
>
> With a Europe aware of the fact that we have an efficient balanced force, adequately supplied with modern weapons, and a reserve available to carry us through initial losses until production can catch up with demand, we should be in no fear of threats or annoyance.

The Chief of Staff left no doubt that he sought "a program of balanced readiness in a sound order of priority." Point-

[3] Staff conference, October 20, 1938, Morgenthau Diary, Bk. 146, pp. 279–94.

ing out that the United States was protected by two oceans and so could not be as seriously threatened by bombing attack as the European powers were, he reasoned that the United States did not need to concentrate upon aerial defense.[4]

General Craig had the support of his newly appointed Deputy Chief of Staff, General George C. Marshall. Marshall believed that if the European situation after the Munich settlement threatened the United States, and he thought it did, then any rearmament expenditures should follow the Army's Protective Mobilization Plan [PMP] of 1937, which pro-rated the expenditures between ground and air forces. In principle, Marshall did not oppose the expansion of the Air Corps (on October 25 Marshall approved an increase of 2,500 aircraft), but he did believe that the President's plan for 10,000 combat planes for the Air Corps appeared seriously out of proportion to what was needed. As one of Marshall's biographers has written, "The Deputy Chief of Staff had too lively an awareness of the total military weakness of the United States in relation to its potential enemies to accept the President's simple thesis that combat planes alone could create an effective deterrent force." [5]

In contrast, the Chief of the Air Corps indicated that he was now ready to plan for an Air Corps larger than his military superiors believed feasible. On October 24 in

[4] "Priority of Requirements to Render the United States Defensively Impregnable during Mobilization," preliminary statement by Chief of Staff (C/S), October 24, 1938, to Director of Budget, Adjutant General File (AG) 580 (10–19–38), National Archives, Record Group 94.

[5] Forrest C. Pogue, *George C. Marshall,* vol. I, *Education of a General, 1880–1939* (New York, 1963), p. 334. See also Watson, *Chief of Staff,* pp. 134–35, note 30.

answer to "verbal orders" Arnold forwarded to the Assistant Secretary of War a

> brief outline of a plan whereby at maximum production the existing industry could produce 10,000 planes in approximately 2 years after receiving orders. The allocation of planes by type to manufacturer is based on facilities now available. . . . The output of each manufacturer is based on operation on a three shift basis.[6]

By October 25, Harry Hopkins had completed his survey for the President on expanding the aircraft industry. General Arnold's notes provide the only evidence of a meeting held at the Treasury which focused on Hopkins' findings. According to the notes, the United States was to try to get an additional 35,000 to 40,000 planes, a goal which the President had cited for the British Air Attaché in late September. The Navy would have 2,000 to 4,000 planes and the Air Corps the remaining 31,000 to 36,000. It was estimated that half of the total could be obtained from the existing aircraft industry. Even though the industry was presently turning out only 2,600 planes a year, Hopkins optimistically predicted that some 20,000 a year could be attained if the industry worked on a three-shift basis and if types already in production were frozen. Hopkins projected a rate of plane production higher than that set by either Captain Kraus in his report to Monnet or the Chief of the Air Corps in his October 24 memo.

Arnold's record of the conference further reveals Hopkins' plans for expanding American aircraft-production

[6] Memo from CAC for Assistant Secretary of War (ASW), October 24, 1938, Arnold Papers, Box 222, Subject file, 1938 Aircraft Production.

facilities for an additional 20,000. Eight to ten new plants would be built at government expense and they would be operated by the War Department. The location of these plants would be subject to War Department's approval, and consideration would be given to labor availability, raw material supply, and proximity to experienced manufacturing facilities. No new facilities were to be constructed near Pittsburgh, Chicago, or Denver, but rather near cities such as Boston which suffered from unemployment more seriously.[7]

On the strength of the report Hopkins gave on October 25, President Roosevelt appointed the Assistant Secretary of War, Louis Johnson, the Assistant Secretary of the Navy, Charles Edison, and a Deputy Administrator of Hopkins' Works Progress Administration, Aubrey Williams, to study ways to increase military aircraft production. Within three days, the committee called for the aircraft industry to raise its production by using three shifts and by freezing the designs they had for the standard types, a recommendation that showed that much advanced planning had been done. The committee believed that the existing production facilities could raise their annual output from 2,600 to 11,000. The committee also recommended building government plants which would turn out an additional 20,000 planes over the next three years for a grand total of 30,000.[8]

The secrecy surrounding these plans was broken on November 6 when *The New York Times* reported that

[7] Arnold's rough and undated notes are written on the reverse of a letter written to him by Lieutenant Colonel George S. Warren, Air Corps, Chief of Finance, dated October 25, 1938. *Ibid.*

[8] Report from Assistant Secretary of Navy, Assistant Secretary of War, and Williams of WPA to President, October 28, 1938, AG 580 (10–19–38).

President Roosevelt was prepared to ask Congress for a "vast air fleet" of from 7,000 to 10,000 planes which would "at least triple the Air Corps' [Baker] goal of 2,320 set in 1935." In addition, Roosevelt would seek full war equipment for a ground army of 400,000. The total cost of this rearmament was estimated to be more than $300 million.[9]

On November 10 the Chief of the Air Corps sent to the Assistant Secretary of War a further estimate of what the military was coming to call "the numbers racket," the quantity of planes needed for the Air Corps. Arnold proposed that the two-year objective for the Army's Protective Mobilization Plan be set at 7,000, of which 2,000 were already in hand. The 7,000 planes would be divided between combat and training types and be backed by an annual production rate of 10,000. Arnold went on to propose that two-thirds of the 7,000 planes be placed on active status and one-third in reserve to replace war losses. The Chief of the Air Corps also forwarded "a method of securing in the shortest space of time [the new] 5,000 planes." Encouraged by response to letters that he wrote to all aircraft producers on October 14, the General predicted these 5,000 could be obtained within eighteen months to two years if existing plants were worked to a maximum. Arnold noted the surplus capacity: "about half of the Glenn Martin production was utilized and nothing was being purchased from Brewster or Grumman."

Arnold sent another memo to Johnson on his "personal ideas of an objective for the Air Force." The General underlined "the need for the President [to call] a special council of land, air, sea forces, State Department and

[9] *The New York Times,* November 6, 1938, p. 1, col. 2; October 16, 1938, p. 31, col. 1, and October 18, 1938, p. 1, col. 2.

industry [in order] to determine the size of each force." He noted what he estimated to be the current military threat to the United States, "Germany has 2,000 bombers with a range of 3,300 miles and so might cross the Atlantic, but this requires bases on the west coast of Africa." He cited Germany's total air strength at about 10,000. Britain had set an objective of 4,000 fighting planes on hand and an annual production rate of 3,500. Italian strength was rated at about 4,000 and production at 2,100 per year. Russian strength was listed at 6,000. The Chief of the Air Corps concluded by repeating his goal of 7,000, two-thirds active and one-third reserve, with a 10,000 production rate.[10]

Arnold's proposal for "a special council" may have prompted Roosevelt to call together his closest civilian advisers on aircraft production—Hopkins, Louis Johnson, and Morgenthau. In the conference held on November 12, the President approved of Hopkins' proposed eight to ten factories to be erected with WPA funds, but Roosevelt suggested that only two operate at a rate of 2,000 combat types a year, leaving the other plants on a standby basis. Roosevelt now set total production at 10,000, which later led Morgenthau to observe, "Every time I have talked to the President the number he has in mind has become less," but the Secretary was encouraged because Roosevelt's earlier goals had seemed unrealistic. Discussion turned to ways to obtain "in the shortest space of time" the 5,000 new planes which the Chief of the Air Corps had just recommended.[11]

On November 14, the President had Hopkins, Johnson,

[10] Memo from CAC for ASW, November 10, 1938, both in AAF File, Document Collection of the Air Force Library.

[11] Blum, *Morgenthau Diaries,* vol. II, p. 47.

Morgenthau, Colonel James H. Burns, who was Johnson's executive assistant, Herman Oliphant, who was Morgenthau's General Counsel, and Solicitor General Robert H. Jackson, who was marked as the next Attorney General, meet with General Arnold, General Malin Craig, and his Deputy, George C. Marshall. The President used this occasion primarily to dissuade Craig and Marshall from their insistence upon a balanced rearmament plan and convince them of the validity of constructing air power with which to influence Hitler. Records of the President's remarks at this conference by General Arnold and by Secretary Morgenthau provide a clear account of the President's thoughts and plans.[12]

Arnold noted Roosevelt's basic argument for the necessity of a large mass of planes and productive capacity: "a well-rounded ground army of even 400,000 could not be considered a deterrent for any foreign power whereas a heavy striking force of aircraft would." The President added a point which appealed particularly to the Chief of the Air Corps, who had strongly sponsored the Flying Fortress: "[Roosevelt] stated long range bombing is now the duty of the Army" and it was up to the Air Corps "to keep anyone from landing in North or South America . . . the United States must be prepared to resist attack on all the Western Hemisphere and to deter landing in either North or South America. We must not be caught napping again as in 1917."

[12] In his memoirs, *Global Mission* (New York, 1949), p. 178, Arnold erroneously cites this meeting as having been held on September 28, 1938. This date appears on Arnold's original notes but appears to have been penciled in after they were written. The General's memorandum on the meeting, written the day after it was held, uses November 14. Arnold also erred in his memoirs by reporting Admiral Stark, The Chief of Naval Operations, as being in attendance.

Roosevelt estimated current strength and the productive capacity of the foreign powers and he used figures a good deal more refined than he had cited some three weeks previously at Hyde Park for Murray and Monnet. Germany had 10,000 planes, of which 7,500 were first line, and possessed a productive capacity for 12,000; Britain had a first-line strength of from 1,500 to 2,200 and a capacity for 4,800, whereas France possessed less than 600 planes that could be put in the air and a capacity for 3,600. The President believed the United States should turn out 20,000 late-model planes, but he explained he was sufficiently realistic to settle for a two-year goal of 10,000, backed by an annual productive capacity of 10,000.

According to Arnold's notes, the President then repeated plans for the construction of 10,000 planes for the Air Corps which he had drawn up with Hopkins and Johnson. Of these 8,000 could be turned out in two years by existing private industry. He believed the United States "must have more plants . . . sufficient to bring annual capacity to 20,000" and he recommended that the government construct seven plants with WPA funds. Roosevelt still wanted only two of the new plants to be put into operation and for them to turn out 1,200 planes a year. The President urged that, to achieve as rapid production as possible, plane designs be frozen for the next two years.

At Louis Johnson's request, Roosevelt broke down the 10,000 planes for the Air Corps to 2,500 trainers, 3,750 combat planes on active duty, and 3,750 on reserve. The President added that he planned to ask Congress for a supplementary budget to initiate the program and, recalling Arnold's memo of November 10, he "figured 5,000 planes would be a good figure . . . to start with." Ultimately, he would seek $2 billion for national defense.[13]

Secretary Morgenthau's notes on the November 14 White House meeting provide further insights into the President's thinking. After Roosevelt cited the figures of European plane production and spelled out his goal of 10,000 for the United States,

> [He] then pointed out that the recrudescense of German power at Munich had completely reoriented our own international relations; that for the first time since the Holy Alliance in 1818 the United States now faced the possibility of an attack on the Atlantic side in both the Northern and Southern Hemispheres.

The President explained that he remained unconvinced by the Army's demands for a balanced rearmament program because Germany's growth of power "demanded our providing immediately a huge air force so that we do not need to have a huge army to follow that air force. Sending a large army abroad was undesirable and politically out of the question." Roosevelt emphasized that the United States would not be given a "period of grace" such as the thirteen months it had in 1917 "to put the first battle plane on the battle front in Europe." Therefore, he insisted, "we must have resources, plans and equipment for putting a large number of planes into actual operation at any time on short notice."

Morgenthau recorded the President's second, and in his opinion "significant," reason why he called for such a large number of planes:

[13] For Arnold's original notes on the back of a manila folder, see Arnold Papers, Miscellaneous Correspondence, 1938. For his full report dated November 15, see AAF File, Document Collection of the Air Force Library. Watson in his *Chief of Staff*, pp. 136–38, used only Arnold's notes.

> I am not sure now that I am proud of what I wrote to Hitler, September 27, 1938 in urging that he sit down around the table and make peace. That may have saved many, many lives now, but that may ultimately result in the loss of many times that number of lives later. When I write to foreign countries I must have something to back up my words. Had we had this summer 5,000 planes and the capacity immediately to produce 10,000 per year, even though I might have had to ask Congress for authority to sell or lend [*sic*] them to the countries in Europe, Hitler would not have dared to take the stand he did.[14]

Roosevelt wondered how to alert the public to the need of building American air strength. He suggested that at the next day's press conference he would announce the aeronautical strengths of Germany and Italy and of Britain and France. Secretary Morgenthau thought this a grave mistake because it would provide complete justification for Prime Minister Chamberlain's appeasement policies. If those figures were to be released, they should come from Europe.[15] But Roosevelt's idea of wanting large numbers of planes "to sell or lend" to Britain and France was received favorably by those at the meeting.[16] George Marshall was the only person who outspokenly disagreed with Roosevelt's policies.[17]

The day after the White House meeting the Assistant Secretary of War, who supported a balanced armed force,

[14] For the above selections from Morgenthau's notes, see Blum, *Morgenthau Diaries,* vol. II, pp. 48–49.

[15] Morgenthau's notes on White House conference November 14, 1938, Morgenthau Diary, Bk. 150, pp. 337–42.

[16] For this conclusion by Colonel Burns, see Watson, *Chief of Staff,* pp. 132–33 and 138–39.

[17] Pogue, *Marshall,* vol. I, p. 323.

requested that General Craig submit estimates of costs for raising plane strength to 10,000, with half on active duty and half on reserve. In addition, costs were requested for the construction of seven aircraft plants with an annual capacity of 1,200. Johnson also asked for a two-year estimate of "essential supplies to equip and maintain the Protection Mobilization Plan Army until production is adequate." [18]

On December 1 the President received a four-point proposal from the Chief of Staff covering these rearmament expenses in excess of the regular fiscal budget for 1940. The total reached some $2 billion. The first and largest item covered a two-year air program for $1.28 billion. More than half of this was allocated to 8,030 new planes, which, with the planes on hand, would raise the Air Corps to 10,000. There was $561 million scheduled for the operation of 50 per cent of this force; the rest would be held in reserve. Another $42 million was set aside for the construction of seven government aircraft factories. The second item was lumped under PMP and totaled $421 million. The third item, for $122 million, would accelerate industrial mobilization, though, as the proposal estimated, "not more than half these sums will be needed the first year." Finally, the Chief of Staff recommended the increase of the Regular Army's ground forces by 58,000 men and the National Guard by 35,000, for a two-year cost of $272 million.[19]

At a meeting on December 10 with the War Department, the President reacted against the Army's four-point

[18] ASW to C/S, November 15, 1938, Arnold Papers, Box 2, Arnold Miscellaneous Correspondence 1938. See also Watson, *Chief of Staff*, p. 139.

[19] ASW memo for the President, December 1, 1938, AG 580 (10–19–38).

proposal. As a result the Assistant Secretary of War immediately requested the Chief of Staff to send up "a justification of the program as submitted to the White House." [20]

Seventeen days later, a fourteen-page memorandum from the Chief of Staff provided the justification. It began,

> Democracy in Europe has weakened before the aggressive tactics of the combined dictatorships. These latter states are penetrating economically and politically into Central and South America. The United States has announced its intention of defending the Western Hemisphere against aggression. . . .
>
> The above developments have greatly increased the requirements for national defense. . . . The Army we have today is far below the strength contemplated by the National Defense Act. . . . At present it is actually not a serious threat to potential enemies.

The memo then repeated the planned expansion of its earlier four-point program, and it went on to argue,

> The requirements set up under the four categories cannot logically be considered separately, but . . . as one indivisible whole.
>
> Air forces are subject to destruction unless their bases are adequately protected by ground forces. . . . All the proposed increases look forward toward . . . a balanced Army. . . .

In the section devoted to air power the memo argued,

> Airplanes will not impress foreign leaders and their general staffs. The absence or weaknesses in the other

[20] ASW memo for C/S, December 10, 1938, *Ibid.*

> two elements required to make an effective air force —facilities and skilled personnel—will be well known and accurarately evaluated by potential enemies. . . . Ultimate rejection of overseas enemies from the Western Hemisphere and the ultimate defense of our own territory rests with the ground forces. To neglect this component is to ignore every lesson of history. . . . The entire program must be considered as an integrated whole. . . . Weakness in any major part of this structure may cause the whole to collapse.[21]

The Chief of Staff backed up this justification with a final statement entitled "Two Year Augmentation Plan."[22] Despite the President's criticism, the Army had made no real modifications or concessions.

In addition to his inability to persuade the Army to give up the idea of a balanced force and concentrate upon aircraft expansion, Roosevelt conflicted with Arnold on how to balance the Air Corps. He wanted combat planes for the support of the European democracies, whereas Arnold maintained he needed training aircraft so he would have sufficient pilots to man the new combat planes. In late November, Arnold reduced the number of war planes in the original plan, which had called for a 10,000-plane air force. Instead of the 7,500 first scheduled, he set the figure at 5,625 and raised the number of trainers from 2,500 to 3,750. Next the General requested additional personnel to man the new planes and called for raising the officer corps from 2,250 to 10,600 and the enlisted men from 19,000 to 90,000.[23] Arnold, in an effort to

[21] C/S memo for ASW, December 17, 1938, *Ibid.*

[22] Watson, *Chief of Staff,* pp. 141–42.

[23] Memos CAC for C/S, November 18 and 28, 1938, AAF File, Major Lyons Project Book, "10,000 Plane Program."

build up a balanced air force, demanded not only planes but also productive capacity, pilots, mechanics, air bases, and an adequate training program. As the General later recalled,

> I had to give [that lesson] to Harry Hopkins, and through him, to the President. The President, though he was still primarily engrossed with the problem of sending planes and material to Britain and France, seemed to understand this.[24]

But the President did not arrive at this understanding easily, and he still resisted the demands by the military for a balance between the ground forces and the air forces. But by late November, when General John J. Pershing argued for a balanced military, Roosevelt had changed: "I am having the General Staff study the ground forces that are necessarily connected with increased air operations." [25]

After receiving the General Staff's "Two Year Augmentation Plan," the President called his military advisers back to the White House and "informed them sharply that, contrary to the confidence they were showing, it was extremely doubtful whether he could ask Congress for more than $500,000,000 in new armament money for the coming fiscal year." By now the Navy was asking for $100 million, the materiel branches of the Army were requesting $200 million for immediate outlay, and the Army's industrial education orders would require $33 million. Unstated amounts were being sought for air bases and pilot training. Roosevelt complained that he originally planned to devote the whole $500 million to aircraft and

[24] Arnold, *Global Mission,* p. 178.

[25] For the exchange of letters between Pershing and the President, see *F.D.R.: His Personal Letters, 1928–1945,* ed. Elliott Roosevelt (New York, 1950), vol. II, pp. 837–38. See also Pogue, *Marshall,* vol. I, p. 335.

that now "he was being offered everything except planes." [26]

At this conference the question was raised whether the United States could effectively use 10,000 combat planes before they became obsolete. The President retorted that if the Air Corps could not use that number, Britain's Royal Air Force could.[27] It is likely that it was at this time that the President argued, "he could not influence Hitler with barracks, runways and schools for mechanics." [28] At any rate after the President had completed his arguments against the War Department's "Two Year Augmentation Plan," the military launched "a careful and thorough discussion of the armed forces' low state and, more particularly, of the futility of producing planes over a long period without producing pilots and crews and air bases at an appropriate rate." It was probably at this time, as General Craig recounted, "the conversation became quite emphatic, and came very close to table pounding," and Marshall backed up his Chief of Staff with some blunt talking.[29] As a result, Roosevelt agreed to find the Navy's $100 million from some other source so that he could focus the $500 million on the Army. He agreed to allot $200 million of that sum to "non-air armaments." Of the remainder, he conceded $120 million for "air bases and other non-plane air items," but the President insisted that the final $180 million be spent only for combat planes "with which to impress Germany." [30]

[26] The account of the White House conference on the "Augmentation Plan" is drawn from the recollection of one of its participants, Colonel Burns, executive assistant to the Assistant Secretary of War, as recounted in Watson, *Chief of Staff*, pp. 142–43.

[27] William Frye, *Marshall: Citizen Soldier* (New York, 1947), p. 249.

[28] Arnold, *Global Mission*, pp. 178–80.

[29] Frye, *Marshall*, p. 250.

[30] Watson, *Chief of Staff*, pp. 142–43.

Roosevelt's plan to devote $500 million to complete 10,000 planes and to create an aircraft potential of twice that figure had been seriously trimmed. For fiscal year 1940 which began in June 1939, he could obtain military approval for only a $180 million supplement sufficient to finance only 3,000 new aircraft. The Air Corps recommended these new aircraft be both combat types and advanced trainers, but the President firmly insisted that they all be combat types and that the funds for trainers would come from some other source.[31] Roosevelt lost on this point as well, however, and the Air Corps was finally authorized to order only 1,593 combat types. These plus 1,425 trainers and 14 miscellaneous types came to a total of 3,032 new planes. The planes on hand and the ones on order would bring the number of Air Corps planes up to 5,500 by the end of 1940. In mid-January the Chief of the Air Corps achieved his balanced air force when $130 million of the $300 million scheduled for the Air Corps was diverted to construction and to increasing personnel. At that time he summed up his opinion for the Chief of Staff:

> The program indicated above and the breakdown of the $300 million as shown is sound and economical and can be efficiently executed. It provides the nucleus of a well-rounded air defense which would be wholly lacking if the whole $300 million were devoted to the procurement of planes.[32]

President Roosevelt also ran into trouble with his plan to use WPA funds to build standby factories for planes. On November 21, representatives from fourteen of the

[31] *Ibid.*, p. 143.
[32] CAC to C/S, January 13, 1939, AG 580 (10–19–38).

leading aircaft producers met at the War Department. They explained that they could produce even more than the 10,000 planes required if they were permitted to "operate according to the most efficient methods in their opinion." As the Chief of Staff was informed, "All seemed very fearful of the effect of the erection of plants for possible governmental operation." Particularly, they feared that their own expansion would be hampered because of the lack of trained management personnel and the bottleneck in skilled labor. Some of the industrialists saw that if they subcontracted components, their factories would become little more than assembly plants.[33]

Despite such reactions from private industry the President continued to explore the possibility of building standby plants. Original estimates set the cost at $8.7 million per plant producing 1,200 planes a year, but as this appeared too high a new study suggested working the plants on two shifts and thus cutting erection costs to $4.5 million. On November 23 the Assistant Secretary of War informed the President, "I am initiating action to construct plants utilizing WPA funds" and listed the seven cities where the plants would be.[34] Although Harry Hopkins approved, it soon became obvious that Congress would balk at using government funds to build aircraft facilities whose production might be for the immediate benefit of foreign countries. Congress was already critical of foreign purchase of American planes, fearing it might involve the United States in a foreign war as well as take materials out of the country when the United States Army

[33] Deputy C/S memo to C/S, November 21, 1938, *Ibid.*

[34] ASW memo for the President, November 23, 1938, Arnold Papers, Box 222, Subject File, Aircraft Production 1938, Planning 10,000 Plane Program.

and Navy needed them to rebuild their nation's defenses.[35] On December 21, General Craig was informed that the elimination of the proposed seven aircraft factories was being considered.[36]

By mid-December President Roosevelt's whole plan to create an arsenal for aircraft in the United States faced serious difficulties. He had been unable to get across to the military either his sense of urgency or his recognition that only vast numbers of planes might deter Hitler. By mid-December Roosevelt was further disappointed when Great Britain declared she would not assist in creating an aircraft industry in North America.

On December 14 Arthur Murray reported to the British Prime Minister the talks he had had in October with the American President. Chamberlain felt it "very encouraging indeed" to have the President's private assurance that Britain "would have the industrial resources of the American nation behind him." As to Roosevelt's statement, which he agreed to publish, "Great Britain could rely upon receiving raw materials from the democracies of the world," Chamberlain admitted,

> It might be most important. There is no question but that in certain circumstances a statement, which really brought it home that the vast resources of the United States would be behind Great Britain, might have a properly deterrent effect.

The Prime Minister was not sure it would influence Hitler, but, as Chamberlain said to Murray, "at any rate, a statement of this kind might certainly have a powerfully deter-

[35] Watson, *Chief of Staff,* p. 133.
[36] ASW memo to C/S, December 21, 1938, AG 580 (10–19–38).

rent effect on the rest of them and on the Army and make them do their best to put a brake on Hitler if his idea looked like bursting out."[37]

Murray's letter to Roosevelt did not give any indication that the Prime Minister had listened to his military advisers in the Air Ministry. On November 12, the Royal Air Force's Plans Branch recommended that orders be placed in the United States because, even if current types were not up to British standards, or produced in sufficient quantity, immediate orders would contribute toward developing the American aircraft industry in time of peace as a "sure and safe 'war potential.' "[38]

By late 1938, only one source of assistance remained for President Roosevelt's goal of 10,000 planes: France. On December 16, Monnet, on his second trip to Washington, reported to the Secretary of the Treasury that his nation had agreed to allot $65 million for the purchase of 1,000 of the latest American planes, to be delivered by July 1939.

[37] Letter from Murray to Roosevelt, December 15, 1938, in Elibank Papers, and quoted in part in Elibank, "Franklin Roosevelt," *Contemporary Review,* June 1955, pp. 366–67.

[38] "American Co-operation with Great Britain in the Event of War with Germany: The Neutrality Act and the War Debt Settlement." November 12, 1938, prepared by Plans Branch, Air Staff, kindly shown to the author by Air Marshal Sir John Slessor following an interview in June 1964. Slessor had been Chief of Plans for the British Air Staff in the fall of 1938.

CHAPTER

4

1,500 Planes a Year for France

BY THE END OF JANUARY 1939, France, through negotiations carried out by Jean Monnet, agreed to purchase 555 American planes.[1] Though 200 of these were Harvard trainers, the remainder were the latest combat models. But, most important for expanding the American arsenal, France signed options for future deliveries which by 1940 would amount to 1,500 planes a year. To reach that goal the French Government agreed for a second time to subsidize the expansion of the American aircraft industry. It extended to the Glenn L. Martin Company $2.25 million, a sum which until 1940 surpassed annual capital investment by the United States Government in its own aircraft industry.

Monnet and his three assistants returned to Washington

[1] Material in this chapter expands John McVickar Haight, Jr., "Les Négociations Relatives aux Achats d'Avions Américains par la France pendant la Période qui Précéda immédiatement la Guerre," *Revue d'Histoire de la Deuxième Guerre Mondiale,* No. 58, April 1965, pp. 1–34.

on December 16, 1938, confident of receiving Roosevelt's aid in their search for war planes. Monnet feared, however, that he would meet the Air Corps' opposition, as well as opposition from the isolationists. He knew that the Chief of the Air Corps, General H. H. Arnold, would be particularly opposed to any diversion of modern planes to France just when it appeared the Air Corps' new expansion program required full use of American capacity. Then too if the isolationists learned of the French mission they would use it as proof of Roosevelt's intentions to involve the United States in a European war.

To avoid stirring the isolationists and the Air Corps, Monnet and his assistants moved around Washington with such discretion that three weeks after their arrival one of their number boasted, "our presence until now is absolutely unknown to the reporters." [2] But on January 23 their success in maintaining secrecy exploded when a secret military plane crashed with Captain Paul Chemidlin, a French observer, on board. By this time, however, Monnet's mission had almost completed its negotiations, despite opposition from the Air Corps.

In his effort to keep his mission secret, Monnet had dealt directly with the Treasury Department, as he had done during October. Monnet's initial contact with the Secretary of the Treasury was hardly encouraging. In a meeting on December 16, attended also by Ambassador Bullitt, Monnet reported he was authorized to purchase 1,000 planes for delivery by the end of July 1939. Morgenthau's concern about France's ability to pay for these planes apparently was allayed by Monnet's announcement

[2] Roger Hoppenot in a personal letter to the Air Minister January 12, 1939, La Chambre Papers, "Commandes Américaines," Doc. no. 7.

that Daladier's government had already allocated the necessary $65 million. Nevertheless, the Secretary raised a new hurdle: the French mission must be cleared through the State Department. When Bullitt objected, the Secretary replied, "all avenues . . . are closed until Mr. Welles [the Under Secretary of State] gives me a green light." Morgenthau raised a second problem when Monnet reported that he planned to solicit loans in the United States for a Canadian corporation which France intended to establish for assembling American planes. The Secretary cited the Johnson Act, which forbade loans to governments which had defaulted on their debts from the last war.[3]

Roosevelt had not changed his mind about aiding the French, and on December 17 he officially informed Welles that Monnet's mission was approved. The President also placed Morgenthau in charge of all foreign orders for munitions and implements of war.[4]

Secretary Morgenthau summarized the situation for his staff some days later:

> Triple confidentially Monnet is back with an aviation commission and with the authority signed by Daladier, the Minister of Air and some third person. They wanted it kept secret and I said I wouldn't receive them unless Mr. Welles called me up and said it was alright [*sic*].
>
> Well, the President called up Welles Friday night and Welles called me, and they asked me to go ahead which we're doing. They want a thousand planes.

[3] Blum, *Morgenthau Diaries,* vol. II, p. 65. For original copy of Monnet's letter of authorization of December 9, 1938, see Morgenthau Diary, Bk. 172, p. 1.

[4] Langer and Gleason, *Challenge to Isolation,* p. 46.

They got the cash. They want them before the first of July and we'll help them all we can.

Of course I told them it all gets down to a question will the President tell them that they can really have the most recent planes. I mean if they buy the usual thing which is released, its not much good.

Morgenthau also reported that Monnet had said that American aviation companies were developing new planes for an Army Air Corps competition, but no orders had been placed as yet. Monnet hoped that his orders could be completed before Congressional appropriations would be available for the Air Corps' new planes.[5]

To help speed French orders the Secretary of the Treasury designated Captain Harry Collins of the Procurement Division as his special representative to deal with Monnet. The Navy again cooperated and on December 18 the Chief of Naval Operations, Admiral Leahy, detailed Captain Kraus, Chief of the Materiel Branch of the Navy's Bureau of Aeronautics, to assist the Procurement Division with the French as he had in October.[6] Collins and Kraus met three times with the French before any official notice was given to the War Department.[7] Even after the Air Corps' negative reaction, Collins and Kraus provided the French with information on the performances of the latest American planes, as well as with contacts with American

[5] Staff conference, December 20, 1938, Morgenthau Diary, Bk. 157, pp. 120–21.

[6] "The Diary of William D. Leahy, 1938," December 19, 1938. (The diary is held by the Manuscript Division, Library of Congress.)

[7] Memorandum by Arnold for Assistant Secretary of War, December 29, 1938, AAF File, 161, Special Papers Pertaining to French and Swedish contracts.

companies, and with a review of contracts, prices, and technical specifications. As the French noted, the American officials "never ceased aiding the mission with their experience throughout all the negotiations." [8]

Captains Collins and Kraus did not find the new French negotiations as routine as they had expected. The technical staff of the French Air Ministry had viewed Monnet's report in November with scepticism; fearing that unless new models would be available immediately, the planes which could be delivered by July 1939 would be obsolete by European standards. Daladier and La Chambre had recognized these fears on December 9, when they cautioned Monnet that "the types and characteristics of the planes . . . correspond to those required by the French Government."

Monnet had been sent off with three assistants: Roger Hoppenot, the Air Minister's civil chef de cabinet, who during the spring had been in charge of financial negotiations with Curtiss-Wright for the 100 P-36s which France had purchased, Colonel Mazer, an engeneur en chef, currently serving on the Air Ministry's Comité de Materiel as an assistant industrial and technical director, and Colonel Paul Jacquin who was selected directly from his command of France's single experimental squadron where he had first-hand experience with the latest French planes and with French aerial tactics. The latter two were obviously provided to be sure obsolete types were not ordered.

On December 17 Monnet and his assistants met with Captains Kraus and Collins, who, as the French later

[8] Final Report, Hoppenot Mission to America, La Chambre Papers, Hoppenot Mission File. Though the Air Ministry officially referred to the mission sent to the United States in December 1939 as the "Hoppenot Mission," M. Hoppenot in June 1961 requested the author to call it the "Monnet Mission."

reported, "together with only two or three leading people know of our presence." The French technicians stated their desire to obtain pursuit planes with a speed of 500 kmh (320 mph) and attack bombers which could match the pursuits then flying in Europe. To their chagrin they learned two days later what the technical staff of the French Air Ministry feared: there were no American planes then in production which could meet these standards. Obviously, the original plan to purchase 1,000 planes was out.[9]

Captain Kraus who was in charge of ordering all naval aircraft and well aware of the ratings of the American planes, immediately questioned the French data indicating the over-all superiority of Germany's latest planes, and was skeptical about French methods of conducting speed tests. Obviously, he had failed to recognize the inferiority of the planes being produced in the United States.[10] His questions and doubts, however, show that he had acted in good faith when he told Monnet in October that the United States could probably produce 1,000 to 1,500 planes before July 1939.

If Kraus and his fellow naval officers were unsure of the comparative strength of American planes, the War Department was even more confused. In the Secretary of

[9] For these initial meetings, see the letter from Hoppenot to La Chambre, January 12, 1939, and Final Report, La Chambre Papers, Hoppenot Mission File. See also Collins' reports to Morgenthau, December 17 and 19, 1938, Morgenthau Diary, Bk. 172, pp. 2–11, and the staff conference, December 20, 1938, *Ibid.*, Bk. 157, pp. 120–21.

[10] During an interview with the author in 1961, M. Hoppenot reported the startled reaction of Collins and Kraus to French demands. For Collins' skepticism on the French speed tests, see Major M. S. Fairchild's "French Diary," AAF File, 334.8, French Mission. (Hereafter cited as Major Fairchild's "French Diary.")

War's annual report for 1938 the Air Corps was quoted as stating "our former technical superiority in aeronautical development is no longer clearly apparent." In direct contradiction the Chief of Staff noted, "The Air Corps is now equipped with planes and materiel equal if not superior to any planes in design, speed and endurance." [11]

The demands of the French technicians made the Americans re-think their approach to French purchases. On December 21, Kraus and Collins told the French about the three experimental planes which as yet were neither in production nor released for foreign inspection or sale. In the initial opinion of the French the Curtiss P-40, a fighter, held promise, as did two twin-engined light bombers, the Martin 167 and the Douglas DB-7. The major obstacle to overcome was the Air Corps' opposition to the release of these planes.

When, later that morning, Captain Collins reported to Morgenthau on the talks with Monnet's mission, the Secretary understood the obstacles and took the issue directly to the White House: "Well Mr. President, you sent the French mission to me. It's entirely out of my line. I'm doing it because you want me to do it. I made it as difficult for them to come here as possible." He added, however, "I want to do everything I can to help." [12] The Secretary then argued for the release of the latest American planes:

> If it's your theory that England and France are our first line of defense . . . let's either give them good stuff or tell them to go home, but don't give them some stuff which the minute it goes up in the air will

[11] Watson, *Chief of Staff,* pp. 129–30.

[12] Blum, *Morgenthau Diaries,* vol. II, pp. 65–66. For Morgenthau's further arguments, see his comments to his staff December 21, 1938, Morgenthau Diary, Bk. 172, pp. 12–15.

> be shot down. No sense in selling them that which we know is out of date.

The President agreed and wrote across the top of Collins' report, which Morgenthau had brought with him, "This is O.K. for reasons of state . . . should be kept as confidential as possible and the French orders filled so as not to interfere with the United States' new orders this spring." [13] Roosevelt also approved of Captain Kraus' furnishing "every consistent facility for inspecting and flying the planes involved." [14]

Early the next morning, December 22, Secretary Morgenthau met Monnet, Collins, and Kraus at his own home and

> made it entirely clear that the President is anxious that every opportunity be given this mission to purchase these planes in such volume as to meet their needs, providing their arrangements can be completed and orders given and deliveries made with sufficient promptness so as not to interfere with U.S. Army orders for the same types of planes.

Monnet was also requested to maintain "absolute secrecy as far as other Governments are concerned" regarding information about the planes.[15]

The next step was to persuade the Secretary of War and the Chief of the Air Corps to revise their release policy for the latest planes, and later that day the President talked

[13] Memo from the Procurement Division to the Secretary of the Treasury (S/T), December 21, 1938, Morgenthau Diary, Bk. 172, p. 19.

[14] Memo, December 21, 1938, *Ibid.*, Bk. 172, p. 16.

[15] Blum, *Morgenthau Diaries,* vol. II, p. 66, and the memo of the conference on December 22, Morgenthau Diary, Bk. 172, p. 24.

with Harry Woodring. In the presence of Sumner Welles and Morgenthau, Woodring agreed to permit the French to inspect the three planes. That evening Morgenthau informed Monnet and his assistants that the planes had been released.[16] However, on December 28, when the members of the French mission met with Kraus and Collins, they were surprised to find that because of the demands of the Air Corps the situation had changed.

After the conference on December 22 with the President, Morgenthau, and Welles, Woodring had informed the Chief of the Air Corps that the three planes were to be released and that an officer should be detailed to work with the French mission. Arnold cooperated by assigning Major M. S. Fairchild, but he protested vigorously against the French "either seeing or flying the Douglas attack bomber." The Air Corps Chief persuaded Woodring to call in General George C. Marshall and to go over to the Treasury with him to present their case together. Meeting with Morgenthau, Admiral Peoples, Collins, and Kraus, Arnold stated, "The P-40 and the Douglas attack bomber are still valuable military secrets if we are to lead in the air. However, it is suggested that the P-40 be released and that the Douglas attack bomber be held secret." He also opposed the move because, "An order at this time for 1,000 planes with a foreign government would prevent fulfillment of our 10,000 plane program within the time limits now assigned." When Morgenthau stated it was the President's desire that "we should do everything possible to aid the French and that included releasing the secret

[16] For the conference after the cabinet meeting, see *Hearings before the Committee on Military Affairs, United States Senate, 76th Congress, 1st Session, on H.R. 3791, Jan. 17–Feb. 2, 1939* (Washington, 1939), p. 112. (Hereafter cited as *Senate Hearings . . . H.R. 3791.*) See also Ickes, *Diary,* vol. II, pp. 531–32.

information about the Douglas DB-7," Arnold was so angered, he asserted that if the President of the United States desired planes of that type to be released to them, the President no longer would have staunch support from the Chief of the Air Corps.[17]

Arnold had already been disturbed on December 23 when he met with Admiral Peoples and his two assistants and discovered that the Treasury had been in contact with the French since October and had provided them with specifications and delivery dates of all "our regular standard articles, and much to my surprise, of the attack bombers which had not as yet been tested or delivered to the Army for test." Deeply offended, the General accused the Navy of "selling the Army down the river." Arnold was partially mollified by the argument that French orders "would help us get into quantity production and that if the American aircraft industry was utilized fully the Air Corps production schedule would not be disturbed." But he was aroused again when he learned that without consulting him "the Navy members" had already arranged conferences with Douglas, Martin, and Curtiss representatives about filling the French orders.[18] When he was informed on December 28 of the details of these conferences and of Monnet's having demanded clearance to see and fly these

[17] For Arnold's summary of his reaction to the President's order and the conference at the Treasury, see his memorandum for the Assistant Secretary of War (ASW) December 29, 1938, AAF File, 161, Special Papers Pertaining to French and Swedish Contracts. See also the letter from S/W to S/T, December 22, 1938, AAF File, 161, French Contracts, and notes on the December 22 conference between the War Department and the Treasury, Morgenthau Diary, Bk. 172, p. 30.

[18] For these details, see the memo from CAC to ASW, December 29, 1938, AAF File, 161, Special Papers Pertaining to French and Swedish contracts.

planes, Arnold bluntly told Kraus and Collins "he could do nothing, give them no information at all about the availability of these planes until the matter had been talked over in the War Department." [19]

Arnold's anger at the French for negotiating behind his back is most understandable. So too is his refusal to turn over to a foreign power an attack bomber which he believed could surpass those in Europe and outfly any pursuit plane currently in the air. It was his duty and responsibility to defend the United States. He recognized that French orders would assist his nation's aircraft industry and develop its production capacity, and, as he wrote in his special report for the Assistant Secretary of War on December 29, he was ready "to do everything possible to help the French get plenty of production type planes." He had pinned great hopes on the Douglas bomber, however, and was anxious not to give it up.

Initially, Arnold had expressed his distrust of the French during the past spring when they first sought to test-fly a P-36, then in the Air Corps' possession. The President had granted permission over Arnold's protest, and after the flight the French had ordered only 100 planes.[20] This limited purchase apparently backed up Arnold's fear that all the French wanted to do was to steal the Air Corps' secrets. Now, in December, Arnold found more grounds for distrust. The General and his advisers, as well as Collins and Kraus, were skeptical about the French calling obsolete the American planes currently in production. Several other things also bothered Arnold. By chance, a representative of the Amiot Company, a French aircraft producer, arrived in Washington in late December

[19] See Major Fairchild's "French Diary," December 28, 1938.

[20] See Chapter 1, p. 12.

with a proposal to construct a factory in the United States for the production of the Amiot 350 which its producer claimed was "the fastest two-engined bomber aircraft built today." Amiot was willing to sell its products to the Air Corps as well as to the French Air Force. That an official French mission was, to Arnold's mind, searching out secrets of the latest American bombers at the same time that Amiot made its proposal compounded the General's suspicion. Next came a request by Air France to buy a four-engined flying boat. Though intended for civilian trans-Atlantic service, this plane was powered by a 1,500 hp. engine which, as Arnold noted, "is the only such engine we have in the United States which has passed the test for general use." After recounting these suspicions in his special report to the Assistant Secretary of War, Arnold concluded, "It is recommended [that] very careful consideration be given the above, and that none of our secret projects be released to the French unless there are reasons of state that make it desirable." [21] Morgenthau had already heard these suspicions and had reacted in an entirely different way: "If you don't trust the French as to spies—I think the French would do a better job of protecting the motor [Allison's new in-line engine] than we could here. We have not done an awfully good job of keeping spies out of our plants." [22]

The Chief of the Air Corps finally agreed to release the Curtiss fighter and the Martin bomber, but he continued to

[21] See the memo from CAC to ASW, December 29, 1938. There was no official contact between Amiot and the Monnet Mission. Arnold first met Pierre Wertheimer, the president of Amiot, and his chief engineer, on December 21 and lunched with them on December 29, 1938. See Major Fairchild's "French Diary."

[22] Staff conference, December 21, 1938, Morgenthau Diary, Bk. 172, pp. 12–15.

insist on retaining the Douglas bomber. The General also claimed that a French order for 1,000 planes could not be completed in less than eighteen months and therefore would interfere with completing the Air Corps' current expansion program. According to Major Fairchild's record of December 30, "Arnold felt that this should be fully explained to the French, particularly as to the [Douglas] 7 B, so we would be fully sure they were really interested in the relatively small production possible under this situation. If they were not interested it would be poor policy to show them our secret stuff and then find out they didn't want it after all."[23] To give the Air Corps time to study production schedules, Morgenthau consented to a delay before the French would be permitted to inspect the latest bombers.[24]

During the last days of December 1938, Morgenthau in turn became irritated by the French mission on four counts. First, he was annoyed that Monnet had turned for advice to a legal firm which had shown little support for the Roosevelt Administration and, at the time, was representing the Franco Government of Spain against the Treasury. Second, Morgenthau was distressed at the French mission's insistence upon secrecy. As Morgenthau stated to his staff, "Personally, I think the less explaining . . . the better . . . unless there is some good legal reason . . . I would rather see the French Government . . . do it openly . . . the minute you try to hide your face it looks suspicious." Roosevelt heard his Secretary out at the cabinet meeting on December 28 and agreed it would be better "if this mission of the French government to buy planes were open and public." Monnet agreed to appeal to

[23] Major Fairchild's "French Diary."

[24] Blum, *Morgenthau Diaries,* vol. II, p. 67.

Daladier for such clearance. Third, Morgenthau was annoyed at Monnet's inability to "show us he's got any money." Morgenthau urged the French to deposit $10 million in the United States as an indication that they could pay cash for the planes, and to complete their plans quickly. Monnet agreed to confer with the French Premier on this matter as well. Fourth, the Secretary was bothered by Monnet's negotiations to establish an assembly plant in Canada as an effort to get around the arms embargo of the Neutrality Act. In his concern Morgenthau called the Frenchman into his office, and, as he later reported to Peoples, Collins, and Kraus,

> I had Monnet perspiring here for an hour . . . if you think that once the French Government goes to war that you are going to get any planes any easier by having a flimsy [Canadian] corporation you are mistaken. I said you have my wind up. I don't like this thing . . . up to now I can go up on the Hill and testify to everything.[25]

Morgenthau was also concerned about the production schedules, which Kraus had sketched for Monnet's technicians on December 28. Deliveries of both the Martin and Douglas bombers could not begin before May 1939 and could not be completed by the end of the year. Arnold had been correct in fearing that production for the French would interfere with the Air Corps' procurement program. Worried, Morgenthau remarked to his staff, "The President of the United States says that we consider the Maginot Line our first line of defense [*sic*] and for that reason

[25] *Ibid.*, vol. II, pp. 67–68; Ickes, *Diary*, vol. II, p. 542; Conferences between Monnet, Morgenthau, and Treasury Staff, December 27 and 28, 1938, Morgenthau Diary, Bk. 172, pp. 38–71.

he wants these people to have this thing. Those are my orders. I think he's right." The Secretary also recognized that the French orders would provide cash with which the manufacturers could build plants, order tools, and hire labor, and that such an expansion would cost the United States nothing. Morgenthau determined to clear the final obstacle to Monnet's mission.[26]

This obstacle was the War Department's refusal to release the Douglas bomber. Finally on December 29, Woodring surrendered and forwarded a memorandum to Morgenthau:

> In accordance with our agreement to the plan for French procurement of United States military planes, based on reasons of state and in response to the proposed schedule of production for French orders, I have instructed General Arnold, the Chief of the Air Corps, United States Army, to furnish the facilities looking towards the purchase of the Martin 166–167, Curtiss P-36 and Douglas 7-B attack bomber. He has been instructed to arrange for the inspection of the planes including the revealing of secret developments in our military air production, there involved.

Woodring, harboring his own distrust of the French mission, added a proviso for the Secretary of the Treasury: "that you . . . be assured financially and otherwise that the proposed inspections and revealing of military secrets are on the basis of a bona fide order to purchase."[27]

Morgenthau was incensed and accused the Secretary of

[26] Blum, *Morgenthau Diaries,* vol. II, pp. 68–69.

[27] Letter from S/W to S/T December 29, 1938, AG File 452 (6–7–38).

War of "putting me on record that I should guarantee whether the French can or cannot pay for those planes." Woodring replied by referring to Morgenthau's request for the release of the new planes:

> Henry, your letter to me was just everything on earth that I didn't intend to do. I was confronted here with Congressmen and Senators just ready to raise hell about all the taxpayers' money that we had for development and experiment being given away . . . in the criticism of the French having flown our other planes [in March and September 1938]. All I wanted to do, Henry, was to protect you.

Morgenthau hotly replied, "I don't want to be protected," and the Secretary of War withdrew his demand for a guarantee. However Woodring then asked what would happen if "after we've taken them out there [to the Douglas plant in California] . . . they walk out on us." Because the French indeed might not want the Douglas attack bomber if deliveries could not be completed by July, Morgenthau agreed that the French would visit only the Curtiss and Martin plants. The Douglas visit would be postponed until after further discussion between the Treasury and War departments. Morgenthau concluded, "Now and furthermore I am going to insist that they announce their mission." [28]

The next day, December 31, Morgenthau reported this latest development to Monnet:

> I want to talk very frankly to you. Our mutually good friend Ambassador Bullitt has put me in an

[28] Telephone conversation between S/T and S/W, December 28, 1938, Morgenthau Diary, Bk. 158, pp. 119–20. See also the letter from S/T to S/W, December 30, 1938, AG File 452 (6–7–38).

> almost impossible position on this work that you have done. I mean the whole United States Army is opposed to what I am doing and I am doing it secretly and I just can't continue, as Secretary of the Treasury, forcing the United States Army to show planes which they say they want for themselves.
>
> Now I am going away Monday night. . . . If I am going to do anything more on this thing, I have got to have this mission in the open . . . if not in the open then I am just going to call up Ambassador Bullitt and he will have to take it and do what he can from this point.

The Secretary then explained the background of his apprehension:

> You know the Regular Army officers . . . if you do something that they don't want and it is done secretly —if it is done openly then they would have nothing on me. . . . I don't mind forcing it if it's in the open. I'll take my chances with the Army . . . they have something on me if it's secret.

Monnet replied he would get a ruling from Paris on publicizing his air mission.[29]

Monnet telephoned the Treasury on January 2 that Paris would welcome a public announcement but it must be delayed until the orders for planes had been placed. The Secretary was not satisfied:

> Well I don't think that [the French] are going to get into any more plants until they get out a public

[29] Blum, *Morgenthau Diaries,* vol. II, p. 69, and the conference between S/T and Monnet, December 31, 1938, Morgenthau Diary, Bk. 172, pp. 80–87.

> statement. . . . As far as the United States Treasury is concerned, we cannot cooperate any further until the French Government makes a public statement. . . . Now if the United States Army wants to offer you that cooperation, that's their business.[30]

Morgenthau then departed for two weeks of vacation, and since Bullitt was also vacationing, Monnet and his mission were left alone to find a way into the Douglas plant to see its attack bomber.

During his talk with Morgenthau on the last day of 1938, Monnet summarized his reason for seeking American planes for France:

> This airplane thing is common to the whole European situation. Germany takes this threatening position because she knows that the other countries are afraid of being bombed . . . and they have not the means of retaliating. The moment the Germans know that the others have a force for retaliating, it may change the whole situation.[31]

Realizing that only the latest types of American planes could influence Germany, Monnet and his mission were determined to get the best planes possible.

The French technicians discovered at first hand the limitation of the American aircraft industry during the first week of January when they accompanied Captain Kraus to the Curtiss-Wright factory in Buffalo. Because of the low production rate of Allison in-line engines, the newest American fighter, the P-40, could not be delivered before May 1940. As a result, the French considered an

[30] Telephone conversation between S/T and Monnet, January 2, 1939, *Ibid.*, Bk. 173, pp. 1–5.

[31] Blum, *Morgenthau Diaries,* vol. II, pp. 69–70.

additional order of P-36s.[32] The production line for this fighter, which France had financed during the past spring, was now operating at its planned capacity of 30 per month and final deliveries for the first French order of 100 were due in March 1939. After some negotiation, Curtiss agreed that if the French ordered an additional 150 planes with deliveries scheduled for the end of July, Curtiss could establish a production rate of 87 per month. The company also agreed to raise the air speed for the second order of P-36s from 485 to 500 kmh, increase the number of machine guns from two to six, and because of Monnet's adroit maneuvering, to reduce the cost per frame by $2,250.[33]

When Monnet's two technicians, Colonel Mazer and Captain Jacquin, visited the Glenn Martin facilities in Baltimore and found that the 166, the twin-engined bomber then in production, could attain a top speed of only 425 kmh, they became more interested in the 167, a lighter and faster model whose speed Martin rated at 490 kmh. Although the prototype was not ready to fly, the French, as Jacquin later stated, "bought it knowing it was ordered by the United States Air Corps . . . if it was good enough for the American Army it was good enough for the French Army." [34] Although on December 28 the Martin Company had stated that deliveries of the 167 could not reach a rate of 25 per month before November 1939, on January 6 the company agreed to produce 35 per month by August if France ordered 115, took out options for an

[32] Letter from Hoppenot to La Chambre, January 12, 1939, La Chambre Papers, Hoppenot Mission File.

[33] Memo of negotiations with Curtiss-Wright for 100 P-36s, no date, *Ibid.*

[34] So General Jacquin stated to the author during an interview in June 1961.

additional 100, and paid $2.25 million to cover the cost of developing the prototype and constructing more factory space. Machine tools for the new production line would become the property of the French Government. The company also agreed to expand production of the latest twin-engined attack bombers to 600 a year if France ordered another 400.[35]

The third combat plane, the Douglas DB-7, which was the Air Corps' favorite, was also a twin-engined attack bomber. It had a speed of 510 kmh and a range of 1,300 km. Though the prototype was already flying, final deliveries for the Air Corps' order of 100 could not be completed before January 1940. Thus, Hoppenot reported, "the mission decided to defer its proposals until the plane was seen." [36]

On January 16 Monnet's mission cabled Paris suggesting that the government order a total of 555 planes, with deliveries scheduled between May and October 1939. Two days later the Air Ministry authorized 100 P-36s, 100 Douglas DB-7s, 115 Martin 167s, as well as 40 Chance Vought naval dive bombers, and 200 North American basic trainers.[37]

Although Monnet received his Air Ministry's authorization, his mission still faced the opposition of the Air Corps to a first-hand inspection of the Douglas DB-7. General Arnold was so adamant about maintaining the secrecy of this plane that on January 7 he ordered that all contact with the French mission cease because, as Major Fairchild, his contact officer with the French, noted, "We had offered

[35] Memo of negotiations for 115 Martin 167-FS, no date, La Chambre Papers, Hoppenot Mission File.

[36] Letter Hoppenot to La Chambre, January 12, 1939, *Ibid.*

[37] Final Report, Hoppenot Mission, *Ibid.*

all there was to offer. . . . There was nothing else left."[38] Monnet and his assistants found no way to break this impasse because their contacts with the White House, Morgenthau and Bullitt, were still vacationing. On January 9 the Ambassador returned and immediately told Roosevelt of Monnet's situation. Shortly thereafter, Bullitt informed Hoppenot, "The President expressed his astonishment that his intentions had been incompletely followed and has called for next Monday [January 16] a meeting of the interested Secretaries to whom he will renew his instructions for complete cooperation."[39]

To help get the ball rolling for the French, on January 10 President Roosevelt called into his office the Secretary of War and both the Chief and Deputy Chief of Staff. Roosevelt reiterated his conviction that "the only check to a world war, which would be understood by Germany, would be the creation of a great [French] air force and a powerful force in this country."[40] By January 16, Roosevelt had taken other steps toward obtaining Congressional approval for American rearmament. In his annual address to Congress on January 4, he called for a revision of the Neutrality Act as a "measure short of war," making it clear that an arms embargo would "give aid to an aggressor and deny it to a victim." The following day he sent to Congress his budget message in which he allotted $1.3

[38] Major Fairchild's "French Diary," January 7, 1939.

[39] Letter from Hoppenot to La Chambre, January 12, 1939, La Chambre Papers. Hoppenot wrote after lunching with Ambassador Bullitt and Monnet. See also Morgenthau's memo of the conference with Bullitt on January 9, and with Bullitt and Monnet on January 12, 1939, Morgenthau Diary, Bk. 173, pp. 6 and 37.

[40] The purport of the President's comments was given by General Marshal to General Kilner, Acting Chief of the Air Corps, January 10, 1939. See "Daily Air Corps Record," January 12, 1939, Box 56, Arnold Papers.

billion for defense, a sum considered "an enormous outlay" at that time. A week later he requested $500 million more as a supplemental appropriation for fiscal year 1939, which would strengthen the "utterly inadequate" condition of the armed forces.[41] As the President had agreed with his military advisers in mid-December, $300 million of this appropriation was allotted for the expansion of the Air Corps, and $180 million of that sum devoted to aircraft purchases under what was now called the 5,500 plane program.

Secretary Morgenthau had returned on January 16, and, at a briefing session in the Treasury to bring him up to date, the Army's opposition to the French air mission came up. Captain Collins, still in charge of the Procurement Division's negotiations with the French, summarized the problem:

> Mr. Secretary, they have not seen in the Army—if they see, they won't admit it—the advisability of the French putting money into tools for putting planes into production which would give them by the fall a much larger average monthly output of these planes, instead of having five or ten made by hand. . . . Now the French are willing to go ahead with Martin and spend some money on additional tools . . . and another million feet of plant. . . . If the Army ever wants any of those planes they'll step in with the plant running to full capacity. . . .

Talk turned to Hopkins' plan of government-financed aircraft factories, and the Secretary restated his opposition,

[41] For text of the annual message and January 12, 1938, a message calling for increase of the Air Corps, see *Public Papers and Addresses of Franklin D. Roosevelt, 1939* (New York, 1941) pp. 3–4 and 70–74. See also Langer and Gleason, *Challenge to Isolation,* p. 48.

"My theory is and my philosophy is to always exhaust [*sic*] what private industry can do first." Discussion also came on delivering to the French every alternate plane that came off American production lines, and Morgenthau was informed that the Navy was willing to follow such a procedure. The talk at this briefing session considered as well the French proposal that the Army defer delivery on the last 100 of its order for P-36s and thus permit France to receive 250 by the end of July 1939. The Secretary also learned that General Motors was considering expanding, at its own expense, production of its Allison motors from 300 to 5,000 a year. But this could happen only if French and British orders were added to those from the United States. The Secretary suggested integrating orders for both the Air Corps and foreign countries with his Procurement Division in charge of distributing orders for all plane production. Although the Treasury's Procurement Division had, under an executive order, the authority to do this work, Morgenthau was not optimistic: "The God-damn people sitting there with all that jealousy over there in the organization [War Department], you can't do it!" [42]

Following this staff conference, Morgenthau proceeded to the White House for a meeting with Woodring, Arnold, Louis Johnson, Charles Edison, Admiral Peoples, Collins, and Kraus. Ambassador Bullitt sat at the President's side. Roosevelt reiterated his wish that every effort be made to assist France. Bullitt spoke of time running out and repeated the President's wish. He specifically called for the release of the Douglas bomber. Secretary Woodring replied that the plane included many secret elements and was constructed partially at the cost of the Govern-

[42] Staff conference on January 16, 1939, Morgenthau Diary, Bk. 173, pp. 9–25.

ment. The President retorted that he was determined to have the Douglas plane released. It was a tense meeting and Roosevelt had his dander up.[43]

When the conference broke up, Secretary Morgenthau, referring to Roosevelt's verbal order to release the plane, said, "Mr. President, I want this in writing." Then, with the help of his assistants, Morgenthau drafted letters to the Secretaries of War, the Navy, and the Treasury, in which he wrote, "you are directed," and implied they had a choice between compliance and resignation. When the White House returned the letters unsigned, however, Ambassador Bullitt used his influence and within three days the letters were signed and forwarded.[44] These letters forced the War Department to back down, and after a meeting on January 19 with representatives of the Treasury and the Navy, General Arnold wired the Air Corps' security officer at the Douglas plant to permit the French to inspect and fly the DB-7, "Less its secret accessories." [45]

At the meeting on January 19, Louis Johnson told Collins "they were willing to cooperate 100% with the President's wishes," yet Collins reported that during a meeting with Johnson four days later, "I watched my step all the way through with him because I knew he was quite mad." As the Treasury representative was about to leave

[43] See the memo on White House conference, January 16, 1939, *Ibid.*, Bk. 173, pp. 9–25; Blum, *Morgenthau Diaries,* vol. II, pp. 70–71. See also *The New York Times,* January 29, 1939, p. 1; February 18, 1939, p. 1; Arthur Kroch, February 21, 1939, p. 18.

[44] See the staff conference held on February 6, 1939, Morgenthau Diary, Bk. 173, pp. 212–13.

[45] For the interdepartmental meeting, see the memo from Collins to Morgenthau dated January 19, 1939, as printed in *Senate Hearings . . . H.R. 3791,* p. 93. This January 19 meeting included Arnold, Woodring, Johnson, Charles Edison, the Assistant Secretary of the Navy, Admiral Peoples, and Collins.

that meeting Johnson's executive assistant, Colonel Burns, still had his doubts: "Do you think these French want to buy any planes, or are they on a fishing expedition?" As Collins reported later, he replied, "I didn't see how anyone who was cognizant of the conditions in France could question the fact that they wanted the planes and wanted them badly." Collins then said to Burns, "I feel this way about it Colonel, if there were a thousand planes on the shelf the French would buy them tonight." Burns replied, "That's rather reassuring because that has not been the opinion that has existed in the War Department." [46]

By this time the Senate Military Affairs Committee had opened its hearings on Roosevelt's call for rearmament and had listened approvingly to the War Department's plans for strengthening the defensive position of the United States.[47] Only a few discordant notes had been struck. Senator Champ Clark, the determined isolationist from Missouri, did not want the new planes turned over to a European nation, but he relaxed when he was assured by the Army Chief of Staff that the War Department had the ultimate say in whether any plane could be released for foreign export.[48] Later, another isolationist, Senator Robert R. Reynolds, of North Carolina, returned to the issue indirectly when he asked Arnold how he would feel about a program involving 10,000 planes. The Senator's worry that such a huge program presaged shipment of excess

[46] Memo from Collins to S/T, January 19, 1939, and telephone conversation between Collins and S/T, January 23, 1939, Morgenthau Diary, Bk. 173, pp. 47 and 55–58.

[47] Besides the record published by the Committee on Military Affairs, much helpful material is found in D. F. Fleming, "Our Choice in Foreign Policy," *Events,* March 1939, pp. 161 ff, and Eliot Janeway, *Struggle for Survival* (New Haven, 1951), pp. 23–37.

[48] For this exchange between Senator Clark and General Craig on January 20, see *Senate Hearings . . . H.R. 3791,* pp. 31–33.

planes to the European democracies appears to have been mollified when the General replied,

> I am for this [5,500 plane] program here, hook, line and sinker because I believe it is a program that is well planned, and one that balances the personnel with the airplanes, and one that answers the problem of the aerial defense of the United States, and I cannot see any need at this time for anything more.[49]

On January 25, the third day of Arnold's testimony, the hearings were abruptly disrupted. What, asked Senator Clark, was a Frenchman doing on a Douglas bomber, "the very latest word in American plane construction," when it crashed on January 23? [50]

That morning, two of Monnet's assistants, Colonel Jacquin and his test pilot, Captain Paul Chemidlin, flew into Los Angeles to inspect the Douglas bomber. They had no need to fly the DB-7, for they had already approved the Martin 167—even though it was not ready to take to the air—and they believed they could fulfill the Air Ministry's requirements by a similar inspection and review of the Douglas plans.[51] After watching a demonstration flight, Chemidlin expressed some skepticism about the plane's capabilities, and the Douglas test pilot became annoyed. According to a report later written by General Arnold, the pilot decided to make "the Frenchman eat his words, or in other words, to give the Frenchman a ride." Upon his invitation Chemidlin climbed into the after cockpit, and they took off. Flying at about 400 feet the pilot feathered the left engine and took a number of sharp right turns. As

[49] *Ibid.*, p. 42. [50] *Ibid.*, p. 64.

[51] Colonel Jacquin gave this explanation to the author during an interview in June 1961.

he swung back over the observers at the airport, the pilot, determined to provide a final exhibition of the maneuverability of his plane, put it into a "very sharp left hand turn" with the dead engine on the lower wing, and then followed this with a snap roll. The maneuver demanded too much and the plane went into a tight spin. The pilot jumped, but he was not high enough for his parachute to have time to open. Chemidlin rode the plane down and miraculously survived, suffering only a broken leg and back injuries. Jacquin rushed up and pushed his way through the crowd of bystanders, so excited that he spoke in French. The secret was out.[52]

The isolationists on the Senate Military Affairs Committee took the Douglas crash as evidence that Roosevelt was secretly extending aid to the European democracies. They were further disturbed to hear that the French inspection of the DB-7 and the flight took place despite Arnold's opposition. Asked on January 25 to explain why he had permitted the flight, the Chief of the Air Corps stated it was "at the direction of the Treasury Department." Feelings within the committee crescendoed. A full investigation was called for, and the major officials who had taken part in the French negotitions were ordered to appear within two days.[53]

Morgenthau was infuriated by Arnold's statement and informed the Secretary of War, "I'm not going to have it smeared all over the front pages that I did this. I know

[52] For an eyewitness account of the crash, see the report of Major K. B. Wolf, Air Corps representative at Douglas Aircraft Company, to CAC, January 24, 1939. See also CAC to ASW, February 1, 1939, AAF File, 161, French Contracts. General Jacquin explained to the author that his inadvertant use of French resulted from his relief at seeing his colleague alive.

[53] *Senate Hearings . . . H.R. 3791,* p. 89.

who signed the order to go out there. We have a copy of it. . . . If the Army thinks they can put me in a hole like this . . . they are mistaken." The Secretary of the Treasury also exploded at the staff meeting that he called for the preparation of his testimony before the Senate Committee: "How many times did I tell you that the Army would try to get me because they want to cover up the mess they're in." All the Secretary's fears about working with the French in secret seemed to be coming true, and he was determined to clear himself.[54]

Roosevelt also was disturbed that Monnet's mission was making front-page news and he determined to meet the isolationists attack head on. First, he gave Morgenthau permission to testify that he had acted on the President's authority, and then Roosevelt borrowed from the Secretary of the Treasury details for his press conference on January 27. Morgenthau was unconcerned that the President was "stealing his stuff," because, as he said to his staff, "what could be better? . . . Good guy to work for." [55]

Before the Senate Military Affairs Committee met on January 27, Roosevelt called in the press and announced his personal approval and support of the sale of planes to France. He attempted to soothe the public by emphasizing this was "a perfectly normal purchase and a perfectly normal testing out of the plane." After all, as he said, neither the Treasury nor the War Department had objected to the French ordering planes from a private company. He explained that legally the DB-7 was "purely a manufacturer's plane" and there had been no way of tell-

[54] Telephone conversation between S/T and S/W on January 29; and staff conference, January 27, 1939, Morgenthau Diary, Bk. 173, pp. 69–71 and 143–78.

[55] Staff conference, January 27, 1939, *Ibid.*, Bk. 172, pp. 143–78.

ing whether the Air Corps would select or reject it. The French order had been considered because "six of the major airplane companies are practically closed up" and one of the largest engine companies, Pratt and Whitney, had just laid off 1,500 men. He had expected the French orders to be completed before the new Air Corps orders could be placed, thereby contributing toward getting the idle plants into production. He explained that using the Treasury Department's Procurement Division as a means to increase American exports was legal as well as normal.[56]

On the same day, in testimony before the Senate Committee, Secretary Morgenthau amplified the President's theme of good business. The French were ready, he said, to spend $65 million in six months. They would pay development costs and put idle plants into production, and "good hard dollars would be put into the worker's pockets." Naturally, the French had wanted planes that could stand up to the Germans', and so the French were permitted to inspect the Martin and Douglas bombers.[57]

The isolationists at the Military Affairs hearings refused to be appeased, because, as Senator Sheridan Downey of California charged, this affair revealed "that our government was cooperating with a foreign government to give that government the prior right to the purchase of military secrets and an airplane, prior to its use or choice by our Government." [58] He was supported by the Chief of Staff. General Craig approved foreign sale of planes which had been in service for a year, but he was concerned about

[56] *Press Conferences of Franklin D. Roosevelt, 1939,* vol. 13, microfilm roll 7, January 27, 1939, p. 90. See also January 31, 1939, pp. 102–3.

[57] Blum, *Morgenthau Diaries,* vol. II, pp. 72–74; *Senate Hearings . . . H.R. 3791,* pp. 91–115.

[58] *Ibid.,* p. 108.

releasing military secrets. The isolationists agreed with the General about the necessity of providing priority for national defense.[59] To do this they proposed to block the sale of the latest types of planes abroad.[60]

Nevertheless, Morgenthau reported to Captain Collins after the Cabinet meeting of January 27, "the President said to proceed as before . . . to go right ahead with the French . . . and let them buy what they want." [61] When Roosevelt and Secretary of the Treasury talked on January 31, the Secretary commented, "for your international speeches to be effective, you must be backed up with the best air fleet in the world." In saying this, the Secretary repeated a point which Roosevelt had made to his military advisers on November 14 when he called for 10,000 planes for the Air Corps. Morgenthau now stressed that the latest French order for 200 bombers was speeding that goal: "we are going to do in less than a year what it normally takes the Army several years." [62]

On Tuesday, January 31, Roosevelt again mentioned his basic reasons for extending aid to France. The isolationist members of the Senate Military Affairs Committee still refused to call off their attacks on such aid, and, in a determined effort to quiet their hullabulloo, Roosevelt invited the entire committee to the White House. A record of what the President said at that meeting was probably never made, but the drift of his remarks was captured in a later account by Joseph Alsop and Robert Kintner. Their

[59] Craig testified January 28, 1939, *Ibid.*, pp. 123–33.

[60] Senator Clark, as well as Senator Gerald P. Nye of South Dakota, scented an alliance with France. See *The New York Times*, January 28, 1939, p. 1, col. 8, and Fleming, "Our Choice in Foreign Policy," *Events*, March 1939, p. 162.

[61] Blum, *Morgenthau Diaries*, vol. II, p. 74.

[62] *Ibid.*, vol. II, p. 76.

description of Roosevelt's deep concern for Europe and the strong words to describe Hitler's ambitions and the threat they posed to the United States fits closely with the evidence of the President's thinking presented here. Certainly, the remark which he allegedly made at that meeting, "the frontiers of the United States are on the Rhine," reflected his comment to Morgenthau in late December: "we consider the Maginot line our first line of defense." [63]

Roosevelt spoke too strongly, however, and the committee, instead of curtailing its investigation, was more convinced that the President was leading the United States down the road to war.[64] A committee member broke the secrecy surrounding the White House meeting and reported Roosevelt's statement. The public's reaction revealed Roosevelt had gone too far. He admitted as much three days later when he denied using the phrase. At the same time, he restated the foreign policy of his Administration in terms which would reassure any American who had been disturbed by the chain of events set off by the crash of the Douglas bomber.

The President retreated from his position of leadership into silence, hopeful the opposition would quiet. The cautionary approach of Secretary Hull and the State Department was put into practice, and the major issue became a revision of the Neutrality Act in time to restrain Hitler from further aggressive action. It was useless for the President to take the lead on this issue, and even the State

[63] Joseph Alsop and Robert Kintner, *American White Paper* (New York, 1940), pp. 30–32. For the President's earlier comment to Morgenthau, see p. 82. For similar comment see also p. 75.

[64] Senator Hiram W. Johnson of California stated to the press on January 31, "Good God, do you not, gentlemen, think the American people have the right to know if they are going down the road to war?" *The New York Times,* February 1, 1939, p. 83.

Department backed away, preferring to rely on Senator Key Pittman of Nevada to maneuver a bill through his Foreign Affairs Committee.[65]

While Roosevelt had been struggling to clear the way for France to buy American planes, Premier Daladier and his Minister for Air had promptly responded to Monnet's cable of January 16 by recommending that 555 planes be purchased. In two days, and before Arnold had granted final clearance for the inspection and flight of the Douglas bomber, the Air Ministry had cabled back its approval.[66] The Air Ministry later raised only one question about the American planes: what about the flying capabilities of the Douglas bomber which had crashed so spectacularly? Colonel Jacquin replied that the accident was "uniquely the fault of the pilot." Indeed, the Captain had gone back after the crash to assure Donald Douglas, the president of the Company, "we are going to buy that plane, it is only necessary now to talk about deliveries." The French accepted the Douglas offer to deliver 100 by January 31, 1940, and options were taken for an additional 100 with a production rate raised to 30 per month.[67] The French turned again to Pratt and Whitney for engines. This was a boon to the company since in late 1939 they had been forced, owing to competition from Allison, to lay off

[65] Divine, *Illusion of Neutrality,* pp. 238–39; Langer and Gleason, *Challenge to Isolation,* pp. 48–51.

[66] Final Report, La Chambre Papers, Hoppenot Mission File. This report includes separate résumés of the negotiations with Curtiss, Martin, Douglas, and Pratt and Whitney. There is also a résumé of the negotiations for the 200 North American trainers which were initiated January 9, 1939, by the Air Attaché in Washington, Colonel René P. G. Weiser.

[67] Memo for the negotiation for 100 Douglas bombers, no date, La Chambre Papers, Hoppenot Mission File. In June 1961, General Jacquin recalled for the author his comments to Mr. Douglas.

workers.[68] Monnet's mission commissioned Pratt and Whitney to produce 795 Twin Wasp R 1830 SC-3 C engines of 1200 hp. As a result, P & W was required to increase its current production by two-thirds, with peak output of 125 per month to be reached by the coming August and the order completed in July 1940.[69]

France agreed to pay $60 million for the 555 planes which it ordered in February. Almost $2.25 million of this went into capital expansion of the Glenn Martin factory. Most significant for the growth of the American aviation industry and France's future orders was the production capacity which was created. As a result of the French orders, Martin foresaw a monthly rate of 50 light bombers, Curtiss a monthly rate of 50 pursuits, and Douglas a monthly rate of 30 bombers. Thus, by 1940 France would have available an annual capacity for 600 pursuits and 960 bombers, totaling more than 1,500 planes a year.

In March 1939, as Jean Monnet was about to leave Washington for Paris, he told Morgenthau, "I appreciate very much the confidence and support you gave me personally and gave us in the French plane affair, and I do think the result of it, mainly due to the support that was given here by you, has had a great effect in France." Monnet added that in addition to the 555 planes which France had ordered, his mission had signed options to bring total deliveries of these attack bombers in 1939 up to 400.[70] Monnet had taken a major step toward securing

[68] "United Aircraft," *Fortune,* March 1941, vol. 23, p. 168.

[69] Letter from Pratt and Whitney to Monnet, January 28, 1939, La Chambre Papers, Hoppenot Mission File. Contract French State and United Aircraft Corporation, February 14, 1939, AAF File, 452.1–3295 Sec.

[70] Conference between S/T and Monnet, March 23, 1939, Morgenthau Diary, Bk. 174, pp. 170–72.

American aid for France and opening the American arsenal. France now possessed "an extensive rapid assembly plant [for 1,500 planes a year] sheltered from enemy attacks while the military builds up its forces." [71]

But Secretary Morgenthau had paid a price in gaining American support for France. As he said to Monnet at their separation in March, "for a month I went through hell." In his efforts to get off the hook which he believed the Army had dropped for him in the Senate Military Affairs Committee, he relied on President Roosevelt, but in their meeting on January 31, the President had accused Morgenthau of going too far in defending his actions to aid the French. As Morgenthau later reported to Monnet, it had been "one of the most unpleasant experiences I ever had." In reply Monnet said, "If it had not been for you . . . this would not have gone through." [72]

[71] "Notes on the Subject of Creating a Foreign Manufacturing Potential," La Chambre Papers, "Commandes Americaines," Doc. no. 1 bis. See p. 26.

[72] For fuller account of Roosevelt's reaction to Morgenthau, see Blum, *Morgenthau Diary,* vol. II, pp. 74–78. See also the conference between S/T and Monnet on March 23, 1939, Morgenthau Diary, Bk. 174, pp. 170–72.

CHAPTER

5

Troubled Interlude: The Prewar Months

FROM FEBRUARY 1939 until September 1939, when World War II commenced, France placed no orders for American planes. Except for exercising options for 1,400 additional aircraft engines, the French contributed nothing toward increasing the American industrial arsenal. These eight months witnessed increasing international tension as Europe sped toward war, and American foreign policy at this time was dominated by the Congressional struggle to revise the Neutrality Act to permit the European democracies to obtain arms on a cash-and-carry basis.[1] In President Roosevelt's estimation, the strongest contribution which his nation could make toward maintaining peace in Europe was to remove the arms embargo because he hoped that Hitler would have to

[1] No attempt will be made here to trace once again the course of the struggle to revise the Neutrality Act between January and July 1939. For the most detailed account, see Robert A. Divine, *The Illusion of Neutrality,* pp. 236–85. See also Langer and Gleason, *Challenge to Isolation,* pp. 136–47.

think twice about launching a war if he knew that the American arsenal lay open to the European democracies.

The President had publicly called for a repeal of the embargo in his State of the Union address in early January 1939, but his personal part in this campaign had been seriously compromised with the revelation that France was being provided with the most advanced American planes. The investigation led by the Senate Military Affairs Committee had become a platform from which isolationist leaders could attack the President for committing the United States to the support of the European democracies and for leading the nation toward another world war. Knowing himself to be compromised in the eyes of the isolationists, the President withdrew. The Chairman of the House Foreign Affairs Committee, Sol Bloom of New York, and the Chairman of the Senate's parallel committee, Key Pittman of Nevada, were given charge of winning approval for the arms embargo. With caution and patience both men began their campaign, and it was not until late June that the issue reached the floor of the House.

Meanwhile, events in Daladier's government made the pattern of American aid for France clearer. First, Daladier had found support for the purchase of American planes. Second, his government wanted to build a medium French bomber, the Amiot 350, in the United States. Third, Daladier wanted to repay France's war debts in an effort to open new sources of credit in the United States. In April came the flurry over the French Air Ministry joining the American Air Corps to expand the production of Allison in-line engines. Finally, in July, France was dismayed by President Roosevelt's failure to repeal the arms embargo. All of these developments, in which France played a part, took place against President Roosevelt's search to revise the Neutrality Act.

Daladier's gratification, when he heard that on January 19 Monnet's mission had been granted clearance to see the Douglas DB-7,[2] can be understood if one considers the lack of progress the French aircraft industry had made toward meeting Plan V. On January 16 the Air Minister and the members of his Comité de Matériel met with the producers of the two new French medium bombers, the Breguet 690 and the Amiot 351, as well as Sauliner, the head of the company producing the Morane 406. Only the Breguet production was keeping its schedule, and would have the first 5 planes ready in February. Amiot was forced to admit that its initial 10 medium bombers scheduled for January would not be ready before mid-April. As for the Morane fighters, not one of the 30 initially scheduled for delivery in September 1938 had been delivered and no more would arrive until March 2, 1939. Obviously, France needed American fighters and bombers.[3]

Not everyone in France responded with enthusiasm to the orders for the Curtiss, Martin, and Douglas planes. When press reports of Chemidlin's crash had alerted the public to the fact that France was negotiating for planes, reactions were mixed. General Maurice Gamelin was dis-

[2] Daladier to St. Quentin, Ambassador of France, in Washington, January 19, 1939, La Chambre Papers, "Commandes Américaines," Doc. no. 8. See also Welles to Roosevelt, January 19, 1939, *FR, 1939,* vol. II, p. 500. Daladier and La Chambre further revealed their attitude toward the reception which the Monnet mission received when they offered to confer the Legion of Honor on Peoples, Collins, and Kraus. (Bullitt, March 9, 1939, State Department unpublished document (SD) 851.248/162, National Archives, Record Group 19.)

[3] Procès-verbal, Comité de Matériel, January 16, 1939, Service Historique de l'Armée de l'Air (SHAA), Box B-104.

turbed that only 600, rather than the 1,000 originally planned, would be ordered. The Chief of Staff for Defense failed to understand that only 600 were ordered because of the inadequacy of American productive capacity rather than the short-sightedness of General Vuillemin.[4] At the other extreme, the Air Committee of the Chamber of Deputies once again refused to approve the purchase of any foreign plane unless it underwent the same technical tests required of French planes. Finally, private financial circles expressed doubts that France possessed sufficient gold reserves to purchase American planes.[5]

Daladier's government immediately moved to scuttle this opposition. On January 29 the Finance Minister, Paul Reynaud, gave a radio broadcast and assured his listeners that gold that had returned to France since his entry into the Ministry would permit France to buy more than 5,000 foreign planes.[6] La Chambre spoke before the Deputies:

> The Air Ministry cannot overlook the attack against the purchase of planes abroad at the time when France has just received whole-hearted cooperation from the great American democracy and its President in supporting orders which had no other object than to secure the cause of peace. . . .

[4] For the meetings of the heads of the armed forces at the Air Ministry held on January 25, 1939, to approve the American orders, see Gamelin, *Servir,* vol. II, p. 389.

[5] "Nouvelles de l'aviation," *L'Intransigeant,* January 27, 1939, p. 4. See also *Le Jour-Echo de Paris,* Léon Bailby, "Do We Need American Planes?" February 2, 1939, p. 1.

[6] *The New York Times,* January 29, 1939, p. 1, col. 7; *L'Intransigeant,* January 30, 1939, "Nouvelles de l'aviation," p. 6. Two weeks later, writing in an article for the *Daily Telegraph* of London, Reynaud stated the figure was 6,000 rather than 5,000. ("Nouvelles de l'aviation," *L'Intransigeant,* February 14, 1939, p. 6.)

He went on to say that although the planes had been ordered without having undergone French tests, trial flights had proven their worth. He said that in a power dive during a recent test flight, a P-36 had reached a speed of 925 kmh. The Air Minister left the Chamber with a strong vote of confidence.[7]

On February 2, La Chambre met with Premier Daladier, Reynaud, and the Foreign Minister, Georges Bonnet, for the final decision on the American orders. La Chambre explained that the goal of 1,000 had not been met because there were "no modern planes which equaled the minimum performance demanded by the Chief of Staff for Air." He emphasized that the Martin and the Douglas, which could attain speeds of 480 kmh, were the best American types and that "at the personal intervention of President Roosevelt, France had been permitted to place its orders even before the American Army placed its own orders." He said further that the cost of the Douglas and Martin bombers closely approximated that of the Amiot 350 and Bloch 174. He brought up the one serious problem: deliveries had been delayed beyond the July 15 deadline. The Minister of Finance remarked that although credits were not easily attainable, he believed the decision was up to the Minister for Air and the Minister for Foreign Affairs. He also noted that "cancellation of these orders about which the American press has made so much noise, would only be exploited against us by Germany and Italy." By the end of the meeting La Chambre had ap-

[7] *Journal Officiel, Débats Parlementaires, Chambre des Députés, 1939,* January 31, pp. 296–301. The opposition had been led by a Communist, Armand Pillot, who feared a reduction in employment and by Pierre Béranger, who apparently spoke for P. L. Weiler, the director of Gnome-Rhone, a French aircraft-engine company, and a consistent opponent of foreign purchases.

proval for the orders, which he had already cabled to Monnet on January 18.[8]

Critics of the government's aerial rearmament who sat on the Senate's Air Committee had been trying to schedule a hearing before the National Defense Committee since the past October, but they had been held off by the Premier until after the announcement that the Martin and Douglas bombers plus 100 more P-36s had been ordered.[9] The hearing finally got under way on February 8. The critics ridiculed the Air Minister's production figures and demanded that the number of planes in his Plan V be doubled so that the total would be raised to 5,000. They called for the mobilization of France's aircraft industry to speed production and criticized the slowness of administrative procedures within the Air Ministry. Influential members of the Air Committee, like Laurent-Eynac, editor of the weekly *L'Air,* and Senator La Grange, who had helped initiate the negotiations for American planes, joined in the attacks. One of the strongest voices was that of the Secretary of the Senate Air Committee, André Maroselli, who, although he grudgingly gave consent to the American purchases, pointed out that they indicated a confession of failure by the Air Minister to develop French production. Despite this opposition, the Senate's National Defense Committee voted its confidence in La Chambre. Undoubtedly, the vote had been favorably influenced by the purchase of American planes.[10]

[8] "Minutes of Conference in Office of the President of the Council on the Subject of Purchase of Planes in the United States," February 2, 1939. La Chambre Papers, "Commandes Américaines," Doc. no. 9.

[9] For the Senate National Defense Committee hearings, see *Le Temps,* February 11, 1939, p. 3, and February 12, 1939, p. 4, and André Maroselli, *Le Sabotage de Notre Aviation: Cause Principale de Notre Défaite* (Paris, 1941), pp. 46–50.

[10] *Ibid.,* pp. 68–72, and La Grange Papers, "The Campaign Led in

Daladier's Government again turned the purchase of American planes to its advantage during a debate in the Senate on foreign policy. Georges Bonnet referred directly to the recent developments across the Atlantic and said, "Never before have the relations between France, England and the United States been better." The Premier in a later address commented, "In the present situation I do not believe that France needs to be worried and I certainly do not believe, as some contend, that France is isolated in the world." Then Daladier spoke of British and American support: "This accord of the democracies provides a fundamental basis for the maintenance of peace in the world." The Senate's voice of confidence was obviously related to the latest exhibition of Franco-American friendship.[11] Several days later Premier Daladier amplified his comment for Ambassador Bullitt when he said, "war would be imminent if it were not for the hesitation created in Germany and Italy by the evolution of opinion in the United States and by the attitude of the President and the American Government."[12]

Despite Daladier's success at purchasing American planes, his government was fully aware of the continuing inferiority of the French Air Force and aircraft production, and the minutes of the Air Ministry's Comité de Matériel

---

the Senate Between 1937 and 1940," p. 132. For a summary of the public debate in France on air defense, see Wilson, Chargé d'Affaires, Paris, to Secretary of State, March 3, 1939, SD 851.248/163.

[11] *Journal Officiel, Débats Parlementaires, Sénat, 1939,* February 7, 1939, pp. 103–8. In his memoirs, Georges Bonnet gave an opposite interpretation of the role of the United States during the winter of 1939. See his *Défense de la Paix, Fin d'une Europe* (Geneva, 1948), pp. 106–8.

[12] Bullitt, February 13, 1939, *FR, 1939,* vol. II, pp. 501–4.

during the late winter and spring of 1939 note them. Most serious was the "motor crisis." France's two aircraft engine producers, Gnome-Rhone and Hispano-Suiza, were still deep in their expansion efforts and this left a serious gap in the production of high horsepower engines. To meet the "motor crisis" the Air Ministry was forced to look abroad. The most obvious source, the United States, was limited both because of the scarcity of dollar exchange and because of the threat of the arms embargo. Guy La Chambre therefore sought to obtain European motors. An order for 50 Koolhaven engines was placed in Holland. A Czechoslovakian firm was scheduled to establish a production line for 50 engines a month, half of which would be Hispano engines of 860 hp and half Gnome-Rhones of 660 hp. Orders were placed in Switzerland for another 25 Hispanos a month. Next, the French turned to Britain for heavier engines. In late February, an order was placed for 500 Rolls-Royce Merlin engines of 1,000 hp. The French also looked to Russia, but the available Soviet engines were the same as those powering the Russian planes which, as Bullitt described them, "were all copies of American models more than three years old which I had procured for the Soviet Government when I had been Ambassador in Moscow." [13]

The French Air Ministry's search for engines led to Germany. In December 1938 Daladier had asked Charles Lindbergh to search out the possibility of French purchases of German aircraft engines. During two visits Lindbergh opened the way for the purchase of 300 to 500 of

[13] For these foreign plane orders, see Peyronnet de Torres, "Nouvelles de l'aviation," *L'Intransigeant,* January 30, February 15 and 18, 1939; Bullitt, February 6, 1939, SD 740.00/568. Wilson, March 3, 1939, SD 851.248/163.

the best engines that Germany manufactured, the Daimler-Benz 601 of 1,250 hp. The French air attaché in Germany was informed that there was a chance of purchasing these engines, thereby supporting the Franco-German diplomatic accord talked about by Foreign Minister Von Ribbentrop during the past December: "it is probable and possible to develop this 'bonne entente' by a technical cooperation between the two air forces." If the new French fighter, the Dewoitine 520, was powered by the German engine, this "would be a move towards peace for it would mean that the two countries would have the same aviation." The attaché talked with General Udet, who headed the materiel section of the Luftwaffe. Udet carried the issue up to General Milch, the Secretary of State in the Air Ministry. In turn, Hermann Goering, the German Air Minister, was consulted, and he won Hitler's approval on the condition that deliveries would begin at the end of 1939 and be paid for in foreign exchange. By February 21 the French Air Minister requested Ambassador Bullitt to sound out American reaction to such a purchase. The United States gave no reply until March 23, and then Hitler's seizure of Prague had compromised the engine deal, but its final demise came when President Roosevelt reacted negatively. Ambassador Bullitt later reported to the White House, "Following our cryptic telephone conversation, the French Minister for Air decided to let the purchase of 300 Daimler-Benz motors die an immediate and natural death." [14]

[14] For the air attaché's report, see Paul Stehlin, *Témoignage pour L'Histoire* (Paris, 1964), pp. 129–32. For Lindbergh's mission, see *The New York Times,* January 17, 1960, p. 1, col. 6. See also the letters from Bullitt to F.D.R. dated February 21 and March 23, 1939, President Secretary's File, Box 5, France, William C. Bullitt, 1936–1940, Roosevelt Library.

One result of the Air Ministry's search for British and German engines was, as La Chambre informed Bullitt in late February, that with so much of France's foreign exchange earmarked for these purchases, the Ministry could not exercise its options for 200 additional Martin and Douglas bombers. Indeed, not until after it let the order for the German engines die did the Air Ministry take up its option for 100 more Martin 167s plus 300 Pratt and Whitney engines with deliveries of the latter to start September 1939 and be completed by August 1940. The Douglas option, however, was not exercised.[15]

The Air Minister finally turned to the United States to find aircraft engines on April 12, when La Chambre reported to Ambassador Bullitt that France was prepared to order 500 Allison in-line engines if General Motors could be persuaded to expand its production lines. Negotiations soon crescendoed but they took place against two other developments which were already under way and which influenced the Allison negotiations.

First, France wanted to repay the war debts to the United States which it had defaulted after 1918. Because of these debts, France had come under the Johnson Act of 1933, which prohibited loans for arms and munitions to any nation that had not paid its debts to the United States. On February 13, when the French Finance Minister authorized the payment of gold for the latest American planes and thought about exercising options for further orders, he called in Ambassador Bullitt to explore the possibility of arranging credit with the American Import-Export Bank or with private banks for as long as five years. Bullitt referred to the debts as well as the Johnson Act and stated that he felt there was not the slightest

[15] Memo, March 31, 1939, AAF File, 161, French Contracts.

chance for such credit. Premier Daladier, who was present, joined in expressing the opinion that "France had acted with extreme stupidity in defaulting on her debt," and the men discussed whether the United States would be prepared to make a debt settlement at this time. The Ambassador said that he believed "France did not at this time have a sufficiently stable financial situation . . . to pay sums . . . large enough to be acceptable to the Congress of the United States as a debt settlement." The French officials asked whether a token payment would be helpful.[16] Washington informed Bullitt, "your reply concerning aircraft credits is approved," and added that "token payment, while it might produce favorable reaction as a gesture of actual acknowledgment of the indebtedness, would not effect Johnson Act prohibition."[17]

On February 21 the Finance Minister stated to the American Ambassador his conviction that "France must make immediately a settlement of her debt to the United States." He proposed that France turn over to the United States some 10 per cent of its 87 billion francs of gold reserves. This, he recognized, was a small sum in American eyes, amounting to roughly $300 million, but it made up 15 per cent of France's war chest. Bullitt replied that Congress had complete control over the debt and was loath at this time to deal with the matter, and he added, "I felt the French offer of $300 million in gold to settle a debt of many billions would probably not be regarded as good business by Congress." France then offered as payment "French possessions which we [United States] might desire for strategic reasons," such as Pacific and Caribbean bases. Ambassador Bullitt reported this development with

[16] Bullitt, February 13, 1939, *FR, 1939,* vol. II, pp. 501–4.

[17] Secretary of State to Bullitt, February 16, 1939, *Ibid.,* II, 504–5.

enthusiasm to President Roosevelt in a private letter: "In any event, will you please get your imagination to work furiously on the subject. I wish to God I could be with you in the White House for one evening. Our inventions would be terrific, if you want any French territory plus 10 billion francs in return for releasing France from the operation of the Johnson Act." [18] This idea had been initiated by Daladier, and he was prepared to send Monnet back to the States to negotiate this settlement as "no one was so well qualified." [19]

On April 4 Monnet was brought into the discussions during a luncheon with Daladier, Reynaud, and Bullitt. They decided to let the question rest with the President, and Bullitt reported to Roosevelt that he could expect a visitor.[20] Monnet was not able to leave for Washington until April 18,[21] and on May 3 the President granted a private interview.[22] Next, the Frenchman talked with Morgenthau on May 8 and again on May 16.[23] Although this effort of the French to settle its war debts had drawn the interest and concern of President Roosevelt, the negotiations were turned aside for fear that they might upset the more important goal: Congressional votes for revision of the arms embargo.

Sensitivity to isolationist opinion also prevented Roose-

[18] Letter from Bullitt to F.D.R., February 22, 1939, President Secretary's File, Box 5, France, William C. Bullitt, 1936–1940, Roosevelt Library.

[19] Cable from Bullitt to F.D.R., March 23, 1939, *Ibid.*

[20] Bullitt memo for F.D.R., April 4, 1939, *Ibid.*

[21] Letter from Daladier to F.D.R., April 18, 1939, President Secretary's File, France, 1933–1939, Roosevelt Library.

[22] Untitled memo, Monnet Papers, File 2a (London, January–March 1939).

[23] For Monnet's talks on the war debts with Secretary Morgenthau on May 8 and 16, see Morgenthau Diary, Bk. 188, pp. 382–88, and Bk. 190, pp. 57–61.

velt from approving another French proposal: the construction in the United States of a factory to produce French light bombers. This proposal had initially been explored in late December 1938 when Pierre Wertheimer, the head of the company manufacturing the Amiot 350, talked with Louis Johnson and General Arnold.[24] Wertheimer's proposal had advanced sufficiently by late February for the Air Ministry's Comité de Matériel to approve of producing the Amiot in the United States, and the Air Minister called upon Senator La Grange to lend his support to this enterprise and accompany Wertheimer to the United States.[25]

On March 6, Ambassador Bullitt was asked to help prepare a favorable reception for Wertheimer and La Grange in Washington. He was told they wanted to establish an Amiot factory in New Orleans, that the American financial house of Kuhn Loeb and Company would put up $3.5 million, and that the French government would order 300 planes if the factory was built. The plan called for deliveries of six planes a day to begin within six months. The Ambassador was also informed that the Secretary of War, as well as Louis Johnson and General Arnold, "were all entirely familiar with this deal and approved it unreservedly." [26] Bullitt's report was taken by Joseph C. Green, the chief of the State Department's arms and munitions control office to the Secretary of War, who was indignant at these advances because he had learned only indirectly of Wertheimer's earlier visit. When Woodring called in Johnson and Arnold they both

[24] See Chapter 4, pp. 79–80.

[25] Procès-verbal, Comité de Matériel, February 21, 1939, SHAA, Box B-104, and "Report to Baudouin, Minister of Foreign Affairs," September 16, 1940, p. 3, La Grange Papers.

[26] Bullitt, March 6, 1939, *FR, 1939,* vol. II, p. 505.

strongly opposed an Amiot factory large enough to turn out 180 planes a month because they considered it would be "disastrous" for the national defense and the interests of the American aircraft industry.[27] As a result, the State Department, again with the President's approval, instructed Bullitt to advise Wertheimer and La Grange to cancel their sailing.[28] Even though La Chambre was reluctant to call the two Frenchmen back, he did try, unsuccessfully, to persuade them not to sail.

La Chambre told Bullitt he had approved the Amiot plan, believing it would be warmly accepted by the American government. The Minister regarded the Amiot 350 as

> the finest fuselage yet designed in France and he felt that in granting permission for the export of its plans and for its sale to the United States Government he was in a small way responding to the gesture of confidence and friendship that the American government had made when it had permitted the sale of the Martins and Douglases to France.

La Chambre added that Daladier had approved the plan "most heartily" and he concluded by saying he was ready to give Wertheimer any orders which the American government might desire.[29]

The Amiot project became such an issue in Washington that it drew the attention of Sumner Welles, who cabled Bullitt on March 10 that he had considered with the War Department the effect the plan would have not only on American aircraft industry and national defense, but also

[27] Green memo, March 6, 1939, SD 851.248/154B.

[28] Secretary of State to Bullitt, March 7, 1939, *FR, 1939,* vol. II, pp. 505–6.

[29] Bullitt, March 8, 1939, SD 851.248/58.

on public and Congressional opinion, if it were known that Wertheimer and La Grange were coming to Washington to discuss the new factory. "We are convinced that it would be most unfortunate should they persist in attempting to carry out their plans." The State Department was also upset because the project seemed "at least in spirit if not in letter a violation of the Johnson Act." [30] When the two Frenchmen arrived in New York, they received a cable from La Chambre urging them to drop the matter. La Grange replied by requesting the Air Minister to have confidence in his "delicate diplomacy." La Chambre, however, did not have the authority to order Wertheimer and the Senator back to France and, as he admitted, "he was not their wet nurse." [31]

Senator La Grange had initiated his "delicate diplomacy" on March 10 with a radiogram from his ship to Mrs. Roosevelt requesting to pay his respects to her and the President on either March 17, 18, or 19.[32] Roosevelt was not inclined to accept a polite social call that could turn into an international incident, and asked Sumner Welles to inform the French Ambassador that the President would not be able to receive La Grange so long as he was in the United States on the Amiot project "although Senator La Grange had been a personal friend of the President for more than twenty-five years." [33] La Grange later recalled that the Ambassador told him that he could not meet the President "because of the difference between

[30] Welles to Bullitt, March 10, 1939, *Ibid.*

[31] Bullitt, March 11, 1939, SD 851.248/160.

[32] For La Grange's cable to Mrs. Roosevelt, see SD 811/4611 France/141. Attached to this cable is the President's note of March 16, 1939, "Explain to La Grange that Mrs. Roosevelt is away and some reason why I cannot see him."

[33] Memo of conversation with the French Ambassador by Welles, March 11, 1939, *FR, 1939,* vol. II, pp. 506–7.

him and Congress on the delivery of modern American planes to France."[34] The Senator and Wertheimer decided to return to France without going to Washington, but the project was kept alive during April. Finally, it was postponed for some two months because, as the American negotiator for the Amiot project said, he realized that in view of the furor stirred up by the purchase of planes by the French, publicity regarding the project might be embarrassing to the Administration.[35]

On May 9, La Chambre attempted to reopen the Amiot project, for, as he informed Ambassador Bullitt, the Bloch 171 prototype for a light bomber which "the French had expected to be as good or better than the Amiot," was a failure. In reply, Roosevelt wrote the Ambassador: "[It is] very inadvisable at this time . . . maybe in two or three months."[36] Once again the President decided this was no time to upset the Congress as it moved toward revision of the Neutrality Act.

Roosevelt was unconcerned about Congressional reaction when an opportunity came for France to assist in enlarging the production of aircraft engines, however. On April 12 the Minister for Air proposed to place an order for 500 Allison in-line engines. The reaction of the War Department and the French solution warrant a brief review because they underscore the forces acting in France and the United States which influenced and interfered

[34] "Report to Baudouin," September 16, 1940, p. 4, La Grange Papers.

[35] See memo of conversation with Sol Rosenblatt by Green, State Department's Munitions Control Officer, April 21, 1939, *FR, 1939*, vol. II, pp. 515–17. For further details on the Amiot project, see SD 851.248/160, 164, 179, and 193.

[36] Letter from Bullitt to F.D.R., May 9, 1939, and the reply, May 24, 1939, President Secretary's File, Box 5, France, William C. Bullitt, 1936–1940, Roosevelt Library.

with further French purchases of American planes and engines.

Shortly after Germany seized Prague, Neville Chamberlain informed the French Foreign Minister that Britain had successfully overcome her air rearmament problems and was producing about 600 planes a month. This permitted British military experts to determine that war with Germany could be conducted without extreme risk. The Prime Minister had expressed dissatisfaction with the rate of French plane production which had not reached the 400 a month that Daladier had predicted. The Foreign Minister admitted that France had produced only about 100 planes in February, but spoke also of the recent purchases in the United States. Chamberlain then presented his evaluation of American aircraft: "the Americans had not given the same attention to military aircraft as to civil aircraft, and that in design their military aircraft were inferior to the British." [37]

In early April, the French Air Minister went to London to explore methods for speeding up French aircraft production with the British Secretary for Air, Sir Kingsley Wood. When he was in London, La Chambre learned that the British Air Ministry, despite Chamberlain's evaluation of American planes, planned, once war broke out, to order all the planes that American industry could produce and to spend between £100 to 500 million in developing United States aircraft capacity. At present, the shortage of dollars laid rigorous limitations on peacetime orders.[38] In contrast,

[37] Record of Anglo-French conversation, March 22, 1939, *Documents on British Foreign Policy, 1919–1939,* Third Series, vol. IV, pp. 462–63.

[38] For the British Air Ministry's plans for war purchases in the U.S., see La Chambre's comments to Bullitt, April 12, 1939, *FR, 1939,* vol. II, pp. 508–9. See also Hall, *North American Supply,* p.

the French Air Ministry had funds which could be used immediately for expanding American aircraft industry, and La Chambre, as well as the British, determined that the major bottle-neck lay with the production of in-line engines. Upon returning from London, the French Air Minister called on the American Ambassador and informed him, "no single act would be of greater assistance to France and England than an immediate great increase in the production of Allison motors." He hoped that a French order for 500 would persuade General Motors to embark on large-scale production. The order, however, could not be placed until one of these engines was shipped to France for tests.[39]

The French Air Minister's proposal drew immediate attention from the military in Washington, whose conclusions were cabled to Bullitt. The Air Corps had funds for 400 engines, but General Motors was shying away from making any capital investment unless it could be assured of orders for a total of 1,200. The Air Minister was informed, "If the French government desires to place an immediate order for one Allison engine [for tests] with the Company, neither the War Department nor the Navy Department would interpose any objection. . . . The engine would be stricken immediately from the list of military secrets and the Department will issue an export license without delay." If France would order 800 engines, General Motors would have sufficient incentive to make its capital investment.[40]

The French Air Minister was delighted. If each engine cost $10,000, he could order 800, for he had $8 million

111, and procès-verbal, Comité de Matériel, April 6, 1939, SHAA, B-104.

[39] Bullitt, April 12, 1939, *FR, 1939*, vol. II, pp. 508–9.

[40] Secretary of State to Bullitt, April 13, 1939, *Ibid.*, vol. II, pp. 509–10. See also Green memo, April 13, 1939, SD 851.248/145.

available for foreign purchases. La Chambre wanted Allison to raise production to 300 a month since it was "almost certain that France and England would be in war at the end of 3 months," and at that point France's monthly needs would amount to 300.[41] But when the Minister requested to see the test engine, delays began. First, General Arnold was reluctant to release an engine that had not first been released to the Air Corps.[42] Then the French insisted that the engine be subjected to special block tests used to test French engines since the United States tests were not rigorous enough. Another problem arose when General Motors revised the delivery schedule and informed the French that it would take fourteen months before engines could be turned out at a rate of 300 a month.[43] La Chambre was disappointed. Ambassador Bullitt cabled, "Could not an appeal be made to General Motors on the ground that it seems a patriotic duty to increase production of Allison engines?" [44] General Motors replied that a definite French order would have direct bearing on the size of their plant expansion, and the Corporation was prepared to raise production on the basis of the Air Corps order for 400 and an order from the French. La Chambre replied that it was legally impossible for him to place orders for this motor until one was inspected in France.[45] The test engine did not arrive in France until May 22 and not until mid-August did the Allison Corporation begin to develop a special coupling

[41] Bullitt, April 14, 1939, *FR, 1939,* vol. II, pp. 510–11.

[42] For the American military's view, see Watson, *Chief of Staff,* p. 302.

[43] Secretary of State to Bullitt, April 15 and 18, 1939, *FR, 1939,* vol. II, pp. 511–13.

[44] Bullitt, April 20, 1939, *Ibid.,* vol. II, p. 513.

[45] See Secretary of State to Bullitt, April 21, 1939, *Ibid.,* vol. II, p. 514, and Bullitt, April 25, 1939, *Ibid.,* vol. II, p. 517.

which would permit block testing.[46] La Chambre's prewar effort to buy Allison engines and expand American manufacturing facilities for in-line engines had failed because of the French opposition to purchasing foreign equipment that would compete with French engines and fuselages.

A significant development which came out of the Allison negotiations, however, resulted from La Chambre's concern about the proportion of deliveries which would be made. The War Department agreed that deliveries would be two-thirds—one-third, if France ordered 800 engines and the Air Corps ordered 400. The department, on April 18, had stated a principle: "Non-interference with available industrial facilities used by the French Government or new industrial facilities created by reason of orders placed by the French with American firms unless such interference were required in the interests of the United States in some unforeseen and extreme emergency." [47] The French Air Ministry was immediately notified of the principle, which had been arrived at a week earlier when the Acting Chief of Staff cleared the way for orders by the French Ministry of War for anti-aircraft gun barrels from Bethlehem Steel and anti-aircraft fire-control equipment from Sperry Gyroscope. In his original statement, General Marshall had been less vague about the grounds for interference, and he had written that French orders would not be interrupted "unless the United States becomes itself involved in war and such interference was subsequently found to be necessary to the best interests of the United States and its allies." [48]

[46] Bullitt, May 26, 1939, and Welles to Bullitt, Aug. 8, 1939, SD 85.248/210 and 245.

[47] Secretary of State to Bullitt, April 18, 1939, *FR, 1939,* vol. II, pp. 512–13.

[48] For Marshall's original statement of April 11, 1939, see AAF File, France 1939, National Archives, Record Group 160.

The issue of using foreign orders to expand United States armament facilities came under intense discussion by the military during the spring and summer of 1939, and a tendency developed to liberalize the release policy. In July, President Roosevelt agreed to have the Army-Navy Munitions Board clear all exports of munitions. Early the next month, both the Air Corps and the Navy modified its policy so an item could be released for sale as soon as it became a production article, thus eliminating the six-month wait after the next production article was turned out.[49]

Despite such steps the Air Corps still jealously guarded its latest planes. When in late May the French Air Ministry, on the basis of information obtained in Europe, requested release of Lockheed's twin-engine fighter, the P-38, the Air Corps reacted quickly and negatively.[50] The welcome extended to French orders for the Allison engine had obviously been a special case. Now that Congress was finally appropriating funds for the 5,500 program, the Air Corps was in no mood to share with France the latest American planes, especially since in May, Lindbergh had pointed out to General Arnold the decisive inferiority of his Air Corps.[51]

[49] For summaries of the release policies, see Watson, *Chief of Staff*, pp. 300–3; AAF File, Lyon Project Book 10-F; and Army Air Force Historical Study, No. 106, "Distribution of Air Materiel to the Allies, 1939–1944," National Archives, Record Group 160.

[50] Bullitt, May 26, 1939, and Secretary of State to Bullitt, May 31, 1939, SD 851.248/210. See also AAF File, 161 French Contracts and AG File 452 (5–31–39).

[51] See Arnold, *Global Mission*, pp. 189–90, and *Army Air Forces in World War II*, vol. 6, *Men and Planes*, eds. W. F. Craven and J. L. Cate (Chicago, 1955), pp. 178–80. See also Army Air Force Historical Study, No. 50, "Materiel Research and Development in the Army Air Arm, 1914–1945," pp. 26–30. For the Milner-Lindbergh Board Report of June 28, 1939, see AAF File, Lyon Project Book 13.

Between February and September 1939 the French Air Ministry made at least one breakthrough in placing orders for American equipment, when options for an additional 1,000 Pratt and Whitney engines were exercised. Significantly, all but 200 of these were scheduled for installation in French frames, primarily the Brequet 691, a light bomber. La Chambre had at last won his campaign, which he had begun the spring of 1938, to overcome the French motor crisis by purchasing American engines for installation in French fuselages. These new orders together with the engines ordered for American frames brought the total of prewar orders that France placed with Pratt and Whitney up to 2,245, fully using that corporation's capacity. As soon as war broke out, La Chambre launched negotiations to double the order by constructing new production lines. While the Air Minister's peace-time efforts were frustrated, the advent of war removed the obstacles to obtaining large numbers of American engines.[52]

While France struggled to order American equipment, President Roosevelt was still fighting his frustrating battle for the revision of the Neutrality Act and the repeal of the arms embargo. His crisis came in late June and early July. On May 1, 1939, the cash-and-carry clause of the Neutrality Act lapsed and as a result Britain and France would not have access to the American arsenal once they became belligerents. The meaning of this was not lost on Georges Bonnet, who requested his Ambassador in Washington to insist on material aid from the United States, adding, "In

[52] See AAF File, 161 French Contracts, for French orders for the Twin Wasp SC3G:350 on June 16, 1939; 200 on July 12, 1939; and 500 on August 26, 1939. See also procès-verbal, Comité de Matériel, April 6, May 9, July 27, August 9 and 23, 1939, SHAA, Box B-104.

the terrible crisis that faces Europe . . . a support from America that is only moral would prove a cruel deception."[53] Bonnet expressed his worries to Ambassador Bullitt who cabled that London also believed that unless the Neutrality Act was amended soon, Hitler might decide that he could attack France and Great Britain without the risk that military supplies from the United States be sent to them.[54]

These cablegrams arrived in Washington as Cordell Hull was hesitating about testifying before the Senate Foreign Affairs Committee for fear that the isolationist members would ask embarrassing questions about American planes and equipment which had already been ordered by Britain and France.[55] Because of the Senate opposition, Roosevelt asked Sol Bloom of the House Foreign Affairs Committee to lead the fight for revision of the Neutrality Act. On May 19 President Roosevelt stated to the House leaders his conviction that a repeal of the arms embargo "would actually prevent the outbreak of war in Europe, or, if it did not, it would make less likely a victory for the powers unfriendly to the United States." [56] The President's remarks only strengthened the fears of the isolationists, who, as a State Department official noted, shared one emotion: "the fear that the President would wish to line up this country in war if England and France should

[53] Georges Bonnet, *Fin D'Une Europe,* p. 59.

[54] See Bullitt, May 10, 1939, *FR, 1939,* vol. I, pp. 184–85. See also Bullitt's other cables of May 10, 1939, SD 740.00/1416; *Memoirs of Cordell Hull,* vol. I, p. 646, and record of conversation with the French ambassador by Pierrepont Moffat, May 10, 1939, *FR, 1939,* vol. I, pp. 656–57.

[55] "Moffat Journals," May 9 and 10, 1939. For this Congressional struggle over the arms embargo, see Divine, *Illusion of Neutrality,* pp. 271–81.

[56] Hull, *Memoirs,* vol. I, p. 643.

become involved with hostilities."[57] Because his support for France's purchase of planes still gave a firm foundation for those fears, the President remained silent during the Congressional debate.

By the end of June, Germany had increased its pressure on Poland to return Danzig and to let the Germans use the Polish Corridor freely. Britain's unilateral treaty of support for Poland had committed the British to fight in its defense, in which case France would inevitably become involved. The French appeasers, wishing to escape this obligation, used the foreign policy of the United States in their campaign, as they had done during the Sudeten crisis in the fall of 1938. On June 24 *Paris Soir* printed an article by Pierre-Étienne Flandin, a former Premier and a leading exponent of appeasement, who asked, "And now where is the United States?" and went on, "war threatens to steep Europe in blood, because the United States remains indifferent and immovable. . . ."[58] The following day Georges Bonnet, in a speech before the convention of Radical Socialists, stated, "If the United States makes it clear that they are on our side when the conflict starts, the specter of war would be banished definitely."[59] Bullitt doubted whether this type of thinking was a plan to make the United States the scapegoat for another Munich, but he warned that such a possibility existed. The Ambassador added that Bonnet's speech had not drawn the press attention in France that it had in the United States because Bonnet had "said only what many Frenchmen have long thought."[60]

After an interview with Premier Daladier on June 28,

[57] "Moffat Journals," May 27, 1939.

[58] *Paris Soir,* June 24, 1939, p. 1.

[59] As quoted in Langer and Gleason, *Challenge to Isolation,* p. 141.

[60] Bullitt, June 27, 1939, SD 740.00/1808.

Bullitt reported the Premier's conviction that Hitler intended to make war that summer and would be prepared to strike any time after July 15. Daladier added,

> he felt Hitler might fear to strike if the negotiations of France and England with the Soviet Union could be concluded successfully before July 15 and if the Neutrality Act in the United States should be altered to permit the shipments of arms, munitions and implements of war, and if the Germans should become convinced that France and England were absolutely determined to fight by the side of Poland.[61]

The French press reported that the balance between war and peace rested with Stalin and Roosevelt, and the press attentively watched the Anglo-French negotiations in Moscow which had been going on throughout the last weeks of June. Here, it seemed, lay the greatest likelihood of success and the strongest defense against war. The press also followed Washington's debate over the repeal of the arms embargo, and most Frenchmen shared the opinion that American arms for Britain and France would deter Hitler.[62] On June 30, during a conversation with Ambassador Bullitt, Alexis Saint Leger of the Foreign Ministry hoped the House of Representatives would revise the Neutrality Act: "The passage of this change undoubtedly would be a large factor in deterring Hitler from making war. The conclusion of the alliance with the Soviet Union would be another such factor." [63]

On July 1, Paris heard that the House of Representa-

[61] Bullitt, June 28, 1939, *FR, 1939,* vol. I, pp. 277–78.

[62] *Le Populaire,* July 1, 1939, p. 1. See also John McVickar Haight, Jr., doctoral dissertation, "Reaction of the Paris Press to the Neutrality Policy of the United States, 1935–1939" (University Microfilms, 1953), pp. 366–95.

[63] Bullitt, June 30, 1939, *FR, 1939,* vol. I, pp. 278–80.

tives had decided to restore the arms embargo to the neutrality legislation. Bullitt reported that members of French political life had been telephoning him constantly to express their opinion that "the vote of the House has increased greatly the chance that Hitler will precipitate war with Poland since he feels certain that he and Mussolini will be able to defeat France, England and Poland unless they receive supplies of munitions and arms from the United States." [64] The editors of the pro-democratic socialist Left, who counted heavily upon Roosevelt's support for Europe's peace, decried the House vote: "It will be received with joy by Hitler and Mussolini." Only the pro-fascist Right in France was pleased. The foreign editor of *L'Action Française* sneered, "The American democracy assumes a heavy responsibility. It brings grist to Adolf Hitler's mill. . . . Alas, since Woodrow Wilson, American foreign policy misleads us." The French press, which prided itself on its many individualistic voices, at least shared a common opinion on the American failure to remove its arms embargo.[65]

The House support for an arms embargo had also shocked President Roosevelt and Secretary Hull, and the American leaders turned to the Senate Foreign Affairs Committee for help. The party line-up divided this committee 10 to 10, leaving the deciding vote to Senator Guy M. Gillette of Iowa. He was a Democrat but he felt a personal animosity toward the President, who had tried to purge him during the last elections. Gillette's negative vote was correctly forecast by *Le Matin,* a large conserva-

[64] Bullitt, July 1, 1939, SD 811.04418/454.

[65] Pierre Brossolette, *Le Populaire,* July 2, 1939, p. 3; Léon Blum, *Ibid.,* July 2, 1939, p. 1; José le Boucher, *L'Action Française,* July 5, 1939, p. 1.

tive Parisian daily and supporter of appeasement.[66] On July 18, President Roosevelt entered the struggle and invited the members of the Senate committee to the White House, but even this effort failed to convince the isolationists of the necessity for revising the Neutrality Act. The meeting came to a head when Senator William E. Borah of Idaho, on the basis of his own private sources, doubted Secretary Hull's prediction that war was in the offing. Vice President Garner brought the conference to a close by turning to the President and saying, "Well, Captain, you haven't got the votes, and that's all there is to it." [67]

The Parisian communist daily, *L'Humanité,* which still supported resistance to Germany, headlined this news: "THE RANSOM OF MUNICH; Roosevelt Has Fallen Victim to the Partisans of Splendid Isolation." Pertinax, an astute commentator, noted, "It is unfortunate at this critical juncture that the news from Washington and Moscow only encourages the two dictators. . . . Our loss is certain." Genevieve Tabouis, another of France's ablest commentators, admitted, "This proves, once again, that the American senators are still far from the Western democracies. . . . It is clear that Anglo-American relations are not as good as we believed." *L'Action Française* remarked with sarcasm:

> America is with us!
> One hundred and twenty million free citizens of the United States burn to help our soldiers! The "gogo" Frenchmen, who have lived on this agreeable convic-

[66] *Le Matin,* July 10, 1939, p. 1.

[67] Alsop and Kintner, *American White Paper,* pp. 44–46. See also Langer and Gleason, *Challenge to Isolation,* pp. 143–45.

> tion, learn brusquely that neutrality will not be revised until "la Saint glin glin."

In contrast, Léon Bailby in his rightest daily caught the seriousness of the American failure:

> To notify the totalitarian countries in advance that they need not count on America . . . is to help Hitler and Mussolini to make calculations and to establish their forecasts.[68]

Whether or not Hitler was influenced by the failure of the United States to repeal its arms embargo cannot be determined here.[69] Nevertheless, the majority of the French thought the German Führer would be influenced, as did those Americans who favored a revision of the Neutrality Act. The President had met a personal defeat at the hands of the Senate Foreign Affairs Committee, and could look forward only to reopening a campaign to revise that act when Congress reconvened in January 1940, or sooner, if war came to Europe in 1939.

Since January 1938 the plans and expectations of Senator La Grange, Guy La Chambre, Premier Daladier, and Jean Monnet had garnered little in the way of combat planes and aid from the United States. Of the 315 light bombers and 200 pursuits, only the latter had been shipped to France before war broke in early September.

[68] *L'Humanité,* July 20, 1939, p. 1; Pertinax, *L'Europe Nouvelle,* July 22, 1939, p. 804; Tabouis, *L'Oeuvre,* July 20, 1939, p. 3; Francis Leger, *L'Action Française,* July 21, 1939, p. 4; Léon Bailby, *Le Jour-Echo,* July 22, 1939, p. 1.

[69] For the latest evaluation, see James V. Compton, *The Swastika and the Eagle: Hitler, The United States and the Origins of World War II* (Boston, 1967), pp. 3–38, 72–75, and 82–83, and Saul Friedlander, *Prelude to Downfall: Hitler and the United States, 1939–1941* (New York, 1967), pp. 15–26.

Despite the efforts of President Roosevelt and Secretary Morgenthau more planes could not be made available simply because the United States had none on hand. These prewar orders, however, opened the way for larger wartime orders by developing procedures for release, and by acquainting the French and the British with American aircraft industry and its techniques of production. Once the war came the Allies were in a position to take fuller advantage of the American arsenal.

CHAPTER

6

War, the Arms Embargo, and Two French Initiatives

THE WAR CRISIS in Europe came to a turning point on August 23, 1939, with the announcement of the Nazi-Soviet Pact.[1] For many Frenchmen this sudden and unexpected desertion by the Soviet Union scuttled the last chance for peace. France was left alone with Britain and Poland to face Germany which, through diplomacy, had secured its eastern front and, once Poland was removed, could amass its superior forces against the European democracies. France needed the arsenal of the United States to offset Germany's aerial superiority, but she would not be able to get at it, nor would any other belligerent, if

[1] Material in this chapter has been taken in part from two articles, by John McVickar Haight, Jr.,: "France's First War Mission to the United States," *Airpower Historian,* vol. XI, no. 1, January 1964, pp. 11–15, and "Jean Monnet and the American Arsenal After the Beginning of the War," *French Society and Culture Since the Old Regime: The Eleutherian Mills Colloquim, 1964, of the Society of French Historical Studies and the Société d'Histoire Moderne,* eds. Evelyn M. Acomb and Marvin L. Brown, Jr. (New York, 1966), pp. 269–83.

an arms embargo was imposed. On September 3, two days after Germany marched into Poland, Britain and France declared war, and President Roosevelt had no choice under law but to impose an embargo. While his spokesmen in Congress "carefully avoided any implication that the purpose of [a repeal of the embargo] was to enable England and France to buy munitions from the United States," [2] this was indeed Roosevelt's goal. It took two months for Congress to repeal the embargo but during that period delivery of planes to France did not seriously suffer because few were ready for shipment before early November anyway. In these months France also took out new orders for some 1,000 combat planes and the French pace was neither desultory leisurely nor sluggish.[3]

The placing of those plane orders was the first of two special initiatives France took that fall of 1939 when Poland went down to quick defeat and the Phony War in the West began. The second came when French leaders authorized Jean Monnet to negotiate with Britain a coordination of the two nations' economies with the primary aim of placing a massive joint order for American planes to ensure aerial superiority over Germany.

France's first initiative grew out of a war council which Premier Daladier called on August 23 after learning of

[2] For quotation, see Divine, *The Illusion of Neutrality,* p. 317. Divine provides the fullest account of the campaign to revise the Neutrality Act.

[3] Langer and Gleason in their *Challenge to Isolation,* pp. 288–91, labeled the Anglo-French efforts to place orders for American planes as not only leisurely, dilatory, and sluggish, but also halting and slow. See also *Hull,* vol. I, pp. 700 and 763. *Fortune,* January 1940, p. 96, in summarizing Allied orders after the repeal of arms embargo noted "the visible war orders are indeed paltry . . . the great war boom seems to be hell-bent for oblivion." See also *The New York Times,* November 7, 1939, p. 51, col. 1.

the Nazi-Soviet Pact. The Premier asked his military advisers whether France was prepared to enter war if Germany attacked Poland. The French ground and naval commanders announced their arms were ready. The Air Minister in turn stated, "the situation of our aircraft ought not restrain the decision of the Government in the same way as it did in 1938." La Chambre added that, as far as fighters were concerned, "the Anglo-French supply is just about equal to that of the German-Italian supply," but that "Our bombers still have not begun major deliveries and this will not begin until early 1940, [however] England has the capacity to carry out heavy bombing of northern Germany." [4] There were, said the Air Minister, sufficient fighters to make daylight bombing of Paris and other French cities extremely risky for the Germans, although night bombing would be rather easy for them because French anti-aircraft

[4] An official French analysis of August 26, 1939, reported modern fighter strength as:

France	442	
England	492	
		934
Germany	900	
Italy	30	
		930

The analysis underlined the deficiency in modern bombers:

France	0	
England	776	
		776
Germany	906	
Italy	434	
		1,340

See La Chambre's testimony, *Événements,* vol. II, pp. 328–29. For corroborative evidence, see Lieutenant Colonel Hayez, "Situation de l'Armée de l'Air en Avions Modernes aux premiers jours de la Guerre, 1939–1945," *Forces Aériennes Françaises,* December 1962, pp. 781–95.

artillery was deficient. Despite this deficiency, Daladier was determined that France would go to war if Germany attacked Poland.[5]

The following day, La Chambre asked the Chief of Staff for Air to verify the Air Minister's analysis of France's capacity for aerial warfare, and General Vuillemin admitted that Allied planes were still numerically inferior to those of the Axis but he predicted,

> In six months, on the condition that the means of production are not weakened by offensive enemy action and the U.S.S.R. does not give active support to the Axis, French and British aviation ought to balance the German and Italian air force.[6]

Nevertheless in August 1939 the French aviation industry had been able to turn out only 285 military planes of which but 150 were fighters. Obviously, such production did not yet cover France's war needs, and on August 26 the Air Minister called his advisers together to determine what should be done.[7] They underlined that France's domestic aircraft industry was already working at full capacity to complete Plan V and that the new production lines would not begin to meet France's requirements for full-scale war for at least seven months. La Chambre's advisers estimated that to fill France's war needs for the

[5] See La Chambre's testimony in *Événements,* vol. II, pp. 327–30, and *Événements, Rapport,* pp. 276–78. See also Daladier's testimony, *Événements,* vol. I, p. 55.

[6] Vuillemin to La Chambre, August 26, 1939, *Ibid.,* vol. II, p. 331.

[7] This meeting was described to the author by La Chambre and Stéphane Thouvenot during interviews in the summer of 1961. As a Colonel in the French Air Force and a member of La Chambre's staff in 1939, Thouvenot took part in this conference at the Air Ministry on August 26.

coming six months an additional 2,800 planes as well as 10,000 engines were required. La Chambre proposed that, despite the threat of an American arms embargo, a new purchasing mission be sent across the Atlantic under Jean Monnet and Colonel Paul Jacquin, and the Minister forewarned Ambassador Bullitt of France's new requirements for planes and engines.[8]

On August 29 La Chambre reported to Premier Daladier that French production facilities were fully utilized and recommended a third air mission to the States. He added, "I am ready . . . to confer with you on this mission," but Daladier quickly replied, "It is useless to talk and lose time, it is better to send the mission at once."[9] Apparently, the Premier had been encouraged by a recent telephone conversation with President Roosevelt concerning additional American planes. Daladier later recalled Roosevelt's saying,

> Do not forget that the majority of American opinion is isolationist. Do not forget the American Senate has embargoed all the arms that you have ordered in the United States. But you can count on it, that I will overcome this opposition and raise the embargo.[10]

Confident that Roosevelt would be able to open the American arsenal to France, the Premier called on Jean Monnet to head this third mission to the United States.

Monnet, however, objected, and in a memorandum of

[8] Bullitt to Secretary of State, August 28, 1939, *FR, 1939,* vol. II, p. 518.

[9] Letter from La Chambre to Daladier, August 29, 1939, a copy of which M. La Chambre presented to the author. Daladier's reply was reported to the author by La Chambre during an interview in June 1963. See also his testimony, *Événements,* vol. II, p. 334.

[10] Daladier's testimony, *Ibid.,* vol. I, p. 60.

September 3 he summarized his reasons for Daladier. According to his information, the 2,800 planes and 10,000 engines which the Air Ministry sought for delivery from the U.S. within the next six months, "surpassed by a good deal the known potential of the American industry." He warned that to resolve this problem, "it is necessary that we have the aid of the American administration and of the President as we had the first time [during the 1938–1939 mission]," and Monnet added, "without doubt this aid can only be obtained after the Neutrality Act is eliminated." Until then, Monnet preferred to stay in Europe to initiate a joint Anglo-French program for American purchases.[11]

La Chambre therefore requested Colonel Jacquin, who had been with Monnet on the last air mission, and Colonel Stéphane Thouvenot, an aeronautical engineer and a member of the Air Minister's personal staff, to undertake the mission. During the last days of August, the two officers were instructed by Daladier and La Chambre to buy every plane and engine that could be delivered to France by next April, but they were to proceed with utmost caution so as not to upset the Congressional debate over the embargo. So that there would be no delay in getting the new orders into production, contracts were to be drawn up as soon as possible. The contracts were to include a clause permitting their cancellation if the embargo were not removed. Because of the Neutrality Act, Daladier wanted his representatives to arrive in the United States before France became a belligerent, and they caught the last plane that left Europe before France declared war on Germany. The two officers believed, as one said later, "We could not lose. Daladier knew perfectly the thinking

[11] Memorandum, September 3, 1939, Monnet Papers, File 2A, Paris, October–November 1939.

of President Roosevelt." [12] To prepare the ground for the Jacquin-Thouvenot mission the Air Minister requested France's Air Attaché in Washington, Colonel René Weiser, to search for suitable planes.[13]

Although President Roosevelt proclaimed the embargo shortly after Jacquin and Thouvenot arrived in Washington, the two officers reported to the American Air Corps, "We are going to try to buy everything." General H. H. Arnold had recently issued a public statement: "Sales to foreign governments will be encouraged with a view to increasing our productive capacity . . . ," [14] but he still opposed selling the latest types of planes. Typically, he turned down Jacquin and Thouvenot's request for Bell's P-39 as this fighter was not scheduled for delivery to the Air Corps until the summer of 1940.[15] Thus while the Air Corps facilitated the sale of planes it no longer wanted, Jacquin, Thouvenot, and Colonel Weiser discovered that no adequate American planes were available for export to France within the next six months. A trans-Atlantic phone call moved the final delivery date to the end of 1940 and opened the way to the order of some 1,000 planes.[16]

[12] During interviews in June 1961, Generals Jacquin and Thouvenot reconstructed for the author the instructions Daladier and La Chambre gave them.

[13] Weiser reported to the State Department August 29, "He was authorized to negotiate for 400 pursuits, 800 combat planes, 1,000 observation planes and 600 bombers for the earliest possible delivery . . . orders to be placed irrespective of the outbreak of war." Secretary of State to Bullitt, August 29, 1939, SD 851.24/72a.

[14] General H. H. Arnold to All Concerned, September 1, 1939, AAF File 452.1-A, Sales of Planes Abroad.

[15] For the French request on October 23, 1939, for the P-39, see AAF File, 452.1, 3295 conference. For the official policy, see "Outline of Policy of War and Navy Departments for Release of Aircraft, Engines . . . and Accessories for Export and Domestic Sale," September 28, 1939, AAF File 452.1, 3295.

[16] As described to the author by General Jacquin.

The French officers were able to obtain only one plane which France had not ordered before, the new Curtiss fighter, the P-40. But if the French wished deliveries in 1940, they would have to pay $940,000 for acceleration charges.[17] Paris agreed to do this, and Jacquin and Thouvenot placed an order for 100 planes. To meet the Air Ministry's request for 600 fighters, they supplemented the P-40s with 550 of the only other American fighter available, the Curtiss P-36. Because of the engine shortage, deliveries of these fighters would not begin until February and a production rate of 65 a month would be reached only in May 1940.

The mission's judgment in placing a new order for the P-36 seemed verified in early November when nine of these fighters, which had been shipped to France earlier, tangled with 27 Messerschmitt 109s. Outnumbered three to one, the French pilots shot down nine Messerschmitts without a loss. Ambassador Bullitt cheered and reported, "In view of the spectacular performances of the P-36s you may well imagine the violence of the desire of the French to obtain more."[18]

For bombers, Jacquin and Thouvenot could obtain only the types which Monnet's mission had ordered during the past winter, the Martin 167 and the Douglas DB-7. Thanks to France's capital investment of $2.25 million during the past January, Glenn Martin had completed a new production line, and now Martin agreed to raise production to 65 a month for an order of 130. After two

[17] "Curtiss Hawk 81A [P-40] Foreign Release History," filed in AAF File, Lyon Project Book 10A, "Foreign Sales (February 1939–March 1940)."

[18] See *L'Air,* November 6, 1939; *The New York Times,* November 7, 1939, p. 1, and Bullitt's dispatch November 7, 1939, SD 740.0011 Eur. War 1939/1946.

months further orders could be placed for an improved Martin bomber similar to the Air Corps' B-26. The French mission also contracted with Douglas Aircraft for 270 additional DB-7s, and the company promised to raise production to 40 a month by July. France's first war orders for planes were completed by 200 North American trainers, all that the French mission could find available for delivery by September 1940.[19]

After the outbreak of war, Jacquin and Thouvenot found that Pratt and Whitney's entire productive capacity of some 200 per month was tied up in filling French as well as British and the American Air Corps' orders. The Air Corps also fully utilized the engine facilities of Curtiss-Wright, which had about the same monthly capacity. The real bottleneck in plane production thus was in engines, but the American manufacturers, fearing a peaceful solution to the current war boom, were "unwilling at their own expense" to create new facilities.[20] Thus the French Air Ministry ordered Jacquin and Thouvenot to finance a doubling of engine production lines for both Pratt and Whitney and Curtiss-Wright at a capital investment of $5 million each. Finally, the French placed an order for 700 Allison engines, but, as these high-horsepower engines

[19] Most helpful in reconstructing the numbers of planes and engines ordered and the acceleration charges have been two charts, facsimiles of which General Thouvenot provided the author: "Memorandum on Premiums for Accelerated Deliveries" and "Plane Orders Abroad (America)." Additional details have been gathered from *The New York Times,* November 4, 1939, p. 1, col. 2.

[20] See the memorandum by Green, Chief of Office of Arms and Munitions Control, State Department, on conversation with a representative of Pratt and Whitney, October 5, 1939, SD 851.248/273. General Jacquin recalled for the author that a top executive of Allison Engine Corporation said to him in the fall of 1939, "Colonel, will this be a long war? If so, then we will go into the business of plane engines."

were just coming into production, none could be delivered before August 1940.

Jacquin and Thouvenot had accomplished their survey and had prepared their agreements for sale by the time Congress repealed the arms embargo in early November. Their orders totaled over 1,000 combat planes plus 200 trainers and more than 5,000 high-powered engines. Although Jacquin and Thouvenot had been unable to meet the Air Minister's original demand for 2,800 fighters and bombers by April 1940, they had fully utilized available capacity for the production of modern planes. Between the spring of 1938 and the end of 1939 France had ordered a total of some 1,600 American war planes. The Air Corps' own orders for bombers and fighters amounted to 200 less. The cost of all the French orders came to $305 million; Congress appropriated $170 million for the Air Corps. The French orders now exceeded those of the British Air Ministry too, even though, once the embargo was raised, Britain purchased 200 more Lockheed Hudsons and 600 additional trainers, which brought total British expenditures to $96.5 million.[21]

The new French contracts expanding the two major American engine producers caught the United States Air Corps by surprise, for General Arnold was unaware of the extent of the orders until *The New York Times* broke the story on November 4.[22] The intensity of the Air Corps reaction was reflected during a meeting called on November 8 by the Assistant Secretary of War, who in turn responded by warning American aircraft manufacturers

[21] For the figures, see "French Purchase Costs as of 3–31–40," Lend Lease, Federal Economic Administration, President's Liaison Committee (LL, FEA, PLC), A 05/3, National Archives, Record Group 169.

[22] *The New York Times,* November 4, 1939, p. 1, col. 2.

that "the interests of national defense require that engine production keep pace with plane production so there would be no difficulties for additional planes for the War and Navy Departments." [23] The problem also prompted President Roosevelt to have General Arnold determine the Air Corps' requirement for planes and "the unused portion of the industry available for foreign orders." At the same time, Arnold was ordered not to make "any decisions regarding the utilization of aeronautical facilities in meeting foreign orders." [24] To forestall any such attempt, Roosevelt decided on November 10 to take from the Army-Navy Munitions Board control of foreign sale of military items and to substitute a liaison committee. The committee, which would consist of the Treasury Department's Director of Procurement, the Army's Quartermaster General and the Paymaster General of the Navy, would report directly to the President.[25] Obviously, Roosevelt was determined to maintain his control of the foreign sale of planes.

Roosevelt was also piqued by the latest French orders for aircraft engines because the orders had not been coordinated with American defense needs or British desires. The President impatiently demanded coordination of all purchases by the Allies.[26] By the time the President's de-

[23] Memorandum by Green, on meeting in the office of the Assistant Secretary of War (ASW), November 8, 1939, SD 711,00111 Armament Control/2279.

[24] Memorandum for Chief of Air Corps (CAC) from ASW, November 10, 1939, AG 452 (11–10–39).

[25] Langer and Gleason, *Challenge to Isolation,* p. 289. For President's approval of this plan on November 10, see also Under Secretary of State, Sumner Welles, to Treasury Department, December 5, 1939, SD 841.24/136.

[26] Secretary of State to Bullitt, November 10, 1939, SD 841.24/105. See also Hall, *North American Supply,* p. 97.

mands arrived in London and Paris, both capitals, due to the efforts of Jean Monnet, were prepared to fulfill them.

Monnet had already launched on September 3 France's second initiative when he urged the French Premier to coordinate the Anglo-French purchase of additional American aircraft. On the basis of first-hand knowledge gained during the past winter in the United States, Monnet recommended that Britain be invited to join France in an air mission which would (a) "immediately order everything available" and (b) "double or treble American aircraft production." To do this he recommended,

> 1. All effective negotiations with American industry should wait until the repeal of the Neutrality Act.
>
> 2. Negotiations should be carried on with the agreement of the President and his Administration, which is possible only after the repeal of the Neutrality Act, not before.
>
> 3. The program should be a joint Anglo-French effort, as it appeared clearly to me in talks I had with President Roosevelt [in January 1939].
>
> 4. Steps should be taken to organize American production so as to obtain rapidly maximum production.[27]

By September 15 Monnet had prepared for Daladier's signature a letter to the British Prime Minister:

> I am preoccupied with the problem of necessary imports by our two countries and the organization

[27] Memo, September 3, 1939, Monnet Papers, File 2A, Paris, October–November 1939.

> which can assure them. . . . I would like to talk with you at one of our next conferences [and] . . . examine whether our present arrangements are adequate for a long war. I am convinced of the necessity of coordinating all measures . . . unity of action ought to be assured and if required common action taken.

Urging that Britain and France avoid the error made in World War I—letting three years pass before establishing the Inter-Allied Organization—the letter continued, "I have instructed Jean Monnet to go to London to talk with you on this question." [28]

When Premier Daladier arrived in England for the Supreme War Council on September 22, he knew that Prime Minister Chamberlain was interested in coordinating Britain's war economy with that of France. Both Governments had begun that spring to discuss the coordination of their economic warfare, food supplies, raw materials, overseas imports, shipping facilities, and finances. On July 6 Chamberlain had approached Daladier about rebuilding the machinery of joint British and French planning and action which had been established in 1917. In August when the French and British governments constituted the Supreme War Council and appointed permanent military representatives from the three services, they did not establish a joint economic council.[29] At the September council meeting, however, Chamberlain agreed "to the necessity to coordinate Allied imports as much as

[28] Draft of letter to Chamberlain, September 15, 1939. A second draft of this letter dated September 20 had little change; it is also located in Monnet Papers, File 2A, Paris, October–November 1939.

[29] W. K. Hancock and M. M. Gowing, *British War Economy: History of the Second World War, United Kingdom Civil Series* (London, 1949), pp. 179–84.

possible, especially arms." He also agreed to receive Monnet as Daladier's representative.[30]

Monnet arrived in London on September 26 and immediately called on Sir Kingsley Wood, the British Secretary for Air. The two men were joined by Prime Minister Chamberlain's representative, Sir Edward Bridges, Secretary of the newly created War Cabinet. Monnet emphasized that French policy was to concentrate Allied purchases in the United States on aircraft, because only in this way could France and Britain gain air supremacy over Germany.[31] Monnet then brought up his main point:

> If, as hoped, American neutrality would open the United States to the purchase of planes, it is important to avoid competition which would be very dangerous and which the American Administration would not tolerate. In the relations, which the French Administration had with the United States during the past winter, the support of the American Administration was indispensable. . . . It is necessary to have a complete idea of the French and English demands on American industry to avoid upsetting the American rearmament program.

The Air Secretary agreed to "as close cooperation as possible" and asked Monnet to work out the preliminaries.[32]

The next day Monnet met with officials in the Ministry of Supply and expanded his ideas both on economic coor-

[30] Memo, "Anglo-French Organization on Supplies for France and Britain," London, September 29, 1939, Monnet Papers, British Supply Council, Anglo-French Coordinating Committee (A-FCC).

[31] Hall, *North American Supply*, p. 117.

[32] Résumé of Negotiations September 20–26, 1939, for an Anglo-French Organization for Supplies, Monnet Papers, File 2A, Paris, October–November 1939.

dination and a balance sheet showing Anglo-French production and war requirements. He found the Minister of Supply, Leslie Brugin, "very open to the idea of permanent and ordered collaboration," and the Minister was prepared to go to France to establish a joint Armaments Council, whose executive committee would be in London.[33] By October 1 Monnet had talked with not only the British Secretaries of Air and Supply but also the top representatives of the Army, Navy, Exchequer, Food, and Economic Warfare and the Shipping Department of the Board of Trade: "These interviews have convinced me that in the great majority the responsible persons of the British Government are anxious to avoid the delays and gropings of the last war in establishing practical cooperation between France and Britain." [34]

Monnet's negotiations bore fruit on October 3 when the British War Cabinet set up the Interdepartmental Committee for Anglo-French Supply and Purchase of War Materials. It included representatives from the Ministries of Treasury, Air, Supply, Food, and Economic Warfare, as well as Shipping, Mines and Petrol departments. The establishment of the committee was the first step toward coordinating Britain's overseas purchases.[35] In contrast, the French delayed until November 2 the establishment of their parallel body, the Comité de Programmes et des Achats Allies.

On October 1 Monnet proposed to Bridges, the Secretary of the War Cabinet, a three-phase organization to coordinate the Anglo-French war effort. He recommended

[33] Memo on meeting at Ministry of Supply, September 27, *Ibid.*

[34] Report to Daladier, October 1, 1939, *Ibid.*

[35] J. Hurstfield, *The Control of Raw Materials: History of the Second World War, United Kingdom Civil Series* (London, 1953), p. 250.

that each of the ministerial councils on armaments and aviation have a permanent executive committee to handle the problems of supply, finance, and shipping. Monnet then suggested a small economic war council, composed of one British and one French minister, which would provide economic coordination. Finally, he urged that all foreign purchases be channeled through a third organization, a single Anglo-French purchasing agency: "Nowhere will this prove more essential than in the United States." Monnet also warned,

> As to finance, the difficulty is going to be the limited resources of gold and foreign exchange of our two countries. Indeed, the problem of financing foreign imports will be an important one which never existed to a similar extent in 1914–18 because we could draw upon the financial resources of the U.S.A. both before 1917 and after.[36]

On October 11 Monnet again met with the British officials in London and laid the final plan for the machinery to coordinate the economic war effort. They agreed to set up joint permanent executive committees for each of the British Ministeries of Treasury, Air, Supply, Food, and Economic Warfare. A coordinating committee would also be established but with only one full-time chairman who "must have the confidence of both governments and, although in no sense an arbitrator, he must, in a capacity of counselor and guide, endeavor to adjust differences and to obtain decisions," and he was to reside in London.[37]

[36] Letter from Monnet to Bridges, October 1, 1939, Monnet Papers, File 2A, Paris, October–November 1939.

[37] British Official Record of Meeting with Monnet, October 11, 1939, in Treasury Library; Present: Sir Horace Wilson, chairman; Sir Frederick Phillips, Treasury; Sir William Broan, Board of Trade;

At the Brighton meeting of the Supreme War Council on October 17 this plan was discussed, and Monnet prepared a letter for Daladier to forward Chamberlain after that meeting:

> We have met at Brighton on the important question of coordination of the economic war effort of our two countries and have agreed that all useful steps be taken not only to establish coordination but also to attain as much common action as possible. Monnet has given me an account of all his talks with the different British Ministers. . . .[38]

Four days later the Prime Minister sent back his government's approval, and he added,

> I am very pleased to learn that M. Monnet has been so satisfied by the discussion he had with our services in London. I should like to take this opportunity of letting you know how much Monnet's appreciation of our problems and his willing cooperation have assisted in the preparation of this important scheme of Anglo-French war effort.[39]

With Britain's approval Monnet now suggested to Daladier three further steps "to assure implementation of the Daladier-Chamberlain accord": (1) coordinate the interested French Ministries, (2) establish inter-allied orders,

---

Sir Frederick Leith-Ross, Ministry of Economic Warfare; Sir Edward Bridges, Secretary of the War Cabinet. Monnet Papers, British Supply Council, A-FCC Formation. See also "Planned Machinery for Coordination of the Anglo-French Economic War Effort." English text dated October 12, and French text dated October 13, 1939, Monnet Papers, File 2A, Paris, October–November 1939.

[38] Draft of a letter from Daladier to Chamberlain dated October 17 and sent October 18, 1939, *Ibid.*

[39] Letter from Chamberlain to Daladier, October 22, 1939, *Ibid.*

and (3) agree with President Roosevelt on the organization of an Anglo-French mission in the United States and make arrangements for the American Administration to cooperate with it.[40]

Since early October, President Roosevelt's Administration had been bringing pressure upon the Allies to coordinate their American purchases. On October 4, Morgenthau appealed directly through the British Embassy in Washington for this goal and requested reports of purchasing plans and financial assets.[41] From the tenth to the thirteenth, during a visit to Washington of members of the newly formed British Supply Board, Morgenthau stressed the need for weekly summaries of orders and deliveries of foodstuffs, raw materials, and manufactured items, and the Secretary left no doubt that the President intended to give all possible help the moment the arms embargo was repealed.[42] Ambassador Sir Ronald Lindsay reported these talks to London and emphasized the need for action as soon as the embargo was repealed. He referred to the progress Jacquin and Thouvenot were making with their air mission and he noted that Roosevelt expected large orders from the French. He warned that London would make an error if either the Administration or American industry gained the impression that Britain did not place substantial orders at once because "the local press was already estimating Allied orders from $3 to 11 billion." [43]

Roosevelt welcomed the news about the steps taken by Daladier and Chamberlain at Brighton toward Anglo-French economic coordination, and upon Ambassador

[40] Note for Daladier, October 23, 1939, *Ibid.*
[41] Hall, *North American Supply,* p. 90.
[42] *Ibid.,* p. 69. [43] *Ibid.,* pp. 69–70.

Bullitt's request the President sent assurance that a joint Allied purchasing commission would be given the same cooperation which Monnet's mission had received ten months ago. Morgenthau was also pleased, although he had second thoughts about Monnet as head of such a commission: "While I am not crazy to have Monnet come over here . . . I suppose I can get along with him as well as I can with any other Frenchman. But . . . heaven only knows what all his connections are." [44]

Meanwhile, in Paris Monnet was pushing toward a final agreement on an Allied purchasing mission, and on October 23 he urged Daladier to select a chief soon, particularly as "the Neutrality Act will certainly be abolished before the end of the week and at that moment or a little later President Roosevelt will count on receiving from the two governments a formal announcement of a common mission." [45]

On October 28, Paris sent Jean Bloch-Lainé to Washington to establish an agency to coordinate French purchasing missions already in the States and to prepare for a joint Anglo-French group under one chief. Until final word came, the French missions were to continue as before in making independent purchases for France, but they were warned against establishing premature ties with "certain American banking firms following the precedent of the last war . . . circumstances are entirely different and . . . the Administration does not desire an intermediary role of this nature to be confided to American financial interests." [46]

[44] Bullitt October 17 and reply October 18, 1939, *FR, 1939,* vol. II, pp. 566–67. See also Blum, *Morgenthau Diaries,* II, 182.

[45] Note for President of Council, October 23, 1939, Monnet Papers, File 2A, Paris, October–November 1939.

[46] Draft of cables to French Ambassador in Washington, René, Comté de Saint Quentin, October 28 and 29, 1939, *Ibid.*

At about the same time that Bloch-Lainé left for Washington, the British requested Arthur Purvis, a Scot and currently a leading Canadian industrialist, to head the British mission in Washington and to coordinate all Britain's purchases in the United States. On October 31, Britain agreed with France to give up British preference for two separate missions and accept a unified purchasing organization. On November 7, the press was finally informed of the new British purchasing arrangements for North America, and a future announcement was promised concerning "arrangements to secure close coordination of British and French purchases in the United States." [47] However, these arrangements were not completed until November 25.

Since Roosevelt's main reason for removing the arms embargo had been to aid the British and the French, he was impatient when the Allies failed to set up a joint-purchasing-committee mission as soon as the embargo was repealed on November 3. In fact, as Congress voted to repeal the embargo, Roosevelt heard that Jacquin and Thouvenot had put in those large orders for American engines. Just what he had feared had happened: a foreign nation had bought up so much American productive capacity that it threatened to interfere with all future orders for planes. Roosevelt informed Purvis that he was "deeply concerned" over the lack of Allied cooperation.[48]

This cooperation had been delayed because, although a general Anglo-French agreement had been worked out at the Supreme War Council on October 17, the final plans to integrate the two nation's war efforts were difficult to

[47] Hall, *North American Supply*, pp. 70–71. For a summary of Purvis' background see *North American Supply*, pp. 74–80.

[48] Secretary of State to Bullitt, November 10, 1939, *FR, 1939*, vol. I, p. 567.

settle. While the British Government moved slowly and carefully toward the goal Monnet and Daladier wanted, France had its own problems. As soon as the Comité des Programmes et des Achats Allies was established in Paris on November 2, it faced several serious issues: (1) each of the ministries was hesitant to relinquish control of the foreign purchasing missions they had already sent abroad; (2) the ministries failed to forward adequate monthly statements of requirements and purchases and thus provide a basis "for discussion of foreign purchases which is the object of the Comité"—in particular, the "important program of aircraft purchases in the United States" had not even figured in the latest monthly statements from the Air Ministry; and (3) the Minister of Finance wanted to exercise control. The Comité reacted strenuously to this latter problem, and it stated that "its object is to adapt French purchases to the general policy of the government on the conduct of the war" and that its duty "is not to assure realization of the program . . . [nor] to mix in budget control, or control foreign exchange."[49]

At the end of October, Monnet had drafted a letter for Daladier to send to Chamberlain, urging that personnel be assigned both to the Coordinating Committee and to the common purchasing mission. The letter concluded, "The French Government is ready to act. . . . I am sending Monnet to you with my views."[50] As of November 8 no final action had been taken because Paris urged that, as the Allied economic organization was centered in London, a

[49] Minutes of Conference Relative to Armaments; Daladier to Members of Comité, no date; memo to Monnet in London, November 8, 1939; memo by Secretary General of Comité, November 9, 1939, Monnet Papers, File 2A, Paris, October–November 1939.

[50] Draft of a letter from Daladier to Chamberlain, October 30, 1939, *Ibid.*

Frenchman chair the Coordinating Committee. In contrast, Sir Horace Wilson, Chamberlain's special adviser on Anglo-French economic coordination, suggested that a former Minister for Air, Lord Swinton, be appointed chairman. But Daladier opposed a politician, preferring that Monnet be given the post. On November 16 "Wilson was sympathetic" and the British accepted Monnet.[51]

By this time Anglo-French agreement had also been reached on a joint purchasing committee in the United States, and both nations agreed that Purvis should be its chief. On November 18 Bullitt cabled President Roosevelt "to find out urgently and ultra-confidentially if Purvis is a person who will receive the same sort of cooperation that was accorded to Monnet last winter."[52] The President's assurance was received on November 20, and three days later in a letter to the Ambassador in Paris, Roosevelt wrote, "What we want is that perfectly possible combination of two head men—one French and one British—who will sleep in the same bed and lay all their cards on the table to prevent crossing wires."[53]

Although the British and French governments delayed public announcement of their economic coordinating bodies until Roosevelt had assured them that he would support Purvis, other matters had to be settled before the next Supreme War Council meeting on November 17. One of these was the definition of duties of the Permanent Executive Committees. By that meeting Monnet had completed

[51] Letter from Monnet to Daladier, November 8, 1939; memo from Monnet to Daladier, November 16, 1939, *Ibid.*

[52] Bullitt, November 18, and reply of November 20, 1939, *FR, 1939,* vol. I, pp. 569–70.

[53] Roosevelt to Bullitt, November 23, 1939, *F.D.R.: His Personal Letters,* vol. II, pp. 959–60.

an eight-page memorandum spelling out these duties. It began:

> 1. In each area to establish a program of the needs of the two countries and to establish an ad hoc inventory of the resources of each country in that field.
>
> 2. To assure the best utilization of the resources and equitable distribution between the two countries.[54]

The Supreme War Council approved these duties, established the Anglo-French Purchasing Commission, naming Purvis chief with Bloch-Lainé second in command, and set up the Anglo-French Economic Coordinating Committee, with Monnet as its chairman.[55] These Supreme Council decisions were not published until November 25, since the French Government wanted to be assured of American cooperation. Once again Bullitt acted as intermediary, and Monnet drafted a cablegram for Daladier asking the White House to extend "the same intimate cooperation which was given by your Administration and in particular by your Procurement Division of the Treasury to the French mission led by Monnet last spring for the purchase of planes." [56] On November 25, when Lon-

[54] Memo from Monnet to Daladier, November 16, 1939; instructions to the Permanent Executive Committees, November 16, 1939, Monnet Papers, File 2A, Paris, October–November 1939. See also Hurstfield, *Control of Raw Materials,* p. 247.

[55] Supreme War Council Agreed Announcement of Anglo-French Economic Agreement on Joint Foreign Purchases, November 17, 1939, Monnet Papers, File 2A, Paris, October–November 1939.

[56] First and second drafts of a cable from Bullitt to Roosevelt (for final draft, see Bullitt to Secretary of State, November 25, 1939, *FR, 1939,* vol. I, p. 570); letter from Wilson to Monnet through René Pleven, November 25, 1939; cable from Daladier to Ambassador Saint Quentin, November 27, 1939, Monnet Papers, File 2A, Paris, October–November 1939.

don and Paris were again assured of Roosevelt's cooperation, they finally released the news of their latest steps toward economic coordination.[57]

The first twelve weeks of war had witnessed a certain success for Daladier's government. France had further opened the American arsenal when its air mission ordered every plane available by the end of 1940 and had gone on to double American aircraft-engine capacity. On the other side of the ocean, Britain and Franch had established the Anglo-French Economic Coordinating Committee and the joint Purchasing Committee to operate in the United States. The pace had not been leisurely, for, as an official British history states, it was remarkable that so much had been accomplished in those three months.[58] Although the deadline for establishing the two committees before the American repeal of the arms embargo had not been met, it had been missed by only three weeks. The prime purpose for establishing Anglo-French economic coordination was to concentrate Allied finances on developing the American capacity to produce planes, and two days before November 25 when Britain and France publicly announced their plans for economic cooperation, Premier Daladier had already launched a new drive for 10,000 planes to be delivered by the fall of 1941.

[57] Projected and final communiqué from Chamberlain and Daladier to press, November 25, 1939, *Ibid.*

[58] Hancock and Gowing, *British War Economy,* pp. 186–87.

CHAPTER

7

10,000 Planes for the Allies

AFTER THE ARMS EMBARGO was repealed and the Anglo-French Purchasing Commission was established in New York, the stage was set, in late November, for the next move to obtain Allied aid from the United States.[1] Leadership in this campaign came particularly from Jean Monnet, who, as chairman of the Anglo-French Economic Coordinating Committee, remained in Paris and London, seeking out ways to overcome the opposition to his goal of doubling and even tripling American aircraft production. Again he was supported by Premier Daladier and Guy La Chambre, while opposition to a joint purchase of American planes centered in Britain.

Across the Atlantic assistance came from President Roosevelt and his Secretary of the Treasury. They evolved a new method for clearing Allied orders and for by-passing the usual obstructions from the War Department and

[1] Material in this chapter was summarized in John McVickar Haight, Jr., "Jean Monnet and the American Arsenal After the Beginning of the War," *French Society and Culture since the Old Regime: The Eleutherian Mills Colloquium, 1964, of the Society for French Historical Studies and the Societé d'Histoire Moderne,* eds. Evelyn M. Acomb and Marvin L. Brown, Jr. (New York, 1966), pp. 269–83.

the Army Air Corps. Arthur Purvis, who was chairman of the Allies' joint purchasing commission and reported directly to Monnet, helped by winning the support of the key individual in American foreign sales, Secretary Morgenthau. The Allies needed strong assistance if they were to make Premier Daladier's goal: 10,000 American planes by the spring of 1941.

Looking toward Monnet's goal, Daladier talked with Ambassador Bullitt on November 23, two days before public announcement of the Anglo-French Economic Coordinating Committee and the joint Purchasing Commission. Monnet, as well as La Chambre, was present at the conference. The Premier informed Bullitt that he wanted to purchase 10,000 planes from the United States to provide France and Britain "absolute dominance in the air" over Germany. Daladier wanted deliveries to begin in early 1940 and to continue until the spring of 1941, but he recognized "this problem was an enormous one," since U.S. factories already "had more orders than they could fill for the year 1940" and "it would be necessary to create enlarged facilities for the production of planes." He suggested that a portion of the automobile industry be converted to the manufacture of planes and engines. As Monnet was setting up the "organization for pooling the resources of France and England," Daladier stated, he would send René Pleven, Monnet's assistant, to the United States to handle the problem of planes. Bullitt told Washington in his report on this conference that he had known Pleven for years and had "as complete confidence in his character and integrity as I have in Monnet's"; nevertheless, Daladier insisted it was essential for Bullitt to accompany Pleven.[2]

[2] Bullitt to Secretary of State, November 23, 1939, *FR, 1939,* vol. II, pp. 520–22.

For those in Washington who were not fully aware of the background of events, Daladier's wish to purchase 10,000 planes must have looked like a desperate effort. It is understandable that Pierrepont Moffat, the chief of the State Department's Division of European affairs, commented after reading Bullitt's dispatch, "[Daladier] painted a lurid picture of what would happen or what he would do if he was not satisfied with the outcome of the trip." [3] Indeed, Daladier threatened to resign if sufficient planes could not be obtained from the United States and to turn the government over to "Bonnet or Flandin, either one of whom would make an early compromise peace with Germany." Such a threat did not bother President Roosevelt because he was fully prepared for Daladier's search for 10,000 planes. Nor was the President disturbed by the Premier's offer "to make every French resource available to obtain these planes . . . Versailles or any other possession of the French Government," since during the past spring Daladier had offered to settle the war debts by transferring French territory to the United States for use as naval and air bases. Indeed, Ambassador Bullitt and the French Premier had discussed in mid-November "the idea of lease or contract" as a method for opening such bases to the Americans.[4]

On November 23 Roosevelt replied to Daladier's request for 10,000 planes. In a letter to Ambassador Bullitt, he wrote,

[3] "The Diplomatic Journals of Jay Pierrepont Moffat, 1919–1943," November 25–26, 1939. Gordon Wright, *France in Modern Times* (Chicago, 1960), p. 506, labels Daladier's request "a desperate effort to remedy the imbalance of France." See also his "Ambassador Bullitt and the Fall of France," *World Politics,* X, October 1957, No. 1, 79.

[4] See the letter from Welles to Bullitt, Nov. 15, 1939, with note, "O.K., F.D.R.," President Secretary's File, Box 3, William C. Bullitt Folder, Roosevelt Library.

> In regard to purchasing, I am ready to handle the whole matter over here if we only knew whom we were talking to. Our objective is the practical one of not interfering with our own military and naval program, and secondly, to prevent prices from rising in this country.

Roosevelt took issue only with Daladier's demand that Bullitt accompany Pleven to the United States, saying that he and Cordell Hull "feel certain that it would be a mistake for you to come over here on any such mission because it would be sure to leak out and it is not the duty of an Ambassador." [5]

Despite the urgency of Daladier's appeal to the President, Paris did not dispatch Pleven to Washington until December 11. This delay indicated that preparations for the mission had not been running smoothly in either France or Britain. As usual, one center of French opposition was located in the Ministry of Finance, where Paul Reynaud stated on November 30, "French resources would just about cover these needs [for imported goods of all sorts during the coming twelve months] without any additional payments whatsoever for additional planes in the United States." In his cable to Washington reporting Reynaud's position, Bullitt stated that Daladier was still prepared to cut all foreign purchases "in order to provide a sufficiently large fund for airplane purchases from the United States." The Premier's feeling had not changed since November 23, when he had remarked to Bullitt, "If Paul Reynaud should make financial objections, Paul Reynaud could resign." [6]

[5] *F.D.R.: His Personal Letters,* vol. II, pp. 959–60. See also the letter from the Secretary of State to Bullitt, November 25, 1939, *FR, 1939,* vol. II, p. 523.

[6] Bullitt, November 23 and 30, 1939, *Ibid.,* vol. II, pp. 523–24 and 520.

Obstacles also arose in the United States when members of the separate French and British purchasing missions hesitated to give up their independence and to come under a joint authority. Colonel Jacquin, who had successfully established contacts with American companies over the past three months, was reluctant to share them with the British Purchasing Commission which had been operating in the United States only since the repeal of the arms embargo. Then, too, as Jean Bloch-Lainé, vice chairman of the Anglo-French Purchasing Commission, complained, "British officials up to now have been preoccupied with keeping open the ordinary channels of commerce between the two countries." Arthur Purvis, the commission's chairman, was aware of these problems and worked with Bloch-Lainé to overcome "this situation which is incompatible with a joint organization." [7]

As a result of the British Government's policy of self-sufficiency of its war industries,[8] Prime Minister Chamberlain hesitated to send a representative along with Pleven. But by December 8 the French had decided to dispatch Pleven to Washington even if London refused to cooperate,[9] and two days later Monnet prepared a letter for Daladier to forward to Chamberlain:

> In the course of our meetings I have spoken of my desire to see our two countries acquire as rapidly as possible aerial supremacy which in my mind will permit us to impose our initiative on the enemy and

[7] Bloch-Lainé to Daladier, December 2 and 13, 1939, Monnet Papers, File 2A, Paris, October–November 1939.

[8] M. M. Postan, *British War Production: History of the Second World War, United Kingdom Civil Series* (London, 1952), pp. 227–30.

[9] Monnet to Purvis, December 8, 1939, Monnet Papers, File 2A, Paris, October–November 1939.

hasten the end of the war. [While I recognize Britain's] great effort to obtain maximum production . . . [and that] our efforts are also at the maximum, I estimate it is indispensable to complement our national production by American imports.

From information furnished me the present American production is almost utilized by earlier orders and the needs of the American army. Thus to obtain the supplementary supplies the potential of American production ought to be augmented on a large scale.

I am interested to know in what condition this would be possible. To this end I am sending Pleven to make a confidential and rapid survey.

He concluded by requesting Britain to join this survey mission, from which a report could be expected by January 15.[10]

The British Prime Minister's reply was summarized by Guy La Chambre:

1. Chamberlain agrees on the need of aerial superiority.

2. However, he believes this can be obtained through the factories in England and the Dominions. This capacity, already large in time of peace, is growing. But its growth depends on machine tools. Great orders for planes in the United States would reduce the possibility of procuring these machines.

[10] Draft of a letter from Daladier to Chamberlain, December 10, 1939, *Ibid.* For an excerpt of the final letter sent on December 11, 1939, see Hall, *North American Supply,* p. 118.

3. Augmentation of productive capacity in the United States could not be attained in 1941 but in 1942.

4. England fears using foreign exchange on large orders in the United States.[11]

Despite the British position, Daladier and La Chambre signed Pleven's orders on December 11. He would leave for America on the first available boat.[12]

The British opposition to Daladier's program is made clearer by several briefs prepared for Chamberlain at the meeting of the Supreme War Council on December 21. One brief prepared by the Treasury emphasized financial obstacles, while the other written in the Air Ministry underlined that Britain planned to lift its own plane production to 2,500 per month and that the machine tools, for which Britain had paid the United States $150 million, were necessary to fulfill this goal. An order for American planes would divert some of these tools to U.S. production and thus slow deliveries from British factories. An official in the British Air Ministry concluded, "The French proposal is really incompatible with our present program." [13]

At the Anglo-French War Council, Daladier mentioned the issue of American planes and how important they were for winning mastery of the air, and, to save as much foreign exchange as possible, the Premier restated his determination to cut all purchases from abroad. Once again the British Prime Minister hesitated and added to his former objections, "American planes are so expensive that

[11] La Chambre to Daladier (no date), Monnet Papers, File 2A, Paris, October–November 1939.

[12] Daladier and La Chambre to Pleven, December 11, 1939, *Ibid.*

[13] Hall, *North American Supply*, pp. 118–19.

the question of financing purchases of planes in the United States was a serious one which the British Government would have to study with care." Daladier reiterated his intention to go ahead. He and his advisers left the council with the impression that, if the French could create facilities in the United States for building a large number of planes, the British would be forced to share the burden of at least half.[14]

The French judged correctly that the British could not disassociate themselves from the Pleven mission, and London did order Colonel J. M. H. Greenly, already in Washington as head of the British Purchasing Mission, to join Pleven's survey mission. Greenly was not to commit his government to financing new productive capacity for additional American planes, however.[15] By December 21, when Pleven had arrived in New York and had met Morgenthau,[16] a number of developments had taken place which facilitated his mission. On December 6, shortly after Arthur Purvis officially reported as the new head of the Anglo-French Purchasing Commission, Roosevelt established the President's Liaison Committee which, as he wrote to the Secretary of War, was to serve "as the exclusive liaison with reference to procurement matters between this Government and interested foreign governments."[17]

[14] For the fullest report of this phase of the Council meeting, see Bullitt, December 21, *FR, 1939,* vol. II, pp. 524–26.

[15] For Greenly's orders, see Hall, *North American Supply,* p. 119.

[16] Conference among Secretary of the Treasury (S/T), Purvis, Pleven, and Collins. December 22, 1939, Morgenthau Diary, Bk. 232, pp. 1–5.

[17] John M. Blum, *Morgenthau Diaries,* vol. II, pp. 111–12; see also Roosevelt's letter to Secretary of War, War Department Archives, War Plans Division, File 4244, National Archives, Record Group 165, and the letters from Welles to Roosevelt, December 4,

The background of this Liaison Committee underscores the problems which the President and Morgenthau had to meet before new foreign orders for planes and munitions of war could be placed in the United States. The committee grew directly out of talks Roosevelt and Morgenthau had had shortly after the repeal of the arms embargo. During the Congressional debate over that revision of the Neutrality Act, Morgenthau, at Roosevelt's request, had informally and secretly been "pinch hitting" to help the French obtain war materials. As Morgenthau announced to his staff on November 8, he had recently obtained for France its order of anti-aircraft searchlights and had done so despite opposition from the Army. Deliveries were arranged so that France would receive every other searchlight that came off the production line and the United States Army would receive the rest. It was a procedure which set an important precedent for future deliveries of American arms and war material to the Allies.

With the repeal of the arms embargo, Morgenthau expected a deluge of British and French war orders. Convinced that these demands would not be given sympathetic treatment by the Army-Navy Munitions Board, the Secretary of the Treasury, with Roosevelt's help, sought control over foreign war orders. The obvious method would be to restore Captain Harry Collins, the Treasury's new Director of Procurement, to the role he had played with Monnet's air mission during the past winter. Some representation of the War and Navy departments would be important to quiet the opposition expected from those quarters. The solution, which Morgenthau proposed to the President on November 7, was ingenious. He suggested a three-man

---

1939, and to the Treasury Department, December 5, 1939, SD 841.24/135a, 136.

liaison committee made up of the Director of Procurement, the Army's Quartermaster General, and the Navy's Paymaster General. This committee was to meet at least weekly, review foreign orders, and report to the White House through a Presidential assistant, William McReynolds. Morgenthau was to be sent a copy of these reports.

The new committee was designed to avoid the opposition of the War Department to foreign sales. Indeed, this was recognized by the conferees in Morgenthau's office on November 8; as McReynolds said,

> Harry [Collins] is going to have a difficult problem on his hands getting these people together, that is getting an agreement. Of course, he won't have any trouble with the Navy on priorities. The only way you can get anything out of these military fellows—in the military line—will be for two members of the Committee to outvote the Army because, God! they won't agree on anything.

The new liaison committee would also aid the Treasury to regularize French and British purchases.[18]

On November 9 Morgenthau turned over to the President a finished recommendation on this liaison committee and, although Roosevelt had approved of the committee, he delayed establishing it until December 6.[19] He hesitated because the War and Navy departments sought to maintain their control over foreign purchases of arms, which

[18] Staff conference, November 8, 1939, Morgenthau Diary, Bk. 221, pp. 358–64.

[19] Conference between F.D.R. and S/T, November 9, 1939, Morgenthau Diary, Bk. 222, pp. 92–95.

since the past July had, with Presidential approval, been placed under the Army-Navy Munitions Board. While the Secretary of War adamantly opposed any arms sales, Louis Johnson recognized, after the repeal of the arms embargo, that the issue deserved broad representation. Thus Johnson proposed a board made up of the Assistant Secretaries from not only the Army and Navy but also from the State, Treasury, and Commerce departments.[20]

On the day before Thanksgiving, at the request of the British and French Ambassadors, Morgenthau officially met Arthur Purvis, but he refused to extend to Purvis the same cooperation that he had extended to Jean Monnet: "I can't do that because I have no such direction from the President." As usual, Morgenthau wanted official orders before sticking his neck out. He did suggest that Lord Lothian, the British Ambassador, "see the President and come to some understanding with him."[21] Lord Lothian, together with Comte René Saint Quentin, the French Ambassador, prompted Roosevelt to issue the order establishing his Liaison Committee under the chairmanship of Captain Collins.[22]

Opposition continued in the War and Navy departments, as well as in the State Department. Each doubted the competence of the Director of Procurement to advise the President on the foreign purchase of arms and muni-

[20] Memo by the Under Secretary of the Treasury, Hanes, of conference in office of ASW, Louis Johnson, November 9, Morgenthau Diary, Bk. 222, p. 45. For the conflict between Woodring and Johnson, see Langer and Gleason, *Challenge to Isolation,* p. 291.

[21] Conference among S/T, Purvis, Collins, etc., November 28, 1939, Morgenthau Diary, Bk. 225, pp. 34–44.

[22] Ambassador Saint Quentin to French Foreign Minister, December 6, 1939, Monnet Papers, File 2A, Paris, October–November 1939. See also the letter from Welles to F.D.R., December 4, 1939, SD, 841.24/135a.

tions.[23] President Roosevelt countered that probably more than 50 per cent of the foreign purchases would "consist of articles and raw and semi-raw materials which are primarily for civilian use." Also the Munitions Board officials would be represented by the Quartermaster General and the Paymaster General on the Liaison Committee, "especially when it comes to purely military or naval materials."

> Finally it must be remembered that we are not at war, that we are trying to keep prices down in this country, that the work of the Committee deals with civilians and that the general fiscal and purchasing policies of the Treasury are definitely involved.
>
> That is why I think I should let the present arrangement stand.[24]

Despite the President's arguments, General Arnold, in particular, remained disturbed because he had no direct voice in the Anglo-French negotiations for American planes. But the President refused to budge. His intention was to bring negotiations for foreign purchases under his direct control in order to clear any obstacles which might

[23] See the joint letter from ASW and Acting S/N Edison to F.D.R. and the telephone conversation between S/T and Collins, December 12, 1939, Morgenthau Diary, Bk. 228, pp. 195–96 and 203. In the State Department, Moffat voiced his opposition and noted, "there is much more to this than meets the eye." ("Moffat Journals," December 19, 1939.) See also the memo by Herbert Feis dated December 18, 1939, SD, 841.24/152 and the conversation between Feis and S/T, December 12, 1939, Morgenthau Diary, Bk. 228, p. 125. For further opposition, see the telephone conversations between S/T and Welles, and between S/T and Collins, December 28, 1939, Morgenthau Diary, Bk. 232, pp. 236–38 and 240. For a summary, see Blum, *Morgenthau Diaries,* vol. II, p. 112.

[24] F.D.R. to S/W, December 13, 1939, Morgenthau Diary, Bk. 228, pp. 200–2.

arise from various branches of the government. Indicative of his position was his answer to a question raised during a cabinet meeting on December 8. When the Postmaster General, James A. Farley, asked if "England and France just wanted airplanes and we wanted them at the same time, would we insist upon deliveries to us?" the President replied that it was a matter of confidential information but "up to a certain number, at any rate, we would let England and France have first call." [25]

While Roosevelt was smoothing the way for the Anglo-French Purchasing Commission and Pleven's survey, Paris learned that negotiations for 10,000 planes would meet serious technical problems. On December 21, when Bullitt reported Daladier's determination to obtain American planes, the State Department called in the Air Corps, whose reaction was summarized in the department's reply to Bullitt: "The American airplane industry is in a position to increase its output considerably and with little delay if engines can be obtained"; engines were not available because of the large recent French orders, however.[26] Next, the State Department sent a cable referring to Daladier's repeated request that Bullitt proceed to the United States to assist Pleven in his survey: "Daladier is asking us to assume greater responsibility than is possible." [27] Although the President had formally approved both dispatches, he showed by his reception of Pleven that he was ready to have the United States assume new and heavier responsibilities in providing planes for the European democracies.

[25] Ickes, *Diary,* vol. III, p. 84.

[26] Secretary of State to Bullitt, December 21, 1939, *FR, 1939,* vol. II, pp. 524–25.

[27] Secretary of State to Bullitt, December 22, 1939, *Ibid.,* vol. II, p. 528.

On December 22, the day after Pleven arrived, he was introduced by Purvis, to Morgenthau and to Captain Collins. Pleven outlined his mission's goal of 10,000 planes and later reported, "Morgenthau wishes to give us all the cooperation possible and entrusted Collins with this cooperation." Although the Secretary recognized that the time factor was essential, he requested that contacts with the aircraft manufacturers and discussion of the expansion of their facilities be postponed for a short time because he was involved with Purvis and the Anglo-French Purchasing Commission on two matters.[28] First, Morgenthau sought a solution to the tax problems raised by Allied capital investments in new facilities to produce war equipment. The other, involving strategic raw materials, gave Purvis his first opportunity to prove himself, and he worked almost daily with Morgenthau. They wanted to stock pile and buy molybdenum, tungsten, and nickle as a step toward economic warfare against Germany.[29] By late December, after the initial ground work for control of raw materials had been laid, Morgenthau was ready to turn to Pleven's appeal for planes. By that time, the Anglo-French mission had also reached an agreement with the Treasury on a tax formula on payments for capital expansion of the American aircraft industry.

On December 29, Morgenthau asked Pleven, Purvis,

[28] Pleven to Daladier, December 23, 1939, Monnet Papers, File 2A, Paris, October–November 1939. See also the notes on the conference among S/T, Purvis, Pleven, and Collins, December 22, 1939, Morgenthau Diary, Bk. 232, pp. 1–5.

[29] For the British side, see Hall, *North American Supply,* pp. 87–89, Hurstfield, *The Control of Raw Materials,* pp. 253–57, and W. N. Medlicott, *Economic Blockade: History of the Second World War, United Kingdom Civil Series,* 2 vols. (London, 1952), vol. I, pp. 367–73. Blum, *Morgenthau Diaries,* vol. II, pp. 122–29, summarizes the Treasury's activities.

and Collins to meet in his office. There, Pleven detailed what kinds of planes he hoped to obtain during 1940. The conversation was continued at the White House and, as Pleven reported, it "was extremely cordial." It touched upon points being discussed by Monnet's Anglo-French Economic Coordinating Committee, the Anglo-French Purchasing Committee, and the American Administration, "especially the Allied requirements of duraluminum." The President also approved of three matters which Pleven had introduced: (1) France would be given priority over the Air Corps in obtaining the initial P-40s which came off the assembly lines, (2) Colonel Jacquin would be permitted to examine the latest American prototypes, and (3) Pleven would be granted permission to study with the manufacturers the ways of increasing production. Purvis expressed the thanks, which Monnet had cabled, of both France and Britain for United States cooperation in the control of the strategic raw materials "as such control might well shorten the war considerably without in any way adding to the suffering of the German people." [30]

In the reports which Purvis made on these talks with Morgenthau and the President, he remarked about the "extremely friendly atmosphere," but he warned on December 31, "They desire to keep secret and official these exchanges of views . . . to avoid stirring the isolationist groups." Then, ten days later, Purvis complained directly to Monnet about a leakage of information, which originated in London, regarding the latest talks with Morgenthau and the President. Purvis' analysis of the situation

[30] Pleven to Daladier, December 31, 1939, Monnet Papers, File 2A, Paris, October–November 1939. See also the notes on conferences in Treasury and White House, December 29, 1939, Morgenthau Diary, Bk. 232, pp. 316–17.

provides unique evidence of Roosevelt's methods in dealing with the British and French:

> The President, using his famous "quarterback" technique and finding in the State Department (as might be expected) a reluctance to take as open action in favor of the Allies as he would like, has turned to Morgenthau as his best channel. . . . Morgenthau is only too happy to play the role.
>
> To take advantage of the evident desire to help, we have to protect the channel, through which help is being given, from too much knowledge on the part of the State Department as to what is going on.
>
> The President is trying to avoid the State Department caution which might be translated quite easily into political opposition.[31]

At the beginning of the new year, Pleven was able to contact the American manufacturers. In a final report dated January 25 he summarized the findings which he and Colonel Jacquin had made with the assistance of Captain Collins: American aircraft industry could not meet Daladier's demand for 10,000 planes by April 1941. As had been foreseen, the major problem lay in the production of engines. Not only was all available capacity fully utilized, but the engine industry was already struggling to double its assembly lines to meet the recent orders placed by the Jacquin-Thouvenot war mission. Pleven reported that even if these assembly lines were doubled again they could turn out only 13,000 engines by October 1941. Thus the total number of planes would have to be reduced to 8,400. Only one-third of this number could be

[31] Purvis to Monnet, December 31, 1939, and January 12, 1940, Monnet Papers, File 2A, Paris, October–November 1939.

delivered before April 1941, and it would take another six months before the remainder would be completed. Pleven had explored getting the Cadillac division of General Motors to produce aircraft engines but "in accord with the American Administration we gave up this solution as the American auto industry has such specialized methods of mass production that neither the tools nor the skilled workers could be rapidly adapted to the production of motors with great power." One solution was to arrange with the Allison division of General Motors, which alone had had experience with aircraft engines over 1,000 hp, to produce Wright as well as Pratt and Whitney engines: "Mr. Sloan, the President of the Company, has informed us that General Motors will do everything to aid the Allied cause." In his report Pleven analyzed the problems faced by the engine industry in expanding its facilities. Twenty thousand workers were needed to be hired and trained. Raw materials assembled and some materials like aluminum, which were in short supply, would require new production units. As for machine tools, an area which troubled the British Government, Pleven reported that no problem existed. Because General Motors purchased so many of these tools, the machine-tool industry kept up a reserve capacity especially for such vital clients as General Motors. This reserve capacity could be tapped.

To speed plane deliveries, Pleven urged the rationalization of American airframe production. He recommended placing orders for fighters only with Curtiss, and selecting only two companies to produce bombers: "Glenn Martin on the east coast and Douglas on the west." These three firms had the best technical means and "Captain Collins has arranged that they will cooperate in avoiding competition for subcontractors, raw materials, machine tools and labor in order to halt the rise in prices which is unacceptable to the American Administration." Between October 1940 and September 30, 1941, each company would be able to turn out 2,800 frames. According to Pleven's estimate, the total costs for frames, engines, and propellors would reach $974 million, with expansion charges costing an additional $509 million. Pleven commented,

> We have been aided in a most cordial manner by the Administration, and the President as well as M. Morgenthau have proved their desire to assist us in every way possible. To avoid all disappointments it is necessary to remember that the United States enters in 1940 into its presidential elections and that, whatever may be the good wishes of the President, Secretary of the Treasury and their collaborators, they are obliged at this time to be extremely discrete to avoid providing the isolationists with any propaganda.[32]

Captain Collins had provided the greatest assistance during Pleven's survey mission. On January 5, 11, and 15 he had arranged a meeting between plane manufacturers and French and British representatives.[33] Morgenthau was

[32] Pleven Report, January 25, 1940, La Chambre Papers, "Commandes Américaines," Doc. no. 13.

[33] For the engine conference of January 5, 1940, see Collins' report to the President, January 8, 1940, Morgenthau Diary, Bk. 233, pp. 394–95. For the January 11, 1939, engine conference at which the Army and Navy were represented, see the memo for Chief of Air Corps (CAC) by Major Lingle, member of the permanent working committee of the Aeronautical Board, January 12, 1940, Arnold Papers, Box 223, Subject File, Aircraft Production, 1939–41. For January 15, 1940, meeting with the airframe producers, see the telephone conversation between S/T and Collins, January 15, 1940, Morgenthau Diary, Bk. 235, pp. 390–91. For Collins' correspondence on these engines and fuselages, see Lend Lease, Federal Economic Administration, President's Liaison Committee (LL, FEA,

kept fully informed of all the negotiations and made his own contributions. Most important was his effort to divert delivery of the first P-40s from the Air Corps to the French. As early as December 22 Morgenthau began to explore such a deferral after a talk with the Chief of the Air Corps. When the Secretary had sought Arnold's support for the new Anglo-French order for 10,000 planes, the General expressed concern about the combat qualities of the P-40 and Morgenthau suggested letting the French test three of the planes in combat against German fighters.[34] During the talk with Pleven on December 29 President Roosevelt had agreed to the prior delivery of the P-40 to the French, and on January 8 Morgenthau pressed the issue. Later, the Secretary reported to Pleven, "I did a magician's trick for you, pulled 25 planes [P-40s] out of the hat." Deliveries, to "be handled like the searchlight thing," would commence in April and be completed by June 30.[35]

Morgenthau's interest in providing combat tests for the P-40 had led him to a conclusion which he reached before his conference with the President. In January the Secretary noted:

> [England and France] should place orders so that they take every other one of the Army and Navy planes now in production that they can use.

PLC), Box 59, General Country File and File C 31/1, National Archives, Record Group 169.

[34] Telephone conversation between S/T and Collins, December 22, 1939, Morgenthau Diary, Bk. 232, pp. 95–98. See also Suggestions Morgenthau sent to Bullitt through the French Financial attaché, Le Roy-Beaulieu, December 29, 1939, *Ibid.*, Bk. 232, pp. 298–306.

[35] Blum, *Morgenthau Diaries*, vol. II, p. 115. In reporting on January 8, 1940, to Purvis by telephone on the P-40s Morgenthau referred to the searchlights he had obtained for France in September, Morgenthau Diary, Bk. 233, pp. 396–99.

> I am afraid they are getting planes now which will be one cycle behind their enemies.[36]

In his final report Pleven referred to this procedure and suggested transferring deliveries from the United States forces to the Allies. He noted that the Army Air Corps in 1939 had ordered 2,400 planes and the Navy 1,200 for delivery in 1940 and during 1941 an additional 3,000 would be delivered and he commented,

> If it is possible to persuade the American Administration to give up a part of the orders placed in 1939 and 1940 for delivery in 1940–1941, the Allied orders, especially for 1940, could be considerably augmented. Expansion costs would be cut. . . . We did not think that we should raise this question without Allied authority . . . it would be preferable that such authority be granted along with the decision to execute in total or in part the program that we have prepared. If this approval is granted, it seems to us that the American Administration would find numerous reasons to accede to it.[37]

Here was the method of speeding deliveries to the Allies which was accepted in March when Pleven and his British associates returned to Washington to implement the Anglo-French order for planes. But in January 1940 this solution was opposed by the Air Corps.

Pleven had spoken warmly in his report of the assistance he had received from Roosevelt's Administration as well as from American industry. The Frenchman cited a comment, which Alfred Sloan, president of General Mo-

[36] Blum, *Morgenthau Diaries,* vol. II, p. 115. The original note is filed in Morgenthau Diary, Bk. 233, p. 377.

[37] Pleven Report, January 25, 1940, La Chambre Papers, "Commandes Américaines," Doc. no. 13.

tors, had made: "If your Governments decide to execute this program, we will do the work, even if we ourselves enter the war." However, Pleven warned that Washington expected that a substantial Allied order would be placed and that it would include both motors and frames. He added,

> We must insist upon the fact that the American leaders, who have shown us such sympathy, count upon the Allied Governments to make a very rapid decision [by February 1, 1940]. . . . The plan has such consequences for the entire aircraft industry that the American government cannot develop its own program as long as the question hangs in suspense.[38]

But Pleven failed to warn, in his report, that Anglo-French orders for planes might meet serious opposition from the American military. The United States Air Corps was indeed deeply disturbed that Pleven wanted to buy more than 13,000 engines and 8,400 airframes. The prospect of having the domestic aircraft industry fully utilized raised a serious specter for General Arnold who was looking forward to further expansion of the Air Force. Perhaps the most remarkable factor about the final Anglo-British order for planes and engines, approved in late March, was that the American Air Corps approved not only an order of that size but also the release of the latest American planes. The Air Corps did not reach this new position easily.

General Arnold heard officially of the extent of Pleven's negotiations for planes and engines on January 11 from an Air Corps representative who attended the conference Collins held for engine producers and Anglo-French

[38] *Ibid.*

representatives. The next day the Chief of the Air Corps forwarded to the Assistant Secretary of War a memo on "possible procurement by Britain and France of vast quantities of planes in this country." The General recommended that in working out this program, an Air Corps officer should be present at all important discussions "to assist in achieving a solution which will be satisfactory to all concerned." [39] His recommendation repeated a demand which first had been made when the President's Liaison Committee had been established in early December. Then the military had foreseen that the new committee might negotiate foreign purchases of American military material behind their backs. Now, again, Arnold thought that solutions were being reached which were not "satisfactory to all concerned."

The Air Corps commander's concern over the negotiations had been stirred several days previously when he learned that President Roosevelt had agreed on January 8 to release 25 P-40s to France. This decision had come on top of a request by the Government of Finland for 40 P-36s, then in use in the Air Corps. While the Navy had satisfied the Finns by releasing 40 Brewster fighters, Arnold was disturbed and wrote to the Secretary of War on January 12: "Any diversion of planes now being manufactured for the United States Army or of planes now in service of the United States Army will delay the completion of the aviation expansion program." He went on to state that, if the P-40s were diverted to the French, the official foreign sales program of the United States would be violated, since then a foreign government would possess a plane superior to the type in Army service. The

[39] CAC memo for ASW, January 12, 1940, Arnold Papers, Box 223, Subject File, Aircraft Production 1939–1941.

General admitted that "it is very desirable to have as many foreign orders as possible placed in the United States as it increases the productive capacity . . . thus making us better prepared for any emergency which may arise," but he added, "such diversions should not be made without careful scrutiny of all factors in the case." [40] In this case he wanted no diversion of the new planes that were ordered in the spring of 1939.

In an effort to quiet the Air Corps' opposition, President Roosevelt called a White House conference on January 17 of Army and Navy personnel as well as the Secretary of the Treasury and his Director of Procurement. The President reviewed the engine situation and underscored that the current planned production of 24,000 engines for 1940 would not meet the American requirement for 20,000 plus the 13,000 required by the Allies. The President then referred to the Anglo-French plan to spend $214 million for these engines plus $65 million for expansion. As Arnold's second in command reported,

> there was a clear indication throughout the entire conference that the President was very much in favor of assisting the foreign powers to every reasonable extent . . . it was clearly set forth that even in our present expansion program, where we could help without seriously interfering, that every effort should be made to help the foreign countries. There was no definite statement of policy as to what extent this help should go but it was merely stated that a little help here and there would be very beneficial.[41]

[40] *Ibid.*

[41] General B. K. Yount, Assistant Chief of Air Corps, memo for CAC, January 17, 1940, Arnold Papers, Box 223, Subject File, Aircraft Production, 1939–1941.

From its tone, Arnold could have interpreted the final portion of this report as indicating that the President had not taken a strong stand. Collins' memo on the conference permits a different interpretation:

> The President stated that he felt that those present understood the necessity for expediting in every way possible deliveries to the Allies, that he wanted them to have his views on the subject and that the matter if necessary would be taken up at a later date.[42]

When Morgenthau reported to Pleven and Purvis on the White House conference which considered means to expand engine production, he was told that a French Air Force officer, who had just arrived to replace Colonel Jacquin as head of France's air mission, had reported that the latest Messerschmitt 109, powered with a 1,200 hp Daimler-Benz engine, "is faster and maneuvers better than the P-36." Since France had nothing to stand up against this new German fighter, Morgenthau replied, "Then naturally you want the P-40." Pleven agreed. This report provided an additional boost to Morgenthau's campaign for the Air Corps to defer deliveries of its latest planes to the Allies and the Secretary began to explore the early release of the Bell P-39, which could attain 400 mph as could both the P-40 and the Me-109.[43]

After Pleven and Colonel Jacquin left on January 18 to report to Paris and London, Morgenthau diverted even more energy toward preparing the way for a large Anglo-

[42] Collins memo, January 17, 1940, LL, FEA, PLC, Box 3, Production and Delivery Program.

[43] Conference among S/T, Purvis, Pleven, Jacquin, and Collins, January 17, 1940, Morgenthau Diary, Bk. 236, pp. 92–98.

French order for aircraft. To obtain first-hand information he toured the factories of Glenn Martin, Bell, and Curtiss as well as the engine plants of Wright, and Pratt and Whitney. Next, he turned his attention to alerting American public opinion. On January 20 the Secretary attended an Air Corps show at Bolling Field and talked to the press about the validity of Allied purchases of planes. When, several days later, the New York *Herald Tribune* countered his remarks by saying he was giving "the British and French a break over our own needs," Morgenthau felt he "was getting on the hot seat again on this air-plane business." To offset such stories, he called in reporters from the *Herald Tribune* and *The New York Times* and told them, "Allied pressures for planes were so great, that Roosevelt had requested him to coordinate domestic and foreign plane procurement to guard against interference with deliveries to the Army and Navy." He went on to emphasize, as he had a year ago, "the desirability of foreign orders as a stimulant to the American economy." [44]

To strengthen his position, Morgenthau suggested that the President make the first public announcement of Collins' Liaison Committee. Roosevelt did so and played up the committee's domestic role of protecting "United States interests in view of the large foreign war orders that are coming on the American market." Morgenthau now felt he could inform the War Department through General George E. Brett, the Chief of the Air Corps' Materiel Division, "As long as the President wants me to do this, I'll have to take the rap I guess." He knew, as he confided

[44] *The New York Times,* January 23, 1940, p. 3 col. 1. For S/T's comments to his staff on January 22, 1940, about the New York *Herald Tribune* article, see Morgenthau Diary, Bk. 237, pp. 2–4 and 116–18.

to his staff, that now when the Army or Air Corps started backbiting, they were "up against the White House." [45]

Next, Morgenthau looked into the problem of machine tools. The machine-tool industry was running behind in its deliveries to the aircraft-engine companies because it had failed to coordinate its domestic and foreign orders. Indeed, the British Government had hesitated to support Daladier's proposal to purchase 10,000 American planes for fear that such an order would divert machine tools ordered for the British aircraft industry. On January 30 Morgenthau brought together representatives of the three aircraft companies as well as the leaders of the National Machine Tool Builders Association. The tool makers agreed to concentrate on American, British, and French orders. In turn, the American engine producers agreed to prepare specific lists of their requirements and shortages of tools. The Secretary then introduced the Anglo-French Purchasing Commission and proposed that its chairman, Arthur Purvis, "be the sole arbiter of machine tool orders in the United States for the Allies." [46] Purvis at last could begin to bring all Allied tool orders under his direct control. Hitherto such orders had been placed helter-skelter by various French and British agencies through private contracts.[47] Purvis now reported to the Secretary, "We have both been asked to say that giving up tools now would be one of the greatest blows to the Allied cause. . . . [London and Paris] would choose against airplane

[45] For White House press release of January 23, 1940, see Morgenthau Diary, Bk. 237, pp. 153–54. See also the telephone conversation between S/T and Brett, January 22, 1940, *Ibid.*, pp. 7–11, and S/T comments to his staff, January 24, 1940, *Ibid.*, pp. 284–88.

[46] Machine-tool conferences, January 30 and 31, 1940, *Ibid.*, Bk. 238, pp. 295–302 and 357–61.

[47] Hall, *North American Supply*, pp. 94–95, and Hall and Wrigley, *Studies of Overseas Supplies*, pp. 72–76.

engines for tools . . . but [we] hope they will not have to."[48] Under Morgenthau's direction the production rate of tools, which was behind schedule, rose rapidly each week, until Pratt and Whitney announced in early May that it had received 93 per cent of its tools.[49]

While Morgenthau was clearing obstacles for a new Anglo-French order for planes, the Army and the Air Corps were marshaling their opposition. At the time Morgenthau had turned to the press and to the White House for support of his efforts, General Arnold forwarded a warning to the Assistant Secretary of War about raising engine production to 32,000 as recommended by the President at the White House conference on January 17. General Arnold estimated that the "situation today is more serious than a year ago because of foreign nationals," and he urged precautionary measures be taken to protect Air Corps delivery schedules. He listed a number of advantages which he believed foreign nations had in purchasing American planes. One was the higher price the French and British paid which permitted the American companies to make earlier deliveries to them and still pay penalties for delayed deliveries to the Air Corps.[50]

On February 2, Arnold received a memorandum from General Brett of the Materiel Division reporting that the present shortage of machine tools and equipment was delaying the expansion of production facilities for Air Corps contracts and that the orders already on hand were leading to shortages of raw materials and trained labor. In

[48] Machine-tool conferences, February 7, 1940, Morgenthau Diary, Bk. 240, pp. 50–69 and 70–75.

[49] For Collins' weekly reports on the machine-tool position during the winter and spring of 1940, see LL, FEA, PLC, File C 31/2.

[50] Memo from CAC to ASW, January 23, 1940, AAF File, Lyon Project Book A.

turn, these were creating "critical difficulties with subcontractors." In Brett's estimation

> the engine situation is extremely critical and this situation cannot be immediately improved if additional export orders are given the engine manufacturers. . . . The tendency will always be for the airplane, and particularly the engine manufacturers, to hold up Air Corps orders in order to become sufficiently tooled up to handle large export orders.[51]

General Arnold did more than make verbal protests against foreign orders; he opposed the release of the latest American planes. On January 22 when Secretary Morgenthau visited the Air Corps exhibit at Bolling Field, he already had talked with General Brett about the release to France of not only the P-40 but also Bell Aircraft's P-39, since they seemed to be the only American planes which could surpass the new German fighter. Morgenthau emphasized that its release to the Allies would boost production.[52] In contrast the Air Corps held that its current order for 93 P-39s would "utilize all existing facilities." [53]

In early February the Anglo-French Purchasing Commission requested performance reports for the P-39 and within two days the Clearance Committee of the Army-Navy Munitions Board released the plane for French and British negotiations. The Air Corps reacted, "It is probable that a period of several months will elapse before tests on the P-39 type plane will have been sufficiently completed to determine . . . if it is to the interest of national defense

[51] Brett to CAC, February 2, 1940, *Ibid.*

[52] Brett memo of talk with Morgenthau at Bolling Field, January 22, 1940, AAF File, Lyon Project Book 10B.

[53] Memo for S/T from Collins, January 27, 1940, Morgenthau Diary, Bk. 238, pp. 111–17.

to recommend actual export of this type of plane. . . . The War and Navy Departments object to its release." [54]

Then suddenly the Air Corps made a startling discovery. All of its new planes, the P-38s and P-39s, the B-25s and B-26s, and the B-17s and B-24s, which had been ordered in the spring and summer of 1939 for the 5,500 plane program, were obsolete. None were combat-worthy according to European standards because none had leak-proof gas tanks, armor, or adequate armaments. A cable, which arrived in early February from the American military attaché in London, forced the Air Corps to recognize the inferiority of its planes:

> Recently the Deputy Chief of British Air Staff stated emphatically that in his opinion if our air force was immediately involved in a task over Germany practically no planes would return because of a lack of protection of gas tanks and personnel, too few defensive guns in each gun emplacement, too few gun emplacements and lack of power operated turrets.[55]

Arnold called his staff together for three days, February 5, 6, and 7, to review the problem. Conferences were held with the major plane producers and it became obvious that the cost of these modifications would be exceedingly high. Bell, for instance, quoted $100,000 to put new tanks into only 30 P-39s. The economy-minded Congress would probably not grant such an amount, particularly as a House Committee had recently reduced the Air Corps

[54] Purvis to Collins, February 2, 1940, and Asst. CAC Yount memo for Asst. C/S G-2, "Release of P-39," February 8, 1940, both in AAF File 452.1, Sale Planes Abroad.

[55] CAC quoted this British comment to Asst. CAC Yount, April 9, 1940, AAF File 381B, War Plans.

request for 496 planes to 57 under the 1941 budget.[56] Here was a serious problem: how could the Air Corps overcome the obsolescence of the new planes which were about to come off the production lines? The solution lay in deferring deliveries of these unmodified planes to the Allies. Once this was recognized the new Anglo-French order would become attractive.

While the American Air Corps slowly came to this conclusion, the French and British governments finally agreed to a joint purchase of a large number of American planes and engines. On January 18 when Pleven left Washington for France, he could claim he was making a joint report with the British, as Colonel Greenly had been officially assigned to his survey mission. However, the Colonel, it seems, had little sympathy with Pleven's conclusions, for on January 6 he remarked to a representative of the State Department that "his Government was not at all certain as yet whether to make extensive purchases" and the American official concluded that the Colonel seemed personally opposed to them, preferring to concentrate on purchases of machine tools.[57]

British opposition toward purchasing American planes was not the only obstacle Pleven faced on his return to Europe. Bullitt had reported on January 9 that both Reynaud and Sir John Simon of the British Exchequer had announced they "positively could not find the dollar exchange to pay for large numbers of planes and materials."

[56] For the conferences of February 5, 6, and 7, 1940, and the conferences with the plane companies, see AAF File, Lyon Project Book 23. For the final cost estimates made at the conference in CAC's office, March 14, 1940, see Brett memo for Arnold, March 14, 1940, AAF File, Lyon Project Book 13.

[57] Memo by Green, Chief of Office of Arms and Munitions Control, January 6, 1940, SD 841.248/371.

The French Finance Minister "is positively opposed to additional purchases of planes." Bullitt added, "La Chambre spoke to Daladier today who reiterated his absolute determination to carry through the order. Daladier's position in France is so strong at the moment that he can put through anything he is really determined to put through." [58]

While the Premier, upon receiving a summary of Pleven's final report, "was most disappointed at the figures and delays," [59] his Minister for Air faced another problem closer to home: members of France's General Staff for Air questioned ordering so many planes and, as one of them remarked, "Maybe the Germans will not attack before 1941. If we order planes now they will become obsolete by then." To this Pleven replied, "There is nothing more obsolete than having no planes," and Colonel Jacquin threw the weight of his technical knowledge behind the Martin and Douglas bombers which in his judgment would meet the combat standards of 1941.[60]

When Pleven and Jacquin flew to London in late January to push their proposals, they also met opposition from the Staff of the Royal Air Force, which opposed focusing the American aircraft industry on only one short-range fighter and only two types of light support bombers. The British like the French Staff were not thoroughly convinced of the wisdom of buying American planes but were willing to explore the possibility of persuading the American Administration to release the latest planes then under production in the United States. The British Air Ministry

[58] Bullitt, January 9, 1940, SD 851.248/318 and 319.

[59] Bullitt, January 17, 1940, SD 851.248/322.

[60] The reaction of the French General Staff for Air is based on personal interviews in the summer of 1961 with M. Pleven and General Jacquin.

in turn doubted, on the basis of British experience, whether the American aviation industry could turn out 8,400 planes by the spring of 1941, and estimated a maximum production of only 4,800. Nevertheless, the Ministry recommended the Pleven plan to the war cabinet and gave three reasons: (1) it would rapidly provide the Allies with aerial superiority, (2) American production would be a valuable insurance against German bombing damage, and (3) such an order would prove to the neutral countries and to Germany that the industry and the United States Government were behind the Allies.[61]

One other obstacle faced Pleven and Jacquin. In determining that the American engine industry could turn out 13,650 high-powered engines by the end of September 1941, they had included some 5,000 which the French Air Ministry had placed under option for use in frames to be built in France. La Chambre could not, because of French production plans, release these engines for installation in American frames. As a result the total number of engines which would be available for the Anglo-French order was reduced to 9,000, and this cut the planes from 8,400 to 5,000.[62]

Aware that these basic problems had to be overcome before Pleven's report could be accepted, Jean Monnet, as head of the Anglo-French Economic Coordinating Committee, sought a final step which would force the decision to make extensive purchases in the United States. He

[61] For the British Air Ministry's reaction, see Hall, *North American Supply*, p. 120.

[62] Letter to La Chambre from Colonel Meny, Chief of French delegation to Anglo-French Executive Committee for Aeronautical Production, February 7, 1940, enclosing note drawn up with Sir Arthur Street and Sir Henry Self. La Chambre Papers, "Commandes Américaines," Doc. no. 14.

realized that if the French Government demanded that the British share equally the financial expense of buying American planes, then Britain could reply that it had already made a much heavier investment than had the French in developing its own plane production and that therefore the purchases from the United States should be met by the French to the extent of matching Britain's over-all investment in plane production. To avoid this Monnet decided to "shock" the British into sharing equally a huge order for American planes with a balance sheet comparing French, British, and German current air strength and production programs for 1940 and 1941.[63]

By mid-February, as a result of this balance sheet, Prime Minister Chamberlain's government finally agreed to join France in a massive order for American planes which would double American aircraft production and provide "absolute dominance in the air" over Germany. It was to take the diplomatic and negotiating skill of Jean Monnet to facilitate this decision and prepare the way for the Anglo-French bonanza of March 1940.

[63] See Monnet's background comment in his note to prepare the conversation of Daladier with Chamberlain, February 27, 1940, Monnet Papers, File 2A, Paris, October–November 1939.

CHAPTER

8

The Anglo-French Bonanza of March 1940

IN MARCH 1940, Britain joined France in placing the largest order for American military planes since 1918. At long last the plans and dreams of President Roosevelt and Secretary Morgenthau as well as of Jean Monnet, Edouard Daladier, and Guy La Chambre came to fruition. Despite the preparatory efforts of these five, the order did not easily receive London's or Washington's approval. However Britain was finally convinced by Monnet's efforts, and it took the authority of President Roosevelt before his War Department and Air Corps would agree. That agreement came only at the price of Allied concessions, but the Allies paid and America's latest planes were released to the two European democracies.

On January 15, ten days before Pleven's report on American aircraft production arrived in Paris,[1] Monnet sensed that it was the time to prove the falsity of Allied

[1] Pleven Report, January 25, 1940, La Chambre Papers, "Commandes Américaines," Doc. no. 13.

optimism about their own plane output, and he proposed his balance-sheet concept that compared British and French air power with that of Germany. A balance sheet would require the Allies, for the first time, both to share exact data on their own aircraft construction and to set these figures against their estimates of German production.[2] To prepare the way for this balance sheet, Monnet drafted a letter which Daladier sent to Chamberlain on January 18:

> This table will be very useful in completing the Pleven-Jacquin-Greenly report. I have learned with great satisfaction that the President and the American Administration have given our mission the most intimate cooperation.[3]

On January 28 and 29 French and British experts finally compared their intelligence estimates of their enemy's aerial strength and drew up their "Report on German Air Force War Potential."[4] Monnet summarized its significance for Sir Arthur Street, Britain's Permanent Secretary for Air:

> The report shows:
> 1. The formidable accumulation of striking power which can be instantly deployed against us.

[2] Monnet to La Chambre, January 15, 1940, Monnet Papers, File 2A, London, January–March 31, 1940. See also the memo by La Chambre, January 15, 1940, File 2A, Comité Coordination Franco-Anglaises (CCF-A).

[3] Daladier to Chamberlain, January 18, 1940, Monnet Papers, File 2A, CCF-A.

[4] For notes on these conferences, the "Report on German Air Force War Potential," and Daladier to Chamberlain, January 18, 1940, Monnet Papers, File 2A, CCF-A. See also, for brief reference, Hancock and Gowing, *British War Economy,* p. 193, note.

> 2. An ability to confront us with a big effort *over a long period.*
>
> 3. The margin of superiority which we have to contend with: which is probably already being reduced but it will take time to establish our supremacy.

Monnet then considered two problems which would result from a sudden or sustained German attack: (1) the effect on public morale and (2) the effect on production facilities. He concluded,

> Under conditions of attack our peoples, in their depth of agony, would draw comfort and courage from the knowledge that the vast resources of America were firmly and surely at their back. . . .
>
> How can we, as their rulers, rest until we have secured for them—even at this late hour—an assurance of an indestructible and continuous production of their vital means of defense.
>
> If French and British factories were destroyed what could they do to attain superiority? We must now create new potential in America which will be productive during this year and thereafter stand ready at our disposal to be brought into immediate use.

Monnet also emphasized that the psychological effect of such a step upon the enemy would be great, for "we would create a vast new potential beyond his reach." Finally, "the effect on opinion in America would be significant. And where we have such good will in such high quarters, let us not hesitate to harness it to our cause." [5] On January 29,

[5] Monnet memo for Street, no date, Monnet Papers, File 2A, CCF-A.

when Monnet discussed implementing Pleven's proposals with the British Air Minister, Sir Kingsley Wood, he again emphasized that American factories were beyond the range of enemy bombers.[6] Monnet's analysis of German air strength and Pleven's report convinced Prime Minister Chamberlain to revise his policy toward American purchases and to join Daladier in ordering large numbers of planes from the United States.

At the Supreme War Council in Paris on February 5 Daladier presented the balance sheet on Allied and German air strength and proposed "we now state our common decision to use the facilities of American industrial production and request our experts to examine this question." The Premier summarized two justifications for the necessary financial expenditure:

> 1. We have before us a formidable accumulation of offensive weapons which can be instantly used against our countries. We are dependent upon our own production to maintain our air forces and gain superiority over the enemy. . . . If the enemy with its superiority systematically destroys our factories, our program will be seriously compromised or destroyed. . . . It is the duty of our two Governments to mobilize American production which represents an indispensable insurance.
>
> 2. The enemy in spite of blockade has the means to continue considerable production for a long time.

Daladier stressed "the urgency of having our decision implemented without delay," and he suggested that President

[6] Note by Monnet on the conversation with Sir Kingsley Wood, night of January 29, 1940, *Ibid.*

Roosevelt and Secretary Morgenthau be informed by the end of the week.[7]

It took eleven days, however, before Arthur Purvis was instructed to contact the American officials. The delay came in part because in Paris the Air Ministry refused to relinquish its options of November 1939 for 5,000 American engines, and as a result the engines available for a joint purchase were reduced. Another cause for the delay was the British air experts' continuing concern about Pleven's plan to limit purchases to available types, the P-40 and the Martin and Douglas bombers. As a result the British insisted that before a final decision was reached another joint survey mission be sent to the States. The British also wanted assurance that the order for planes would not delay deliveries of prior Allied orders for machine tools and raw materials. Finally, the British Treasury raised the issue of paying Washington any taxes on capital investment in the American aircraft industry.[8]

The British demands disturbed Premier Daladier, and he sent Pleven back to London to determine whether the reservations implied "action or merely further discussion." [9] This was a serious political issue for the Premier because he and his Air Minister were again under

[7] See Daladier's note, "American Motors and Planes: Comparison Allied-German Forces, Use of American Production Facilities. Resolution Presented to Supreme Council," February 5, Monnet Papers, File 2A, London, January–March 1940. See also La Chambre to Daladier, February 7, summarizing proceedings of Supreme War Council on February 5, La Chambre Papers, "Commandes Américaines," Doc. no. 15.

[8] The original British draft of the cable for Monnet to send to Purvis was forwarded to Paris by Chamberlain for Daladier's approval, February 10, 1940, Monnet Papers, File 3A, January–February 1940.

[9] See Pleven's memo of the conference with Street, February 14, 1940, La Chambre Papers, 1940.

attack for the lag in French aircraft production. La Chambre had attempted to quiet the critics on January 10 when he appeared before the Air Committee of the Chamber of Deputies. A week later he spoke to the Defense Committee of the Senate. He reported the inventory of modern planes on hand and claimed, "The modernization of fighters ended last July 1. Today there are 1,810 modern fighters."[10] He predicted that France would have 5,540 planes by next July. The opposition refused to be quieted, however, and, as one Senator wrote, "tried to cut through the official figures to what was useful."[11] The debate over the French air power became so critical that Premier Daladier took it to the Chamber of Deputies on February 9. The Air Minister began by stating that France possessed 745 front-line fighters, and continued, "With our British ally we can match Germany, even if its [four] air fleets are used against us." Premier Daladier told the Deputies, "I have brought to France the potential of American aviation," and when he praised President Roosevelt, he was welcomed with "strong applause from extreme left to right." The Premier noted that American pursuits were already in operation and that bombers "have crossed the Atlantic under strong escort and are being assembled with more to follow." Daladier went on:

> I have said several times to the Council of Ministers, "It is necessary to buy 10,000 planes." That repre-

[10] For La Chambre's statement before the Chamber's Air Committee on January 10, 1940, see General Maurice Gamelin, *Servir,* I, 282. For the Air Minister's "Inventory of Planes" presented to the Defense Committee of the Senate on January 17, 1940, see La Grange Papers.

[11] André Maroselli, *Le Sabotage de Notre Aviation: Cause Principale de Notre Défaite* (Paris, 1941), pp. 96–102. See also General Paul Armengaud, *Batailles Politiques, et Militaires sur L'Europe. Témoignages, 1932–1940* (Paris, 1948), pp. 86–88.

> sents a sum perhaps in excess of French gold reserves. I do not know if we can go that far . . . [but] I have been informed by Chamberlain personally that he is in complete accord with us. . . . Now England and France, once again pooling their resources, will obtain from the American Government and industry the increase of forces which I recognize with the opposition is indispensable for victory.[12]

Applause greeted Daladier but the air issue remained and became one of the factors that brought his downfall in March and the succession of Paul Reynaud as Premier of France.

A key point which Daladier used in his defense before the Chamber of Deputies was a massive Anglo-French order for American planes. Thus on February 10, when he learned of the British reservations concerning instructions for Arthur Purvis in Washington, the Premier sensed a "malentendu." Apparently, he was appeased when Sir Arthur Street assured Pleven, "Great Britain intends to participate. . . . British participation will be substantial."[13] Daladier acquiesed, and on February 16 Monnet dispatched instructions to Purvis in Washington.[14]

A copy of this cable of instructions was also sent by the Premier to his Minister of Finance, who once again reacted sharply. Reynaud wrote that $500 million for the French share of the joint aircraft order would reduce

[12] In April 1948, the minutes of this meeting were published separately as *Comité Secret, February 9, 1940, Journal Officiel, Débats Parlementaires, Chambre des Députes* (Paris, 1948), see especially pp. 11–12, 26, and 46–48.

[13] Letter from Street to Pleven, February 14, 1940, Monnet Papers, File 2A, London, January–March 1940.

[14] Monnet to Purvis, February 16, 1940, Monnet Papers, British Supply Council File, Correspondence, American Planes, February 1940.

France's gold reserves which "are the gage to the resistance of the country during the war and an essential element of its reconstructive powers after victory." [15] The Premier replied,

> The problem is to conduct the war to victory . . . to do this it is not only necessary to reduce severely non-essential purchases but create new resources by intensification of exports and by placing all our existing resources at the service of the country. It is necessary to create beyond the reach of the enemy the centers for production of vital and irreplacable elements for our National Defense. This is the case for the creation in the United States of a new potential for aircraft production.[16]

Daladier again refused to permit Reynaud's opposition to interfere and on February 22 ordered Pleven and Colonel Jacquin to return to the United States to join a British Air mission under Sir Henry Self and "submit concrete proposals for execution of the order of February 16." [17]

On February 22 in Washington, Purvis reported to Morgenthau that the new air missions were dispatched and showed Morgenthau Monnet's February 16 cable which stated the intention of France and Britain to place a large order and listing the three reservations concerning numbers and types, taxes, and machine tools. The Secretary was elated: "It may be the deciding factor in having the Allies win the war." [18] When Purvis mentioned he wanted

[15] Reynaud to Daladier, February 16, 1940, *Ibid.*

[16] Daladier to Reynaud, February 19, 1940, *Ibid.*

[17] Instructions signed by Daladier and La Chambre for Pleven and Jacquin, February 22, 1940, Monnet Papers, File 3A, CCF-A.

[18] Penciled note by Morgenthau to Mrs. Klotz, February 21, 1940, Morgenthau Diary, Bk. 242, p. 106.

information on the latest types of planes and accessories, like the new superchargers, and agreed to make a press announcement, Morgenthau called in representatives of the machine-tool industry and engine producers, who had been meeting earlier in "a very good cooperative spirit" with the Secretary. He now outlined the Allied order and remarked,

> I think this is good business for you manufacturers. It's good business from the standpoint of national defense because it enables us to key up our airplane production to a basis that in case the time should come—and we all hope it won't—if we should need this production for ourselves, it's here. . . . All I can say to you is I would not be sitting here for the President, looking at it from domestic economy and national defense if we did not think it was good to take these orders.[19]

On February 24 the newspapers announced the Anglo-French Purchasing Commission: "Allies to Spend Billion in U.S. on New Planes, Will Take Our Surplus, All Aircraft Above Defense Needs Will Be Bought." [20] No order could be implemented, however, until the French and British air mission landed.

Pleven and Jacquin arrived on March 4 in Washington, where they met the British mission under Sir Henry Self. Self had served since 1937 as the British Treasury's special coordinator of all aircraft purchases for the Air Ministry

[19] Conference among S/T, Purvis, Bloch-Lainé, Collins, etc., February 21, 1940, Morgenthau Diary, Bk. 242, pp. 68–96. See also radiogram from S/T to F.D.R. aboard the U.S.S. Tuscalosa, February 21, 1940, *Ibid.*, p. 99.

[20] *The New York Times,* February 24, 1940, p. 4, col. 2.

and had made two previous exploratory trips to the United States in the spring and late summer of 1938. He was backed by Air Commander George R. A. Baker, who for the past five years had been in charge of developing new weapons, armor, gasoline tanks, and particularly power turrets for the R.A.F. They were respected by Pleven and Jacquin, were backed by their governments, and were supported by Arthur Purvis. Together with the French members they made an extremely able team of negotiators.[21]

According to a report cabled back to Paris from Washington Pleven and Jacquin met with the British air mission immediately after their arrival, and reviewed Pleven's plan of the past January to rationalize American aircraft production on large orders of just three types. They agreed that because deliveries would not commence until 1941, these planes would be obsolete as they could not meet the projected European combat speeds of 400 mph. Then they reviewed what they knew about the aircraft being built for the Air Corps under its 5,500 plane program. On March 7, the members of the joint air mission, and Purvis and Bloch-Lainé, met with Morgenthau and requested release of the latest planes and engines plus information about the "results of service and manufacturers' trials of airplanes with details of performance and handling qualities." Morgenthau assured them that appropriate releases would be given and proposed that they meet in New York City with the "motor and propeller people . . . to establish the exact number that can be delivered to us by type and month . . . and with this information we could then determine

[21] During separate conversations with the author in the summer of 1961, all four men recalled with pleasure the closeness of their teamwork during the spring of 1940 in Washington.

the quantities and types of planes." In reporting this progress to Paris, the French representatives were still uncertain as to whether France desired to claim the engine options which had been taken out during the past fall. They cabled, "Our talks would certainly be aided if we could notify the engine manufacturers of the motors which the French Air Ministry desired to exercise its options and use for French air frames." [22]

A result of the meeting in New York with representatives of the three major engine companies was that the Allies reviewed figures and delivery dates which Pleven and Jacquin had discussed in their January meeting with the companies; a total of 13,690 engines was to be delivered by the end of September 1941.[23]

Although the Allied mission had begun auspiciously, General Arnold soon stated his opposition to the foreign sale of advanced types of American planes. On March 5, members of the aviation subcommittee of the House Military Affairs Committee triggered Arnold's reactions by questioning the $20 million rise in costs for 2,100 planes ordered under the 5,500 program. Arnold traced the problem back to large Allied orders and the resulting increase in cost of materials. He also stated that domestic companies were reluctant to delay Anglo-French orders in order to complete the American program for fear of losing

[22] Conference among S/T, Purvis, Pleven, Self, and Collins, March 7, 1940, Morgenthau Diary, Bk. 246, pp. 78–100. See also Jacquin and Pleven report to Air Minister, March 11, 1940, La Chambre Papers, "Commandes Américaines," Doc. no. 18. For Purvis' request for American releases as well as Morgenthau's assurances, see Hall, *North American Supply*, p. 122.

[23] Memo from Collins for S/T on the meeting with Allied Air Commission, March 8, 1940, Lend Lease, Federal Economic Administration, President's Liaison Committee (LL, FEA, PLC), File C/32/2, National Archives, Record Group 169.

Allied business.[24] Two days later, Arnold spoke before the House Appropriations Committee about his concern over foreign orders. Queried whether these orders interfered with deliveries to the Air Corps, the General hedged by saying some deliveries were ahead of schedule and others behind: it was still too early to ascertain the final results. When one of the committee brought up a rumor that foreign buyers were offering bonuses for accelerated plane deliveries, Arnold replied, "I can't put my finger on anything definite. I have heard the rumor." But he went on to explain that early deliveries could be obtained if a foreign power paid the 15 per cent penalty charged by the Air Corps for delay of deliveries. Questioned whether there was an Air Corps representative on the President's Liaison Committee, which had been coordinating all foreign plane orders, Arnold answered, "No sir, not directly from the Air Corps . . . it would be impossible to know everything unless this was so." Asked whether his Air Corps was waiving delivery in favor of a foreign government, Arnold answered negatively and cited the official policy, "Aircraft will not be released for export until they have become identified as production articles." [25]

On March 9 *Business Week* summarized additional opposition to Allied plane orders. The plane makers themselves were unwilling to be stampeded into expansion, fearing a postwar slump. The magazine spelled out the War Department's opposition to Pleven's original plan to

[24] *The New York Times,* March 6, 1940, p. 7, col. 4. During lunch on March 6, 1940, with Morgenthau, Arnold, and Collins, Admiral Towers denied Arnold's claim of increased costs. Morgenthau Diary, Bk. 245, pp. 383–85.

[25] *U.S. Congress, House of Representatives, Hearings on H.R. 9209, 76th Congress, 3rd sessions* (Washington, 1940), pp. 475–78.

freeze plane designs and concentrate production in only three companies. It reported that some Army personnel wanted to delay foreign sales until Air Corps needs were filled, and, if the Administration favored "giving our best to the Allies," the Army wanted Britain and France to be made to pay for the necessary expansion of our aircraft industry. The Army was displeased over Morgenthau's use of the President's Liaison Committee to by-pass the Army-Navy Munition Board's control over the export of planes, and the Secretary of the Treasury was criticized because his concern for aircraft-engine production seemed aimed less at aiding the Army and Navy expansion than at speeding production for the Allies. In contrast, while the White House favored such aid, it did not create the impression of being unneutral.[26]

Favorable news about the Allied search for American planes came on March 11 when the press reported that sources in the War Department were considering the release of Bell's P-39 and a modified Curtiss P-40 or P-46 with a speed of 400 mph, "which the French have wanted." The department had rebuffed a request for Lockheed's P-38 with a speed of 420 mph. It was also reported that the latest Douglas and Consolidated light bombers and even the Boeing B-17 would be released because "new types now nearing completion will be superior." [27] These events were in opposition to the beliefs of Harry Woodring, who announced at this time,

> I continue, as for several years, to absolutely disapprove of the sale of any surplus U.S. Army property. I insist, regardless of any higher authority directions,

[26] *Business Week,* March 9, 1940, p. 15.

[27] *The New York Times,* March 11, 1940, p. 2, col. 2; March 12, 1940, p. 6, col. 1.

> that if Army surplus is to be sold, it only be sold by this government to another neutral government. . . .[28]

Morgenthau knew the War Department would raise obstacles to the release of 1941 types to the Allies and so he attempted to arrange a meeting with the Chief of the Air Corps, the Deputy Chief of the Navy's Bureau of Aeronautics, Captain Towers, and the President. As Morgenthau told Purvis, "I figured he could grease the way if he told them first." The meeting took place March 11.[29] Opposition was still strong and on March 13, Senator Robert La Follette of Wisconsin introduced a resolution calling for an investigation by the Senate Military Affairs Committee to determine whether foreign purchases were "delaying the equipping of our armed forces." [30] The increasing tempo of opposition to the Allied search for planes disturbed Secretary Morgenthau so much that on March 12 he went to the White House to complain because, as he later reported to his staff, "My effectiveness was just being ruined by Johnson and Arnold." The Secretary explained to the President that for both strategic reasons and for business recovery the Allied order was the "most important thing in Washington. And if he wanted me to do this thing, he would just have to do something." Roosevelt realized how the new Anglo-French order would expand the aircraft industry's floor space and labor force. The President also saw the domestic value. "These foreign

[28] For the full quote, see Watson, *Chief of Staff,* p. 304.

[29] Telephone conversation between S/T and Purvis, March 11, 1940, Morgenthau Diary, Bk. 246, pp. 282–92.

[30] For La Follette's Senate resolution, see *The New York Times,* March 14, 1940, p. 13, col. 1. For La Follette's request of March 23, 1940, to Woodring for supporting evidence, see AAF File 425.1-B.

orders mean prosperity in this country and we can't elect a Democratic Party unless we get prosperity. . . ." Referring directly to the propaganda the Chief of the Air Corps was turning out, Roosevelt remarked, "Well, if Arnold won't conform maybe we will have to move him out of town." As Morgenthau later commented, "the President was swell. It was . . . just the question of either backing me up or not and it shows when the President wants to he can take two hours to get a thing straightened out." [31]

To support Morgenthau's efforts, Roosevelt took two steps. First, he called in his press secretary, Steven Early, and his military aide, General Edwin M. "Pa" Watson. He told General Watson to instruct Johnson to cease his opposition to the President's Liaison Committee and henceforth permit "no publicity from the War Department except from the central bureau . . . he can't see the press any more." Then, to counteract the damage already done in the press, Roosevelt requested that Early put out a release denying that "problems of plane procurement for our forces had been made more complex by foreign orders" and adding that these orders had resulted in an expansion of the aircraft industry.[32]

As a second step to support Morgenthau, Roosevelt decided to talk to the military. He called a conference of the key Army and Navy personnel. According to General Arnold's report of this conference the President listed a series of decisions. First came two points which the Chief of the Air Corps favored: (1) no military planes would be released for foreign sale until a better model was avail-

[31] Blum, *Morgenthau Diaries,* vol. II, pp. 117–18.

[32] For Early's press release, see *The New York Times,* March 13, 1940, p. 8, col. 1.

able for the Army or Navy, and (2) closer coordination would be developed between "the Morgenthau Committee and the Army and Navy." The next two dealt with issues which must have caused Arnold embarrassment: (3) greater care would be exercised in releasing publicity on foreign sales, and (4) more thought would be given to questions from Congressional committees before answers were made. The final point dealt with expansion of production: (5) "Every effort would be made to increase the availability of this industry for national defense. The Army and Navy should benefit in their productions in some way from the foreign sales." [33]

However, Arnold did not fully report Roosevelt's irritation as Morgenthau did: "Oh boy, did General Arnold get it." [34] The General's own personal notes, which he took down on the back of a used envelope, reveal the strength of Roosevelt's feelings: "[The President] expressed himself dissatisfied with the manner in which questions had been answered, particularly by War Department witnesses. Then looking directly at me he said there were places to which officers who did not 'play ball' might be sent, such as Guam." [35] Roosevelt's warning was lost neither upon Arnold nor the others at the conference. Even Secretary Woodring changed his tune.

At the same time the White House launched a campaign in Congress to undo the damage created by criticism

[33] CAC to ASW, March 14, 1940, AAF File, Lyons Project Book 10F, Tab. 6.

[34] Blum, *Morgenthau Diaries,* vol. II, p. 117.

[35] Handwritten record by Arnold of Conference, White House, March 13, 1940, Arnold Papers Box 223, Subject File Aircraft Production, 1939–1941. In his *Global Warfare* (New York, 1949), p. 186, Arnold recalls the President's threat but erroneously associates it with a previous conference in January 1939 when the French sought their second order for planes.

of the sale of foreign planes. Secretary Morgenthau passed on to the Senate Majority leader, Alben Barkley, the series of figures which he had brought over to the White House on March 12 when he appealed to the President for assistance. These figures indicated that previous Anglo-French orders had tripled the labor force in the American aircraft industry and the pending order would quadruple it. Prior to March 1940, orders had doubled the floor space and the new order would raise the figure from 3.1 million to more than 4.1 million square feet. Before Allied purchases had begun the aircraft industry had been able to turn out 7,290 engines annually. Now the figure was 19,280 and the new program would raise this to 29,280 a year.[36]

The press of March 14 was provided with data supporting the Allied proposal to buy large numbers of planes. *The New York Times* reported that Germany had a monthly production rate of 3,000 combat planes and was seriously outproducing the Allies. During 1940 the United States would reach a rate of 1,000 military planes a month, of which 300 would go to the Allies in an effort to help match the Luftwaffe. The *Times* also reported the P-40 would go 15 mph slower than the new Messerschmitt 109 which could fly at 400 mph, but an advanced model of the Curtiss fighter, the P-46, would surpass such a speed.[37] A vice president of Curtiss-Wright, Arthur Nutt, announced to the press that the sale of P-40s to the Allies would "more likely prove a boon than a loss to the Army." He had been prompted to make this statement because the Chairman of the aviation subcommittee of the House Mili-

[36] Hall, *North American Supply,* p. 122. See also the telephone conversation between Morgenthau and Purvis on "the battle of Washington," March 13, 1940, Morgenthau Diary, Bk, 247, pp. 25–28.

[37] *The New York Times,* March 14, 1940, p. 12, col. 3.

tary Affairs Committee had been so disturbed by reports that France would receive P-40s before delivery to American tactical squadrons, that he threatened to launch immediately an investigation as to whether the Army was "giving its secrets away." Curtiss-Wright's spokesman rebutted,

> Both Britain and Germany have pursuits right now that are as fast and perform as well as the P-40. If we sold them [Britain and France] every one the Army expected to get, it would make way for developing here something faster and better. . . . As things are today those planes will be obsolescent by the time they reach the front.

In conclusion, Nutt boasted, "We will have something for the U.S. Army that can fly rings around them." [38]

All this information about the combat worthiness of the P-40 had a purpose. President Roosevelt, in late December, had agreed to defer to France the first 25 P-40s due to be delivered to the Air Corps in April 1940. In November 1939 the French had placed an order for 100 of these fighters with deliveries to commence in August, and the deferment of 25 from the Air Corps would permit the French Air Force to test this plane in combat. General Arnold had protested the deferment, and a long series of conferences began, ending in a compromise: the first 25 would go to the Air Corps and the next 5 to France. The issue had come up during the Congressional hearings and now the White House was attempting to justify its earlier decision on the grounds that a deferment of the first P-40s

[38] *Washington Post,* March 15, 1940. The copy in the Air Force files has written on it, "Notes for General Arnold 3–15–40 answer this." AAF File 452.1, Release of Planes to France, Spaatz.

would permit later delivery of more advanced models. It was a basis for a policy which was shortly to come to the rescue of the Air Corps. Morgenthau also made his contribution to the campaign to convince Congress and the public of the validity of the Allied plane orders. Speaking as Secretary of the Treasury, he denied rumors of the aircraft industry receiving high profits on foreign sales by stating that the Treasury had been enforcing the Vinson-Trammel Act which limited profits on military aircraft and other military material to a blanket 12 per cent.[39]

The President had called his White House conference and launched the press campaign at a most strategic time. The next day, March 14, a meeting was held in the office of the Chairman of the President's Liaison Committee where the British and French air missions together with Purvis presented their program to the Army and Navy. Pleven reported that he was not interested in purchasing the types considered in January, the P-40, the Douglas DB-7A and Martin 167. The French in 1938 and in 1939 had purchased planes off the drawing boards for which no prototypes were available, and now both the British and French were anxious to do likewise for planes and engines that would be available in 1941. Thus clearance was requested for the P-38, P-39, P-46 and "generally any other type of fighter which would be serviceable in 1941 when speeds would be not less than 400 mph." "As combat would be taking place by that time at high altitudes," release of the latest types of superchargers for engines was requested. Pleven continued, "We believe that new types of bombers have been developed by the American Army and Navy and we would also wish to have information on those including big four engine bombers and dive bomb-

[39] *The New York Times,* March 15, 1940, p. 2, col. 4.

ers." The Frenchman argued that his nation had large capital investments in American plant facilities for which no return "can be realized unless the Army and Navy release late models and types of airplane engines." He cited as a precedent the release to France in January 1939 of the Martin 167.

After Sir Henry Self had supported Pleven's plea, Admiral Towers stated that the request went beyond the authority of anyone present and "is higher than the Aeronautical Board." The Air Corps representative at the meeting, General Brett, agreed and made two requests of the Allies: (1) that the Air Corps obtain reports on combat performances of any plane released, and (2) in return for releasing the latest American engines, Britain should sell to the Air Corps two of the new Merlin in-line engines built by Rolls Royce and currently powering the British Spitfire.[40]

As the conference ended, Admiral Towers told Captain Collins that he "realized thoroughly their desire for the latest aviation material . . . [and approved] forwarding all information concerning plans and specifications of any existing or proposed planes and engines." That evening he told Collins that the Secretary of the Navy, Charles Edison, and the Chief of Naval Operations, Admiral Stark, also agreed.[41] Future opposition would come from only the War Department.

[40] Notes by Collins on Meeting President Liaison Committee March 14, 1940, LL, FEA, PLC, B/10/2; Collins memo for the President March 14, 1940, *Ibid.*, C/4/0; for Air Corps Notes on this Meeting, see Lyon Project Book 10 B, and AAF File 452.1, Release of Planes to France, Spaatz. See also memo on the meeting prepared for the President by McReynolds, Morgenthau Diary, Bk. 247, pp. 81–82.

[41] Collins memo for S/T, March 15, 1940, LL, FEA, PLC, C/40/1.

On the day that the French and British had met with the Army and Navy to request release of the latest American planes, General Brett filed a report with General Arnold concerning the problem that all the new Air Corps planes on order lacked self-sealing gas tanks, armor for pilots, and sufficient armaments.[42] Arnold had been aware for several months that these planes would not be combat-worthy without modifications, but Brett's final estimated costs must have shaken the General. With Congress squeezing every possible dollar out of the Air Corps budget, there was little chance to obtain the $800,000 needed to modernize only twelve of each type. Arnold quickly became less ill-disposed to work out a new release policy when he recognized he could use the Anglo-French order to his advantage. By deferring deliveries of the new planes to the Allies he could provide them with planes sooner, and in doing so the Air Corps could "off-load" types it did not want. In addition, Arnold and his staff recognized that they might force the plane companies, and indirectly the Allies, to cover the cost of modifying the deferred planes. Also, the Allies might help pay the cost of research and development for the new type of planes which the Air Corps had been paying over the past years. These additional funds could be used to develop more advanced models. On March 14 Arnold and Brett outlined this policy to Morgenthau, who later reported to Collins, "I'm thoroughly in accord with it."[43]

By March 15, two days after the White House conference, the Air Corps staff had completed its release pro-

[42] Brett to CAC, March 14, 1940, AAF File, Lyon Project Book 13.

[43] Telephone conversation between Collins and S/T, March 14, 1940, Morgenthau Diaries, Bk. 247, pp. 75–79.

posal. As the press had predicted, the Bell P-39 and the Curtiss P-40 were on the release list. In line with Air Corps policy of retaining models "with performance characteristics superior to the model offered for foreign sale . . . either by refinement of design or superior engines," it refused to turn over a newly developed turbo-supercharger which would enable the Bell fighter to fly faster than the released model. Three other new fighters, developed by Republic and North American, were also kept secret. As for light bombers, the Air Corps was more generous because all of them had been in the air for a number of months. The staff thus proposed to release three new types, the Douglas A-20, which was the American model of the DB-7, the Martin B-26 and North American's B-25. The staff also approved release of both heavy bombers, the B-24 and B-17. Finally, the proposal deferred to the Allies deliveries on approximately one-half of the 1,247 combat planes still to be delivered to the Air Corps.[44]

This proposal was forwarded to the Secretary of War on March 18. The next seven days witnessed a flurry of activity as a final version of the release policy was hammered out. Following a meeting in the Chief of Staff's office on March 19, General Arnold was ready to admit "the overwhelming advantages" of the new release policy: (1) the development of improved methods of quantity production, (2) the building up of an aircraft industry "that can compete with foreign competition for planes in normal times," (3) foreign capital to expand the industry which the government could utilize in an emergency, (4) the training of key personnel in production, and (5) the introduction of American standards and practices abroad.

[44] Memo for S/W, March 18, 1940, forwarding "Review of Status of U.S. and Foreign Plane Orders for Release for Foreign Export," March 15, 1940, AAF File, Lyon Project Book 10F, Tab. 8.

These advantages offset the dangers of an overexpansion of the aircraft industry: the adverse effect on deliveries to the Air Corps and the danger of "jobbers and promoters" gaining control of critical raw materials and airplane components.[45]

Also on March 19 General Marshall, the Chief of Staff, persuaded the Secretary of War to cooperate. Woodring did so, but with a number of conditions: (1) no military secret or secret development would be divulged; (2) no plane would be released until a "superior plane is actually in the process of manufacture for the War Department"; and (3) "no delivery delays would be tolerated." No deferral would be permitted until the manufacturers accepted change orders to provide "refined models of a more advanced type." Restriction was placed on releasing a manufacturer's own designs without War Department permission. Such a provision aimed at blocking the maneuver which Roosevelt and Morgenthau had used in January 1939 when the latest Douglas and Martin prototypes were turned over to the French. Finally "foreign orders must be for quantity production." [46] Earlier Arnold had spelled out these conditions for Collins of the President's Liaison Committee who in turn commented to Secretary Morgenthau, "I think at last they're trying to find an out so they can throw everything wide open and at the same time save their faces." [47]

[45] Minutes of meeting in C/S office March 19, 1940, War Department (WD) File, Chief of Staff Miscellaneous Conferences, 1938–1942, National Archives, Record Group 165. Arnold used these same points later in testimony before a Congressional committee. See "Questions and Answers, March 1940," AAF File, 452.1–3295, Sale of Planes Abroad.

[46] Minutes of meeting in C/S office March 19, 1940, WD File, C/S Miscellaneous Conferences, 1938–1942.

[47] Telephone conversation between Collins and S/T, March 19, 1940, Morgenthau Diary, Bk. 248, pp. 67–68.

Meanwhile, President Roosevelt continued the effort to win public and Congressional support for selling large numbers of American planes to the Allies. As the House Military Affairs Committee and Senator La Follette prepared to launch their separate inquiries into such sales, Roosevelt spoke to the press about the value of British and French purchases. Emphasizing the economic argument, he stated his preference for foreign orders being placed in the United States because they increased domestic production, giving vital aid to the nation's defenses. He said the recent threefold expansion of plane and engine production was impossible without foreign aid and he insisted on continuing the sales of planes abroad. As to the release of latest models the President stated his criterion was "sell 'em one they'd buy." Questioned whether he favored giving away our "very latest models such as the Aircobra [P-39]," he retorted, "Is it our latest model?" He labeled talk of lost military secrets "bunk" and cited the P-40 which he had first seen in 1938 and subsequently had noted pictures, drawings, and cross-sections in various technical magazines. The President was at his best and, as the press later reported, he "was credited for halting plans for Congressional hearings." [48]

On March 20, the President also called the Army Chief of Staff to the White House. Morgenthau later reported to Purvis, "The President gave General Marshall his orders today of what he wanted in regard to planes for the Allies. . . . I think [the Army] has got to come through." [49] Arnold, however, was not willing to approve a new re-

[48] Memo from Schwarz to Morgenthau, March 19, 1940, "F.D.R.'s Press Conference," LL, FEA, PLC, A/04/1; *The New York Times,* March 20, 1940, p. 13, col. 1, and March 21, 1940, p. 12, col. 5.

[49] Telephone conversation between Purvis and S/T, March 20, 1940, Morgenthau Diary, Bk. 248, p. 102.

lease policy without gaining every advantage possible for his Air Corps, and so on March 20 the General sent additional conditions to the Secretary of War: each type and model should be considered as a special case; a seat on the Liaison Committee should be given to a War Department representative to ensure that improved designs, performances, or models be available before a plane be cleared for foreign sale. A further condition was that General Brett be authorized to arrange with the manufacturers "so as to secure the very best performances for the United States Army." Arnold's note indicated that cooperation with the Liaison Committee was beginning.[50]

On March 21, Arnold accompanied the Chief of Staff, General Marshall, to the White House to discuss considerations of "tremendous importance to the national defense of this country." They considered the possibility that the rapid developments of planes under combat conditions "threatens our Army with having some 1,500 planes now under contract approaching obsolescence at the time of delivery." These had been ordered in 1939 under the 5,500 Program "as a necessary reserve against the then limited production of this country." Marshall now recommended:

> we utilize the urgent necessity of the foreign governments for military planes by accepting a delay in the delivery dates for reserve planes, releasing the actual planes for sale to foreign countries and securing the advantage of exchange orders so as to give us planes of superior performance to those under construction for the Air Corps. This requires no additional funds and no changes of law.

[50] CAC memo for S/W, March 20, 1940, AAF File, Lyon Project, Foreign Sale Procedure.

Recognizing that "we are confronted with limitations in funds for ordering more planes," Roosevelt and Marshall discussed measures for expanding production "particularly for the latest models because this in reality will constitute our war reserve." Marshall repeated arguments he had developed in the fall of 1938, when he had recognized that a policy of building planes to store until required by war conditions posed the dilemma of obsolescence which could be met by only developing the domestic aircraft industry to such an extent that production would fill foreseeable American needs. Now, in the spring of 1940, it seemed the new British and French orders would expand American production toward the required amount.[51]

Following this White House meeting, Marshall forwarded to the Secretary of War his official recommendation for the release of "our late military types" and stated that this could be done "without jeopardizing the military interest." In the General's judgment the releases were "in harmony with the production of pilots in the Expansion Program." Marshall stated one major requirement, the full quota of operating planes would be available by June 30, 1941.[52]

The following day, Woodring, having reluctantly accepted the new release policy, met with his Assistant Secretary, as well as Generals Arnold and Marshall, to discuss the planes and equipment to be released. They differed on the superchargers. While Louis Johnson favored the re-

[51] "Expression of policy made to the President by General Marshall and General Arnold March 21 and handed to General Brett," *Ibid.* For the development of Marshall's thinking on reserve planes, see William Frye, *Marshall: Citizen Soldier* (New York, 1947), p. 274.

[52] Memo from C/S to S/W, March 21, 1940, AAF File, Lyon Project, Foreign Sale Procedure.

lease of the most advanced turbo model, Woodring hesitated and proposed that only the less-efficient, two-speed, two-stage supercharger be sold. In an effort to settle the question, General Marshall contacted the White House and discovered that the President opposed making a clear-cut decision, preferring to settle each case on its own merits. Although the heads of the War Department agreed to add the P-38 and other late models to the list of released planes, the problem of the superchargers had not yet been solved.[53]

On March 21 General Brett spelled out details of the new release policy for Captain Collins. The Air Corps had won valuable concessions. Heading the list was, "no military secret will be divulged or released." Then came a goal toward which Arnold had been working since the opening of hostilities in Europe: "Foreign Governments must agree to furnish the Army and Navy full and complete information on comparative suitability, design, equipment, and combat performance of American made planes." Stimulation of productive capacity for new types and models "is imperative." The armed services would be protected against "interference with delivery of equipment necessary for our defense needs." Finally, "prior to action by the War and Navy Departments, manufacturers will be required to negotiate . . . change orders . . . [to ensure] that improved types of planes are delivered."[54] The Air Corps' conditions for the new release policy were complete except for General Arnold's addition of another, important

[53] Report on meeting in Collins office, 11:00 a.m., March 22, 1940 by Lieutenant Colonel Orlando Ward, WD File, C/S Miscellaneous Conferences, 1938–1942. See also Watson, *Chief of Staff,* p. 305.

[54] Memo from Brett to Collins, March 21, 1940, AAF File, Lyon Project, Foreign Sale Procedure.

condition: the contractor "at no further expense [will] carry out the desires of the United States Government as regards present contracts and a given program for research and development." [55]

Arnold summarized these conditions in his letter to General Brett, the Chief of the Materiel Division, assigning him to negotiations with the President's Liaison Committee, and added "In my opinion it will be exceedingly difficult to justify before Congress and the people of the United States any releases which do not conform to the above fundamentals." Arnold's next statement indicated he had not lost his distrust and suspicions:

> In these deliberations if you find that you cannot come to an agreement with either the aircraft companies or the Liaison Committee which conforms to the principles outlined herewith, you will make the statement that: "you do not have the authority to proceed further and will have to get additional instructions from your superiors in the War Department."

Arnold concluded by adding one more demand, which would, if followed through, establish the Air Corps' final control over the fate of its planes: "All cases will be brought to the attention of the Chief of the Air Corps . . . before clearance is given to the Liaison Committee and go ahead is given to the industry concerned." [56]

Following his meeting with General Brett on March 23, Captain Collins informed Morgenthau that he had found Arnold's principles for release "thoroughly logical

[55] CAC to Secretary Clearance Committee, Army-Navy Munitions Board, March 23, 1940, AAF File, Lyon Project Book 10A.

[56] Arnold to Brett, March 23, 1940, AAF File, Lyon Project, Foreign Sales Procedure.

and sound." Collins showed that he had his own distrust and suspicion when he informed Morgenthau that he should "rest assured that the Treasury Department will not get maneuvered into any position which will release the Army or Navy of any of their responsibilities." [57] By Monday, March 25, the details of the new release policy were completed and the President accepted the policy as the government's.[58] In the meantime, the Anglo-French Purchasing Commission had made progress toward determining what type and how many engines and planes could be delivered by the deadline of October 1941.

Four days earlier, on March 21, when President Roosevelt had met with his Chief of Staff and the Chief of the Air Corps and listened to Marshall's arguments about releasing the latest models and deferring reserve planes, the Anglo-French air mission had every reason to believe the President would approve a new release policy. Pleven cabled Paris and Self cabled London recommending the breakdown in orders of American planes. The British ordered 2,400 planes and the French 2,100.[59]

Pleven's and Self's cables were followed by a supporting message from Arthur Purvis to Monnet's Economic Coordinating Committee in London: "Bloch-Lainé and I feel the program can be achieved—even though major difficulties are bound to be encountered. . . . Morgenthau assured me yesterday we need not worry in regard to the outcome of our application in regard to the releases."

[57] Collins to S/T, March 23, 1940, LL, FEA, PLC, C/40/1.

[58] "Government Policy on Aircraft Foreign Sales, March 25, 1940," *Ibid.* Final copy "Outline of Policy of War and Navy Department for Release of Aircraft . . . for Export and Domestic Sale" is also filed in *Ibid.* For the President's approval, see Collins report to S/T, Morgenthau Diary, Bk. 249, p. 54B.

[59] Cables from Self to Street, March 21 and 22, 1940, Monnet Papers, File 3A, CCF-A.

Purvis estimated the capital expenditure at $15 million for engines and $2.5 million for frames: "all of this is included in the $614 million total figure." Purvis requested that a decision be reached by April 1. The day before, Morgenthau had arranged a meeting of the chairman of the Allied Purchasing Commission and representatives of the Army, Navy, and Aluminum Corporation of America, and now Purvis reported, "Alcoa agreed to supply ingot aluminum to the extent of the requirements of the new aviation program . . . as regards machine tools, we are assured by the engine makers that the new program presents no difficulties." [60]

By March 26 the Anglo-French Executive Committee for Air Production and Supply met in London to review the proposal which had arrived from Washington and had advised their respective Air Ministries, "to recommend to the Allied Governments its broad acceptance as a whole . . . as that scheme provides a well-considered and reliable plan." [61]

In Paris, Guy La Chambre did not have the opportunity of officially approving the new American purchases toward which he had been working for the past two years. Political fortune had swung against Daladier and in mid-March he had lost by one vote the confidence of the Chamber of Deputies. While Daladier remained as Minister of Defense in Paul Reynaud's new cabinet, La Chambre had to relinquish his Ministry to one of his

[60] Purvis to Monnet, March 21, 1940, *Ibid.* For the minutes of the meeting of Purvis, Morgenthau, and Alcoa on March 21, see Morgenthau Diary, Bk. 248, pp. 349–83. See also the memo by Collins on talk with Purvis, March 20, 1940, LL, FEA, PLC, C/40/1.

[61] "U.S. Aircraft Potential, Views of Anglo-French Executive Committee for Air Production and Supply," March 26, Monnet Papers, File 2A, London, January–March 1940.

sternest critics, Laurent-Eynac. The opportunity of obtaining the large number of American planes appeared so advantageous that the new Minister readily extended his approval.[62]

The British Air Ministry approved and so by March 29 when the Supreme War Council met in London, it gave the final word. The Allied missions in Washington were ordered to proceed, "subject to release by the United States of aircraft types contemplated." The council added a major condition: "In case exports of aircraft from the United States become impossible or unnecessary, the Allied governments attach great importance to the introduction of break or safeguarding clauses." This condition gave concern to the American companies, but they had to accept it. Confirmation was also extended to the French order for the 4,050 engines on option. The council finally extended the Allied Government's "warm appreciation to Pleven, Jacquin and Self" and added that it would like Morgenthau "to be aware of their gratitude for his very valuable and friendly offices and of their confidence that these will continue to be available throughout the execution of the scheme." [63]

As the Secretary of the Treasury had predicted, the Allies did not have to worry about the releases. In fact, on March 27, the House Military Affairs heard four of the War Department's major figures support the new release policy. Though the Secretary of War privately opposed this new policy, he testified publicly on the advantages of accepting deferred deliveries in order to obtain improved

[62] La Chambre testimony, *Événements,* vol. II, p. 335.

[63] Draft of cable from Monnet to Purvis, no date, Monnet Papers, File 2A, London, January–March 1940. See also Hall, *North American Supply,* p. 121.

models for the Air Corps. Assistant Secretary Johnson took a wider view, stating this sale "would permit the Allies to gain air parity with Germany" and even repeated his prediction of a few days previous that by the end of 1940, production of American planes would have reached 30,000 to 40,000. The committee was impressed with General Marshall's unqualified endorsement, "I urge it, I recommend it, and I would be deeply concerned if we didn't do it. I consider it of vital importance for national defense." The Chief of Staff explained his major point about holding down the number of reserve planes and thus avoid "loading up with obsolescent craft." He even spoke about reducing the "objective we had set for next year [5,500] to about 3,500 planes, but if the Allies stop buying, then we must have the reserves."

For his part, Arnold marshaled all the arguments that had been developed within the War Department to support the release program. Answering a series of direct questions, Arnold found himself contradicting the vigorous criticisms he had made earlier concerning the foreign purchase of military planes, in particular he denied that these purchases had disrupted plane deliveries to the Air Corps.[64] When the *Washington Times Herald* on April 4 published Arnold's previous testimony of March 7 to the House Appropriations Committee and headlined its article "Arnold Blasts Allies Plane Sales by U.S.," the General reiterated his conversion: "the new policy will operate to the advantage of the Army Air Corps and thereby the National Defense." [65] The strength of the War Depart-

[64] *The New York Times,* March 28, 1940, p. 1, col. 2, March 29, 1940, p. 3, col. 1; stenographic copy of the statements by S/W and CAC to the House Military Affairs Committee, March 27, 1940, AAF File, Lyons Project Book 10A.

[65] *Washington Times Herald,* April 4, 1940, p. 1. For Arnold's reply, see Public Relations Branch, G-2, April 5, 1940, AAF File

ment's defense had another effect. Senator La Follette's proposal to investigate foreign sales was defeated 5 to 4 in the Senate Committee.[66] Henceforth opponents would have a difficult time raising further Congressional opposition to Roosevelt's latest plans to aid the Allies.

One argument which carried weight in the War Department was expressed by Louis Johnson to a Treasury Department official: "If war threatens us, we will take all this newly developed factory capacity for our own use—exactly as we did in 1917." [67] In contrast, Sir Henry Self cabled London on March 21 that if the Allies financed an expansion of American aircraft-engine production "this output would be available for the Allies for the duration of the war." The grounds for future tension between the United States and Britain were being prepared.[68]

The War Department's united support before Congress for the sale of planes abroad did not reflect complete conversion. The Air Corps was ready to make the most out of their concession, and Woodring was determined to exact a price for "championing" Roosevelt's new policy. The eruption came April 11 over the issue of having the Allies pay a share of the development costs for the new planes released to them.

By April 1, the government had finally reached a decision on the material to be released to the Allies. In contrast to Arnold's initial list of March 15, all the latest

---

452.1–3295. Arnold again defended the new release policy in a major address at the National Aerial Round-up of the American Legion at Indianapolis, April 28, 1940, for text, see AAF File, Lyon Project Book 51.

[66] Collins report to S/T, March 28, 1940, LL, FEA, PLC, C/40/1, and *The New York Times,* March 29, 1940, p. 3, col. 1.

[67] Memo for S/T by John Sullivan, March 26, 1940, Morgenthau Diary, Bk. 249, p. 63.

[68] Cable from Self to Street, March 21, 1940, Monnet Papers, File 3A, CCF-A.

types of fighters were included. This permitted negotiations with Lockheed for the P-38, with Republic for the P-44 and P-47, types which had been previously withheld because they were considered "highly experimental" and needed to be "tested before export." Release was also extended for the two-stage, two-speed superchargers. Because Woodring "would definitely not approve the release of the Flying Fortresses," decision was withheld on the four-engine bombers as well as the turbo-supercharger.[69]

By the time the Anglo-French Purchasing Commission was given the official United States reply to its request of March 14 for the release of the latest American planes, the Supreme War Council had met in Paris and approved the orders as outlined by Self and Pleven.[70] Purvis was so pleased when he received the news that he telephoned Morgenthau who, in turn, called the President, who agreed, "it was good news." [71] While the French and British mission worked over the final contracts for planes and engines, the Air Corps continued to seek every benefit possible. In early April, Arnold proposed that he be granted "blanket authority over releases to the Anglo-French Purchasing Commission," claiming this authority "for purposes of standardization of production, expedition, prosecution of negotiations and contractual agree-

[69] Adjutant General to Quarter Master General, WD Representative, President's Liaison Committee, April 1, 1940, AAF File, Lyons Project, Foreign Sale Procedure; Collins to Purvis, April 2, 1940, LL, FEA, PLC, C/40/1.

[70] Monnet to Purvis, March 30, 1940, Monnet Papers, File 3A, CCF-A. For the final figures, see the chart on Anglo-French Orders for American Planes, April 1940, *Ibid.* For schedule of deliveries, see "Commandes Américaines, Prévisions de Livraisons." Copy given the author by General Thouvenot.

[71] S/T memo of the telephone conversation with Purvis, April 1, 1940, Morgenthau Diary, Bk. 250, pp. 65–66.

ments."[72] The purpose of this proposal was revealed when two Air Corps officers appeared at the State Department to request the right to search every modification of the planes ordered by foreign governments. The danger, as they explained, was that these governments might require "changes in original specifications as to leak-proof tanks, armor, etc., which would permit exported planes to match ones to be produced for the Air Corps."[73]

A new problem for the Allies stemmed from the Air Corps' efforts to have the aircraft industry underwrite the cost of modifications, plus research and development. General Brett had initiated the change order or modification program at meetings with the frame makers on March 27 and with the engine manufacturers two days later. He informed them that no release for foreign sale would be granted until it was determined that improved types would be delivered to the Air Corps. He was supported by Admiral Towers who pointed out "that legally the Government must receive benefits for any concessions made in existing contracts . . . it is essential that the Industry cooperate in putting the policy in effect, that in the final analysis it was the taxpayer that must be satisfied with the basis upon which the Government released its late model aircraft."[74]

The Air Corps then attempted to determine the amount

[72] CAC memo for ASW, April 4, 1940, AAF File 452.1–3929B, Sale of Planes Abroad.

[73] Conference of Yost of Munitions Control Office of the State Department with Majors Lyon and Lingle, April 5, 1940, AAF File, Lyon Project Book 10F.

[74] Lyon notes on the conference with plane companies in Collins' office, March 27, 1940, AAF File, Lyon Project, Foreign Sale Procedure; Collins memo for S/T, March 27 and March 29, 1940, LL, FEA, PLC, C/40/1.

of money it had expended in developing the latest American planes, costs which were to be charged off to Britain and France. There was no question that the Air Corps would try to squeeze out as high a price as possible and this stirred French and British opposition.[75] The Air Corps demands also deeply irritated some of the manufacturers. For one, Donald Douglas, president of the Douglas Aircraft, informed General Brett of his disapproval of "your recapturing money from an Allied order. It appears to me that the order from the Allies is very clear and has no bearing on your order." Brett disagreed and Douglas went on to say, "It is impossible and we will drop the whole proposition. I will not exact money out of the Allied contract on something they had nothing to do with." [76]

Troubles came to a head as the chairman of the Allied purchasing mission prepared to sign plane and engine contracts. On April 9, Morgenthau called the Assistant Secretary of War to determine whether Woodring had signed the release. Johnson reported that the Secretary of War had not only refused since April 1 to release the latest models and the turbo supercharger but was now threatening to tell the House Military Affairs Committee that he firmly opposed the new policy. Once again Roosevelt intervened directly and Woodring was in effect instructed "either to go along with the program or resign." [77]

[75] Brett memo on the telephone conversation with Collins, April 8, 1940, AAF File, Lyon Project, Foreign Sale Procedure.

[76] Excerpts from the telephone conversation between General Brett and Mr. Donald Douglas, Santa Monica, California, April 10, 1940, AAF File, Lyon Project Book 10F. For Douglas' position, see also the telephone conversation between S/T and ASW, April 13, 1940, Morgenthau Diary, Bk. 254, p. 169. For a similar stand, see the telegram of R. H. Fleet, president of Consolidated Aircraft, to President Roosevelt, May 3, 1940, AAF File, 452.1–3295H.

[77] Blum, *Morgenthau Diaries,* II, 119–20.

He yielded. On April 10 Morgenthau informed Purvis he could now complete the contracts for the 2,440 fighters and 2,160 bombers.[78]

Even though the contracts had been signed, the final charges for research and development came up for discussion with Allied representatives on April 11. They were disturbed when Brett demanded that the Bell Corporation provide leak-proof fuel tanks, protective armor, and armament at no cost to the government. In addition, Bell was to manufacture and deliver one experimental model with a speed of 440 mph, and Bell was to recoup almost the entire cost of $510,000 from the Allies.[79] Sir Henry Self and Pleven protested and produced a statement of contributions which the Allied governments already had made and were planning to make toward expanding the United States Aircraft industry. Prior to March 31, 1940, France had invested more than $23.8 million and Britain $940,000. They estimated that for the new Anglo-French order an additional $37 million would be expended in capital costs, with the bulk of capital investments going to the engine companies. Self and Pleven included in that total $10 million for "increasing capacity of sub-contractors and suppliers of accessories and equipment such as carburetors, magnetos, armament, etc." They also claimed their government had contributed financially toward developing the planes which they had purchased prior to

[78] Conference among S/T, Purvis, Pleven, Self, and Collins, April 10, 1940, Morgenthau Diary, Bk. 253, pp. 109–41.

[79] Collins memo for S/T on meeting with Self, Pleven, Brett, Kraus, and Bell, April 11, 1940, LL, FEA, PLC, B/10/4. Figures for Bell costs were taken from unsigned note for Arnold, "Reference to negotiations for Export Sale of Aircraft under New Policy," April 22, 1940, AAF File, 452.1–3295G Sale of Planes Abroad. This note also includes details on charges to other companies.

April 1940 and that "very important technical contributions have been made by experts of the French and British Commissions from the war experience to the redesigning of many aircraft." They concluded by suggesting that "the creation of this additional capacity to the military preparedness programme of the United States which, according to declarations of Administration policy, is a factor of recognized importance." [80]

When Morgenthau was informed of the Allied reaction, he informed Captain Collins that he was not prepared to have them

> come and weep on my shoulder. . . . That was one of the principles layed down when these releases were made. . . . That's the cheapest money they have ever laid out. If that's all the War Department wants to charge up, the Allies are God damn lucky! I'll get rough.

Turning to the extra charge of $510,000 made for Bell's P-39, Morgenthau exclaimed, "The fastest plane in the air! Cheap! My heavens! I think the Army is very reasonable." The Secretary's distrust of the British returned and he

[80] "Statement of Expenditure Incurred by French and British Governments for Expansion of Capacity of the U.S. Aircraft Industry, April 11, 1940," presented to the author by General Jacquin and identified by him as being prepared by Purvis. The official figures which the Allied Purchasing Commission reported in early May 1940 were the same except for the $10 million for accessories. The total remained $37 million with the difference made up by an additional contract with Curtiss-Wright for more engines at a capital cost of $7.8 million for expansion and $3.6 for training and "other items." See also memo initialed ABP (Purvis), "Expenditures Incurred . . ." May 10, 1940, LL, FEA, PLC, Box 15, Airplanes and Engines 1940.

worried that they might duck out of signing a contract after "I've turned myself inside out and the President has too." [81]

At 9:00 a.m. on April 12, Louis Johnson, Brett, Collins, Burns, and Lyon met with Morgenthau. Johnson spelt out the Army position which was unmoved by the Allies protest: "We must have improvements in the existing models of planes [and] the War Department expected foreign purchases to pay a fair proportion of the cost of development of new models and equipment." He added "Congress expected the War Department to procure planes with improved characteristics over those released for export." The development costs for all the aircraft companies were estimated to come between $6 million and $7 million.[82]

Next, Morgenthau met with the Anglo-French Purchasing Commission about the development costs. Pleven remarked that a leading American aircraft manufacturer had warned earlier, "You might have to pay a pound of flesh," and the Frenchman went on to object to any such payment because every time the French spent a million dollars for something "which is not actually our expense, it reduced by twenty-five the number of pursuit planes" they could buy. Secretary Morgenthau explained the situation. He cited the problem the administration had had during the past fall lifting the arms embargo and noted there were "a great many people in this country who think we shouldn't . . . sell you armaments." There were also "people in our

[81] Telephone conversation between S/T and Collins, April 11, 1940, Morgenthau Diary, Bk. 253, pp. 312–20.

[82] Lyon notes on the conference in the office of S/T, April 12, 1940, AAF File, Lyon Project Book 10F. See also record of this conference, Morgenthau Diary, Bk. 254, pp. 8–10.

Army who are not pro-Ally. . . ."[83] The Allies agreed to pay $7 million for development costs.

It was, as Pleven remarked many years later, a hard deal but one had to give here and there; "you could not bother Roosevelt all the time." Sir Henry Self's reaction was summed up in a cable he sent back to London some months later. He had been asked to certify that the prices of the April 1940 orders had been fair and reasonable, to which he replied, "Prices I paid most unfair and most unreasonable, but best I could get."[84]

Purvis, Pleven, and Self were realists and although they found the research and development charges hard to swallow, they did not permit this maneuver by the Air Corps to block their efforts. The 4,600 planes and 13,000 engines now on order would make a vital contribution. If the planes deferred by the Air Corps could not be put into combat, their early delivery to the Allies would be useful for training. Although the Air Ministries criticized their missions in the United States for seeking quantity rather than quality, Pleven and Self knew that by ordering the types available they would later be able to obtain improved models. The Allied missions were also criticized by their governments for exceeding their authorizations for capital expenditures, but Pleven agreed with Sir Henry's cable answering this criticism, "Error admitted but not regretted."[85] The two men knew that by financing the expansion of the American aircraft industry France and Britain had developed an annual production rate for 12,000 planes and 20,000 engines. As the British Air

[83] Blum, *Morgenthau Diaries,* vol. II, pp. 120–21, and Morgenthau Diary, Bk. 254, pp. 14–28.

[84] Statements to the author by M. Pleven in July 1961 and by Sir Henry Self, February 1964.

[85] Comment by Sir Henry Self to the author, August 1961.

Mission reported in mid-May, Allied orders and options "will give us complete control of the situation." [86] The French and British missions had in fact laid the foundation for all later war-time supplies to the Allies for "at no time in the war did Britain get more than 1,000 planes a month." [87] Purvis, Pleven, and Self also recognized that if either of the Allies could not utilize these orders, then United States rearmament for active combat would be greatly increased.

Roosevelt was well aware of the significance of the Allied order.[88] Since the Munich crisis he had promoted French and British assistance in building up in the United States a productive capacity of 20,000 planes. The contribution of the two nations far surpassed that of Roosevelt's government, which was still seriously hampered by an economy-minded Congress.

Jean Monnet knew the significance of the Anglo-French order, having carried the burden in Europe for winning approval of, as well as implementing, Roosevelt's concept of obtaining Anglo-French assistance in building the aircraft industry. In Paris, Daladier could not claim full credit for the order he had launched in November 1939, and ironically much credit went to Reynaud, who had long opposed French purchase of American planes, but now as Premier approved. In Britain a hard core of Monnet's associates also congratulated themselves on overcoming the reluctance of Chamberlain's government to help open the American arsenal.

Even General Arnold was pleased with the Allies'

[86] Hall, *North American Supply,* p. 122.

[87] Hall and Wrigley, *Studies of Overseas Supply,* p. 30.

[88] For the reactions of Morgenthau, Roosevelt, and Marshall, see Blum, *Morgenthau Diaries,* vol. II, p. 122.

order. Indeed, the Air Corps had benefited the most. It had "off-loaded" obsolete planes and would replace them with modified models. What better answer could Arnold have found to that problem of obsolescence? The Allied development contribution of $7 million meant that Arnold was spared having to approach Congress for appropriations to cover the cost of either the modifications or the development of new models which could attain a speed of 450 mph. Then too, an Air Corps representative now sat with the President's Liaison Committee and gained first-hand information about future foreign requests for planes. American flyers could visit the European combat theaters and even more important, American planes would be battle-tested. Finally, the British had agreed to ship a Merlin engine to the United States.[89]

Delayed deliveries continued to plague the Air Corps through 1941. As an official history reported,

> When the attack on Pearl Harbor came . . . the Air Corps certainly was not prepared for war . . . it had fewer than 3,000 tactical planes on hand of which a large number were unfit for modern combat. . . . Not one of the new plants authorized after June 1940 and designed to build combat planes had yet produced a single plane and none were destined for full production before 1943.[90]

In such a light, the Anglo-French order of March 1940, together with the Allies' contribution of $37 million toward capital expansion, becomes enormously significant.

[89] Brett to CAC, "Status of Airplane Deliveries as of April 20, 1940," April 26, 1940, AAF File, Lyon Project Book 23.

[90] "The Expansion of Industrial Facilities under Army Air Force Auspices 1940–45," Army Air Force Historical Study, no. 40, p. 107, National Archives, Record Group 18.

General Marshall had been correct: foreign orders had increased aircraft capacity four times. Allied orders between 1938 and the spring of 1940 had doubled engine production, the bottleneck of the industry, and that the order in March had redoubled those facilities. Anglo-French orders had also increased twice over the productive personnel employed by the American aircraft industry, raising the number from 55,000 to 120,000, and British and French capital expenditure enlarged the factory space by more than 6 million square feet. A report in 1941 stated, "Manufacturing facilities, trained personnel, and a backlog of orders are the essential requirements for rapid expansion." [91]

The Allies' contributions conditioned the expansion of Ameican plane production until after Pearl Harbor. If the U.S. Air Corps was short combat planes in December 1941, it would have been even shorter except for the British and French contracts before Dunkirk. The Anglo-French order of March 1940 was considered a bonanza in London and Paris. Indeed, it proved an even greater boon for the United States. Sir Henry Self may not have been exaggerating when he called the March order "the focal stage of the whole Allied war effort." [92]

[91] See the letter from Henry L. Stimson, Secretary of War, to Senator Alben W. Barkley, February 17, 1941, and the attached memorandum, "Part Played by Early British and French Orders in Developing American Aircraft Engine and Airplane Production Facilities," AAF File, Lyon Project Book 57, Tab. 27. See also Edward R. Stettinius, *Lend-Lease: Weapon of Victory* (New York, 1944), pp. 18–24.

[92] Comment by Sir Henry Self to the author, February 1964.

CHAPTER

9

Postlude: The Battle of France

THE BATTLE OF FRANCE during May and June 1940 came as a tragic postlude to France's efforts to buy military planes from the United States. Deliveries of recent Anglo-French order could not begin until the next September, and the last of the planes ordered back in the spring of 1938 and January 1939 were still trickling into France. Their total of 555 American combat types, combined with the quantities France had produced, were insufficient to stem the tide of German tanks and bombers. Thus Franco-American communications during the Battle were peppered with constant pleas from Premier Reynaud for planes and more planes, until finally, as France neared its collapse, he dramatically called for "clouds of planes." In doing so Reynaud, who as Minister of the Treasury had placed many obstacles in the way of French purchases of American aircraft, and who knew that the United States possessed no combat-worthy planes, attempted to shift part of the responsibility for France's defeat onto the shoulders of the United

States and, more particularly, those of Franklin D. Roosevelt. One other point stands out in the story of French appeals for American aid during the Battle of France.[1] President Roosevelt, as never before, revealed himself ready and willing to give "unstinted aid" not only to France but also to Britain.[2]

Roosevelt and Henry Morgenthau had been prying open "for a year and a half," as the Secretary noted in late May 1940, the American arsenal for the Allies. Now, as France faced the overwhelming power of the German armies, the two Americans doubled their efforts to aid the European democracies. The fundamental obstacle was American industry which had not focused on arms production, and it took the President's call to Congress on May 16 to launch rearmament. Because of the deficiency of production the President and Morgenthau in their search for planes, arms and munitions for France and Britain had to turn to material held in stock by the Army and Navy. Because both Services were focusing upon their new expansion, they reacted against diverting equipment to the Allies. As the tide of German conquest rushed ahead and the British Army lost its arms at Dunkirk, the American military saw that the frontiers of the United

[1] For a fuller account of the American response to France's appeals for aid during May and June 1940, see Langer and Gleason, *Challenge to Isolation,* pp. 480–93 and 497–544; Hull, *Memoirs,* vol. I, pp. 761–800; Watson, *Chief of Staff,* pp. 305–12; Hall, *North American Supply,* pp. 127–69. For an excellent up-to-date summary, see Philip Goodhart, *Fifty Ships That Saved the World: The Foundation of the Anglo-American Alliance* (London, 1965), pp. 53–72. For the latest accounts of the Battle of France, see Alistair Horne, *To Lose a Battle: France 1940* (Boston, 1969); Guy Chapman, *Why France Fell: The Defeat of the French Army in 1940* (New York, 1968); and Andre Beaufre, *Le Drame de 1940* (Paris, 1965).

[2] This conclusion was advanced by Langer and Gleason in *Challenge to Isolation,* pp. 471–72, 480, and 503.

States did lie on the other side of the Atlantic. Indeed, when in mid-June Secretary Morgenthau stated, "I would like to see those people do all the fighting over there and give them everything," Admiral Harold R. Stark, the Chief of Naval Operations, remarked, "You and me both." [3] By that time the Army's Chief of Staff General George C. Marshall had already indicated agreement by his own actions.

Premier Reynaud launched his first desperate appeal for American planes on May 15. He informed the American President that the Germans had broken through at Sedan and warned, through Ambassador Bullitt, that "the battle certainly would be lost quickly unless the troops could be protected from German attacks from the air." On the same day Britain's newly appointed Prime Minister, Winston Churchill, issued his initial request for American planes, arms and destroyers.[4] The Allied negotiations for this equipment were carried out in Washington through the Anglo-French Purchasing Commission and on the evening that the initial French and British appeals for aid arrived, Arthur Purvis discussed them first with Morgenthau at his home and then by phone with the President. Their talk turned to the transfer of planes to the Allies, and Roosevelt suggested pushing the planes across the Canadian border in order to avoid the Neutrality Act's prohibition of flights by warplanes out of the United States. Since he was involved in the negotiations during the past March, Purvis knew what American planes were in production and which types were held by the Army and Navy. He was

[3] Conference re: Allied Purchasing Committee, June 12, 1940, attended by Harry Woodring, General Marshall, Admiral Stark, *et al.*, Morgenthau Diary, Bk. 272, pp. 12–45.

[4] See Bullitt, May 15, 1940, *FR, 1940,* vol. I, pp. 220–22, and Winston Churchill, *The Second World War,* vol. II, *Their Finest Hour* (Boston, 1949), pp. 24–25.

fully aware that those available for transfer would be of little use over the European battlefields "because they did not have proper armor or leakproof gasoline tanks." Nevertheless, he urged upon the President the immediate release of as many as possible.[5]

The Secretary of the Treasury, having been asked once again by the President to oversee and assist the Allied negotiations for American equipment, called in representatives of the Army Air Corps and the Navy's Bureau of Aeronautics. They reported that the maximum number of first-line combat planes due for delivery over the next three months amounted to only 125. The new Curtiss fighter, the P-40, would be delayed because of malfunctioning of the new Allison in-line engines and only 25 could be expected in May. The only other plane available was the P-36, and the Air Corps had on hand by mid-May 1940 about three-quarters of its 1938 order for 200.[6] Moreover, General Arnold had again become possessive of every plane scheduled to be delivered to his command, and he was able to persuade General Marshall of the danger not only of diverting the P-40s but also of turning over the P-36s. The Air Corps' 160 of the latter fighter had but two machine guns, lacked armor, and, as Arnold emphasized, they could contribute little to the Allied cause particularly as 100 planes would be only a three days' supply in the European combat zone. In contrast, these planes were vital to the Air Corps' training program and their ship-

[5] See Morgenthau's notes of May 16, 1940, on his talk with Purvis, Morgenthau Diary, Bk. 262, pp. 312–14. For Roosevelt's remarks by phone to Purvis, see Hall, *North American Supply,* p. 78.

[6] Conference among S/T, General George H. Brett, Chief of Air Corps' Material Division, and Captain Sydney Kraus in charge of purchasing aircraft for the Navy's Aeronautical Bureau, May 16, 1940, AAF File, Lyon Project Book 10B, Conferences on Foreign Releases, January–December 1940.

ment across the Atlantic would, as General Marshall summarized, "set us back six months on the pilot end." In turn, Arnold lamented, "It would throw away everything we had." [7]

General Marshall realized, however, that "it is a military decision to us that the Allies succeed in stopping the flood," so he continued searching for arms and munitions which could be considered surplus to the nation's defense. On May 22, the Allied leaders again appealed for military equipment,[8] and Purvis filed a detailed list of all Allied requirements for arms, planes, machine tools, special steels, alloys, and explosives.[9] As the Army and Navy sought legal ways to release material from stocks on hand, Purvis appealed directly to Morgenthau:

> It does seem to me now that, good heavens, any help they can give may be a valuable thing for this side as well as the other . . . the fire is burning and I do hope the legalities—Lawyers are so awfully good at finding loopholes in their shoes.

The Secretary replied, "My dear Arthur, I have felt this way for a year and a half." [10]

On May 22 the Chief of Staff returned to the Treasury and reviewed with Morgenthau ways in which the Army could assist the Allies. Marshall reported that as far as planes went, the answer was an absolute No. Of the 754 fighters which the Army and Navy had ordered in 1939,

[7] Conference among S/T, Marshall, Arnold, May 17, 1940, Morgenthau Diary, Bk. 263, pp. 241–47.

[8] For Reynaud's appeal of May 18, 1940, see *FR, 1940,* vol. I, pp. 228–30; and for Churchill's cables of May 18 and 20, see his *Their Finest Hour,* p. 56.

[9] For the Allied list of materials required, see Morgenthau Diary, Bk. 264, pp. 215–30. See also Hall, *North American Supply,* p. 131.

[10] Telephone conversation between S/T and Purvis, May 21, 1940, Morgenthau Diary, Bk. 264, pp. 241–43.

405 had already been released in March 1940 for early delivery to France and Britain. The situation for bombers was more serious because even fewer bombers were available for the Air Corps. As for anti-aircraft or anti-tank guns no ammunition was available and there would be none for the next six months. However, the Chief of Ordnance had found some material he considered surplus to national defense. His list included 500,000 Enfield rifles together with 100 million rounds of ammunition, 35,000 machine guns and automatic rifles, 500 mortars, and, most important in the eyes of the Allies for use as anti-tank guns, 500 75 mm artillery pieces with 1 million rounds.[11]

The President quickly approved, but the difficulty of finding a legal loophole through which these arms could be released remained. Finally, at the height of the Dunkirk evacuation, a way was found under an act of 1919, which disposed of surplus World War I material. The log jam was broken. On June 3 the Army's list was turned over to Purvis who reported that the Allies would take "the whole damned lot." [12] When informed, President Roosevelt delightedly instructed Morgenthau "to give it an extra push every morning and every evening until it is on board ship." [13] The windup conference came on June 5, just after the evacuation of Dunkirk, when, as Churchill later wrote, "Never has a great nation been so naked before her foes." [14] Small wonder that Purvis gave priority to the 75 mm guns, and of the 348 ready for immediate

[11] Blum, *Morgenthau Diaries,* vol. II, pp. 151–52. See also the memo from Chief of Staff for S/T, May 22, 1940, War Department File, Office of Chief of Staff File 15270, National Archives, Record Group 165.

[12] Telephone conversation between S/T and Purvis, June 3, 1940, Morgenthau Diary, Bk. 268, pp. 170–75.

[13] Blum, *Morgenthau Diaries,* vol. II, p. 155.

[14] Churchill, *Their Finest Hour,* p. 145.

shipment, 300 were sent to France with all the ammunition in an effort to halt the German armies now massing for their sweep toward Paris and central France.[15] Diverted to British ports before France surrendered, these artillery pieces joined the other stocks of surplus American arms which began to move across the Atlantic by June 11. It was an enormous task which was not completed until the end of July.[16]

As France and Britain called for aid and the United States turned over arms from available stocks, American planes were committed to action in the Battle of France. Their performance must have helped to prompt Premier Reynaud to renew his request for more planes on June 5, just as the German armies turned south and launched their attacks toward Paris.

The combat record of these planes against the Luftwaffe, particularly the record of the Martin and Douglas attack bombers, would have been even greater if they had been delivered earlier to French tactical squadrons for training. Of the 555 American combat planes which France had purchased in the spring of 1938 and the following winter, the only ones which had been delivered by September 1939 when war came to France were the 200 Curtiss Hawks or P-36s and, as noted above,[17] they had their special moment of glory during the early months of the Phony War.

In contrast to Curtiss-Wright, Glenn Martin and Douglas could not meet their original schedules so that no bombers were ready for shipment by September 5 when President Roosevelt implemented the American Neutral-

[15] Blum, *Morgenthau Diaries,* vol. II, p. 154.

[16] For problems of shipping the arms and munitions across the Atlantic, see Goodhart, *Fifty Ships that Saved the World,* pp. 61–62.

[17] See Chapter 6, p. 139.

ity Act and proclaimed an embargo on all arms destined for the European belligerents. By November 3, when Congress finally repealed the embargo, the shipment of war planes to France had in fact suffered little delay from the embargo. When the planes could finally be shipped, no Douglas bombers were ready; Glenn Martin had made deliveries. In early November, 50 of the 215 Martin bombers were ready to go. None were shipped until December 5, however, because not enough French ships were available to carry them.

As early as October 7, 1939, the French Minister for Air Guy La Chambre had reminded his Materiel Committee in Paris of the projected arrival of American planes at a rate of 40 per month and of the plans to have them assembled in northern France.[18] By October 23 the Air Ministry requested the head of France's third air mission to the United States, Colonel Paul Jacquin, to determine probable shipping dates, and five days later the French Director General of Transport was warned to be prepared for monthly shipments of 25 to 30 Douglas bombers from the west coast and 30 Martins from the east coast.[19] Deliveries of the latter were to begin by November 1.[20]

At the end of October, Colonel Jacquin cabled that Glenn Martin had beaten its schedule and that 50 bombers were being stockpiled in New York and "can be sent by the next boat after the raising of the embargo." La Chambre immediately informed the interested Ministries

[18] Procès-verbal, Comité de Matériel, October 7, 1939, Box B/104, Service Historique de l'Armée de l'Air at Versailles (SHAA).

[19] Cable from La Chambre to Jacquin, October 23, 1939, as cited in the memo on the Transport to France of Aeronautical Materiel Ordered in U.S., no author, no date, Monnet Papers, File 2A, Paris, October–November 1939.

[20] Memo from La Chambre to Director General of Transport, October 28, 1939, *Ibid.*

in Paris: "Materiel actually ready is more important than indicated in earlier note." Premier Daladier then entered the picture with orders for naval convoys to protect the shipments of these planes. By November 4, the French laid plans for a convoy of five ships in November and another of five in December, and Jacquin was requested to delay shipments until the convoys were formed. By November 7 it was hoped that within a fortnight the initial convoy would sail for France. On November 9, a report from New York confirmed that 52 Martins and 54 North American trainers were crated and ready for shipment and by the end of the month there would be an additional 19 Douglas bombers, 5 more trainers and as well the first 20 of the 40 Chance Vought dive bombers. On November 13 Bloch-Lainé, the recently arrived head of the French Purchasing Commission in the United States, sent an urgent appeal for a solution to the shipping problem. By then not only were there a total of 130 planes already stacked up but Glenn Martin was also planning to ship an additional 3 per day. To compound the situation 315 trucks were beginning to arrive on the docks for shipment to France as well as other material ordered by the various French Ministries. Bloch-Lainé urged an examination of the problem by "highest government authority." [21]

Such an examination finally took place on November 22, when Premier Daladier met with his Ministers for Air, Armaments, Marine, and Merchant Marine. To La Chambre's distress, the Merchant Marine Minister announced the cancellation of the 5-ship convoy scheduled for November. None could be formed until early December and then only 3 ships would be available. However, these were larger and faster ships than the ones formerly

[21] See the summary of events attached to the memo from La Chambre to Director General of Transport, October 28, 1939, *Ibid.*

scheduled and could carry 50 to 60 planes each. A second shipment could be made by the end of December. Thus, in early 1940 some 300 would be landed in France. Admiral Darlan agreed to provide protection by his Navy, "if conditions permit." Finally, the Premier set priorities for the order of shipments: planes and aircraft engines would come first, followed by machine tools, trucks, and then raw materials.[22]

The Air Minister's efforts to speed delivery of the American bombers to combat squadrons was further delayed by a crucial decision of the French Government in November to have the American planes diverted from their original assembly points near Brest, La Havre, and Bordeaux to a new one in Casablanca. This decision came in part from Admiral Darlan's conviction that convoys to this destination would be less exposed to German submarine attack. Then too it was felt that winter weather conditions in Morocco would be more favorable than in northern France for rapid assemblage of the aircraft. Furthermore there would be less danger of the Luftwaffe's bombers or fighters. To make this shift to Casablanca a crash program was implemented. However when the first convoy arrived on Christmas Day small progress had been made.[23]

The arrival of 93 Martins, 8 Douglases and 40 North American trainers on December 25 must have brightened that day for M. La Chambre, but the planes caused headaches for those assigned to the chore of readying them for flight. Colonel Stéphane Thouvenot, who had just returned to Paris from France's third air mission to the United States, was given the chief responsibility. Testify-

[22] Notes on a meeting held in the office of Premier Daladier, November 22, 1939, *Ibid.*

[23] See La Chambre's testimony on Darlan's role in shifting assemblage to North Africa, *Les Événements,* vol. II, p. 322.

ing before the Riom trial in 1942, he recalled that by late 1939 new hangars had not been completed in Casablanca to provide shelter for the assembly lines and in fact were not ready until the following March. Machine tools were lacking. Labor was woefully inadequate, comprised at first of unskilled Arabs supervised by a few trained Frenchmen until some fifty American mechanics arrived. The fuselages and wings of the bombers had been efficiently packaged in four boxes to a plane, but a plane as complex as the Martin and Douglas bombers required many hours to assemble. The process of assemblage was complicated because the American engines and propellors were boxed and shipped separately while earlier shipments of engines had gone first to France and then had to be transshipped to North Africa. But even more serious delays were caused by the shortage of French-supplied accessories such as machine guns, bomb racks, radios, and inter-communications systems. Inadequate production of these items in France and confused shipping schedules played havoc with the efforts in Casablanca to turn out completed Martins and Douglases.[24]

As time went by, the production rate of the Casablanca assembly lines slowly rose. The first 3 Martins were completed in mid-January, but only a total of 6 was turned out by January 22 and they had to wait for French accessories.[25] Before all the initial 93 Martins were assembled a second convoy had arrived on February 15 carrying 81

[24] For the Casablanca problems, see "Assemblage of American Planes," report by Stéphane Thouvenot prepared for the Riom Court, Private Papers of Stéphane Thouvenot. See also the report by R. E. Kettler of Hamilton Propellor division of United Aircraft, April 18, 1940, forwarded by the American Consul General at Casablanca to Washington, SD 851.248/367.

[25] For initial Martin completions and Douglas tool problem, see procès-verbal, Comité de Matériel, January 10, 1940, Box B/104, SHAA.

more Martins, and 32 Douglases.[26] At the time the third convoy sailed into North Africa on April 8, serious problems were still plaguing the personnel trying to put the American planes together. As can be seen from a report at the end of March, 29 bombers still remained in their crates. By that date only 34 Martins, 7 Douglases and 13 North American trainers had been fully completed and turned over to the French Air Force. The condition of the others was as follows: [27]

	Glenn Martin	*Douglas*	*North American*
Still in cases	19	10	0
In process of assemblage	37	12	0
Awaiting repairs	6	0	1
Assembled but lacking French accessories	42	1	3
Awaiting final assembly	30	1	4
In process of transfer to French Air Force	6	1	15
Transferred to French Air Force	34	7	13
Total received in Casablanca by March 31, 1940	174	32	36

[26] For convoy deliveries to Casablanca from December 1939 through June 1940, see annex to "Assemblage of American Planes," Thouvenot Papers.

[27] Report by Commander of French Air Force in North Africa to Minister of Air, March 28, 1940, Materiel Américaine, Box D1/488, SHAA.

The third convoy on April 8 brought 35 more Douglases and 31 Martins. With that shipment all of the 215 Martin bombers ordered in January 1939 had finally crossed the Atlantic. Even the 9 which had been on an early shipment to France had now been transshipped to Morocco. In contrast only 75 of the 100 Douglases had been delivered to Casablanca. It was not until May 10 that 20 more of them arrived. On that day, as the German armies launched their attack, the French Air Force had received only 137 fully assembled Glenn Martin and 29 Douglas bombers. Of the Martins, 64 were assigned to active duty, 11 were stationed in the colonies and 52 were on ready reserve. Of the Douglases, 24 were accounted for by four bombing squadrons with the remainder unassigned.[28]

By June 15, when effective air combat in France ceased, the status of American planes in France was as follows: [29]

	Glenn Martin	*Douglas*	*North American*
Still in cases	11	6	0
In process of assemblage	30	39	2
Transferred to French Air Force	182	55	38
Received in Casablanca	223	100	40

The additional 8 Martins beyond the 215 of the January 1939 order initiated deliveries on the contracts signed during the past fall by France's third air mission.

[28] "Situation des Avions," May 10, 1940, procès-verbal, Comité de Matériel, May 14, 1940, Box B/104, SHAA.

[29] See delivery schedule annexed to "Assemblage of American Planes," Thouvenot Papers.

The short time span between initial deliveries of these American-made planes to active tactical units and the German invasion meant that the French pilots, crews, and ground personnel had little opportunity to adjust to their new equipment. The best-prepared squadrons were those which received the 40 Martins turned over to the French Air Force by the first of April, but even they had only some 40 days of flying time before the German attack. The squadrons assigned the Douglases were in a worse predicament because as late as May 1, only 25 had been delivered to the Air Force.[30] It takes time and intensive training before air crews master new flying equipment, but time and training were limited that spring of 1940 for the crews of both of the American bombers. Nevertheless, the Martins went into their first action on May 22 with the Douglases committed to battle nine days later.

The combat record of the American-made planes in the Battle of France reveals how these aircraft met their ultimate test and indicates one reason why Premier Reynaud was so interested in obtaining more planes from across the Atlantic. The Martin and Douglas attack bombers proved their superiority to French-made bombers and, once committed to battle, carried a larger share of missions. In turn, the Curtiss Hawk fighters won a respectable number of air victories. In sorry contrast, the forty Chance Vought dive bombers, ordered during the winter and fall of 1939, proved tragically deficient.

By May 10 and the start of the German attack upon France, 4 groups of French fighters were equipped with Curtiss Hawks or P-36s. By then these groups were well trained and battle-tested. Until early May, when the first group of France's latest fighters, the Dewoitine 520, were assigned to combat units, the American-made planes with

[30] See chart, "Avions pris en compte," *Événements,* vol. II, p. 337.

their maximum speed of 490 kmh were the fastest in the French Air Force.[31] Although they could not match the most recent Messerschmitt 109s, they continued to be a threat to the Luftwaffe's bombers.

On May 10, the 4 Curtiss groups had been assigned for some months to the North East Zone of France's air defenses.[32] Thus they were ready for action when German planes hit French airfields with the dawn that first day of battle. One Hawk group claimed 3 fighters and 8 bombers.[33] While the sorties of the Curtiss Hawks cannot be detailed, nor their total losses determined during the Battle of France, these planes were heavily and constantly engaged and achieved many and even some notable victories.

An impressive victory was scored on May 12 when a group claimed 22 enemy planes of which 16 were Stuka dive bombers or Junker 87s.[34] Two days later another important victory came when a second group claimed 5 Messerschmitt 110s, the twin-engined fighter and fastest German combat plane.[35] As during that engagement of the past fall when 9 Hawks shot down 9 out of 27 Me-109s, Curtiss maneuverability and rate of climb paid off, but again the German pilots, once burned, used the superior speed of their Me-110s to avoid combat with the Curtiss fighters. The Hawks could still tackle German bombers, and on May 18 one group scored 6 Heinkel 111s, Germany's best attack bomber.[36]

On May 25 a group of Curtiss fighters joined two other French fighter groups and fittingly flew cover for an early

[31] Lieutenant Colonel Salesse, *L'Aviation de chasse française en 1939–1940: L'Aviation française au combat* (Paris, 1955), p. 78.
[32] *Ibid.*, pp. 76–77 and 191–93. [33] *Ibid.*, p. 83.
[34] *Ibid.*, p. 91. [35] *Ibid.*, p. 97. [36] *Ibid.*, p. 107.

Martin bomber attack on German elements near Abbeville.[37] This was one of the first escort missions flown by the Hawks and henceforth they were assigned to such missions and to fly air defense for the ground armies. As a result, their opportunities for victories over German planes declined.

A more interesting and notable record than the P-36s' was achieved by the American attack bombers, the Glenn Martin 167s and Douglas DB-7s: they soon proved their superiority to all French-made bombers. Initially, in the Battle of France, the French relied for low-level bombing attacks upon two planes produced by the French aircraft industry, the Liore 45 and Brequet 693. By May 1 the French Air Force had received 192 of the former and 98 of the latter.[38] Since the beginning of 1940 there had been sufficient numbers of each to provide training for at least six squadrons and so the French pilots and crews were better prepared to enter battle than those equipped with the Martins and Douglases. Nevertheless the initial losses they suffered were staggering.

The Brequet 693s received their first baptism of fire on May 12. Of a flight of 18, 8 failed to return and the remainder suffered heavy flak damage. On the same day, Britain's Royal Air Force suffered similar casualties. It had counted heavily upon the twin-engined Blenheim as an attack bomber but, on May 12, 6 of a flight of 9 failed to return from an attack upon German forces crossing the Maastricht bridges in Belgium.[39] On the following day a flight of 12 Liore 45s attacked columns near Dinant.

[37] *Ibid.*, p. 120.

[38] See the chart, "Avions pris en compte," *Evénements,* vol. II, p. 337.

[39] P. Paquier, *L'Aviation de bombardement française en 1939–1940: L'Aviation française au combat* (Paris, 1948), pp. 38–40.

Although all of them returned, every one had been damaged by anti-aircraft fire. Then on the fourteenth, serious losses were sustained again. First, a flight of 9 Brequets protected by French fighters flew to the Meuse River; all but one returned, but 5 had been hit by anti-aircraft fire. Early that afternoon, 13 Amiot 143s and 6 Liore 45s struck at Sedan. All were hit by flak and 5 were lost. After that the old, slow, and vulnerable Amiots were relegated to night attacks.[40] In turn, the British bombers suffered heavily. On May 14, the Royal Air Force sent out 67 of its medium bombers, Blenheims together with Fairey Battles, the other British attack bomber, and only 32 returned. The remainder were crippled by anti-aircraft fire. Henceforth the British bombers were also relegated to night work.[41] From May 15 through 20, the Liore 45s were called upon to fly 74 sorties and their losses amounted to 11. The Brequets fared better, losing 5 out of 59 sorties.[42] There was no question that France had to call upon every available plane and so the Glenn Martins were committed to action.

When the Battle of France opened, the Martins were assigned to the Air Force's Zone of the Alps in two groups made up of two squadrons of six planes each for a total of 24. A third Martin group was in North Africa with a fourth in the process of being equipped with this type of bomber. The fifth group of Martins was in Syria. Five other French Air Force groups in North Africa were also in the process of shifting over to the Douglas bombers but none were as yet fully equipped. By May 22, the two

[40] *Ibid.*, p. 48. [41] *Ibid.*, pp. 51–52.

[42] See "Missions de Bombardement de Jour, effectuées par l'aviation françaises sur le théâtre nord-est entre le 10 mai 1940 et le 25 juin 1940," *Événements*, vol. II, pp. 346–51.

groups of Martins in the Alps Zone were shifted into the active North East Zone of French air defense to join ten other bomber groups. They went into action that day.[43] The initial Douglas groups did not fly in combat until nine days later.

The first Martin bombers were sent out against enemy columns near Cambrai. Two attacks were launched with twelve planes or two squadrons each. In the first mission only two planes located their target. The others found cloud cover too thick. The second flight was more successful and all planes completed their mission. However, one was shot down and four were so damaged by anti-aircraft fire that they returned with their bomb loads. The Martins had been "blooded," but they had proved themselves in action to be tough planes capable of taking heavy punishment. One even returned with its co-pilot at the controls after its nose section had been shot away and its pilot killed.[44] Their record compared well with the only other French Air Force bombers flying that day. These were two flights of Brequets 693 of 8 each, of which 3 were lost.[45]

On the next day the weather was so poor only a handful of French- or American-made bombers flew. Then on May 24, 30 Martins in two flights hit enemy elements near Arras while one flight of 9 Brequets was engaged. Four of the Martins were shot down, one a victim of German fighters and one falling to anti-aircraft fire. The loss of the other two was undetermined.[46] Apparently a lesson had been learned that day, for such a high casualty rate was never again sustained by the Martins. Almost daily they

[43] Paquier, *L'aviation de bombardement,* pp. 205–07.

[44] "Missions de Bombardement de Jour," *Événements,* vol. II, p. 347.

[45] *Ibid.,* p. 347. [46] *Ibid.,* p. 347.

continued to fly low-level missions, strafing and bombing columns on the highways and bridges over rivers and canals, as well as assemblies of German tanks. Down through the evacuation of Dunkirk the Martins carried their fair share of missions, sometimes making up more than 50 per cent of the bombers sent out each day.[47]

By May 31 three groups of Douglas bombers had come up from North Africa and one went into action that day strafing roads near Saint Quentin. Losses amounted to a grim 4 out of 12. At the same time, 9 out of 23 Liore 45s were shot down.[48] The bad weather of the next four days kept the bombers grounded and then on June 5, as German columns crossed the Somme and headed toward Paris, 12 Douglases were sent against tanks near Elancours. This time only one failed to return.[49] Their crews had learned their tactical lessons quickly and thereafter losses never reached more than one a day.

As the German armies began to move south, Premier Reynaud turned again to the United States. The Premier's appeal came as Paris was threatened and Britain refused to send more fighter squadrons across the Channel.[50] During a telephone conversation with President Roosevelt, Reynaud pleaded, "We need immediately all the planes of your Army and Navy that you in any way can procure for us. Can you stretch your hand across the ocean to help us save civilization? Can you in one way or another, be it directly or indirectly, send us planes completely equipped for battle?"[51]

Reynaud's plea for planes did not come on the spur of

[47] *Ibid.*, p. 349. [48] *Ibid.*, p. 347. [49] *Ibid.*, p. 348.

[50] See Bullitt to Secretary of State, June 5, 1940, *FR, 1940,* vol. I, pp. 240–41.

[51] Reynaud, *La France a sauvé l'Europe,* vol. II, pp. 186–87. See also Langer and Gleason, *Challenge to Isolation,* pp. 512–13.

the moment, but had been in preparation since May 24, when Jean Monnet's assistant, René Pleven, drew up a memorandum addressed to the French Premier. The memo urged the Allies to seek "as many planes as possible to be able to sustain the losses resulting from combat" and to call on the United States for a release of its P-36s, P-40s, and the bombers on order. This memo argued that the U.S. Government should be sympathetic to the Allied request because of the Allies' capital investment of $60 million in the American aircraft industry plus the $7 million paid during the spring "as a friendly gesture" toward the development of new types for the U.S. Army. France recognized that the diversion of planes "would cause a tremendous inconvenience to the Army," but, "if thanks to the planes received now, the Allies are able to master the situation the sacrifice made by the United States Army would have no evil consequences for the defense of the United States." Then, if the Allies were defeated, the 5,000 planes which were on their order plus the large sources of production created by France and Britain would become available to the United States.[52]

The next day the memorandum was given to the Minister for Air, Laurent-Eynac, who passed it on to the Premier as a basis for another appeal to Roosevelt. On May 26, Monnet backed up this maneuver with a special note to Reynaud: "Given the urgency of our needs, new interventions ought to be made through Churchill and yourself. It is important that these personal interventions be synchronized." A list of American aircraft in stock was annexed to the memo, which noted that even though some of these

[52] Memorandum Pleven to Reynaud, English copy dated May 24, French copy dated May 25, 1940, Monnet Papers, File 3A, Comité Coordination Franco-Anglaises.

were obsolete they could help sustain the losses in combat. The annex listed as well all the planes which the United States Army had on order.[53] On June 3 the list of American planes was passed on to Paul Baudouin, who was soon to be appointed secretary of Premier Reynaud's war cabinet. Baudouin reported to Monnet "that following certain telephone conversations, chances appear good to receive immediately aerial material belonging to the American Army and Navy." [54] Premier Reynaud's telephone call on June 5 to President Roosevelt culminated this series of recommendations from Monnet's office in London and, according to Bullitt's report to the President, "Reynaud [was] enormously pleased by his conversation with you on the telephone this evening." [55] When the Premier proposed that the United States release some of its obsolete planes, he received an affirmative reply.

Again Secretary Morgenthau handled the negotiations. This time he turned to the Chief of Naval Operations and asked whether the Navy could start with "their oldest dive bombers . . . the very oldest?" and return them to the manufacturer in exchange for later delivery of more modern ones.[56] Admiral Stark agreed and orders went out for 50 obsolete Curtiss dive bombers of the SBC4 type, to be turned in to that company's plant at Buffalo. The dive

[53] Unsigned note with Annex on American planes, May 26, 1940. Internal evidence indicates it was written by Monnet for Reynaud. See also the note from Monnet to Bridges, Secretary of the British War Cabinet, *Ibid.*

[54] Note on the available American aircraft for Baudouin, June 3, 1940, and the memo on the telephone conversation with Baudouin on the same day, *Ibid.*

[55] Bullitt, June 5, 1940, *FR, 1940*, vol. I, pp. 240–41.

[56] Conference among S/T, Purvis, Bloch-Lainé, and Colonel Jacquin, together with Donald Nelson and Philip Young, the newly appointed chairman of the President's Liaison Committee, June 5, 1940, Morgenthau Diary, Bk. 269, pp. 18–36.

bombers were then to be flown to an airport on the Canadian-Maine border and there they would be pushed across to Canadian pilots. A French aircraft carrier, the *Bearn,* was already in Halifax loading 40 assembled P-36s, ordered by France in the past November, and there would be "lots of room for the dive bombers." [57]

Two days later the Army followed suit. Morgenthau had called a conference with General Marshall and Admiral Stark to let them know that Roosevelt planned to announce the release of the arms as well as the old Navy dive bombers. At the end of the discussion the Secretary turned to the Chief of Staff and said, "While you are all in such a good humor and so generous, what about those 93 A-17As [a twin-engined attack bomber] . . . ?" and General Marshall replied, "They are being concentrated." Morgenthau, obviously surprised, asked, "Are you going through with it?" To which the General replied, "Yes." [58] When the Secretary informed Purvis that these obsolete Northrop A-17As were being assembled on June 10 and that bombs for the American planes had also been located, the head of the Anglo-French Purchasing Committee blurted out in gratitude, "You can't tell what this means abroad. It just means everything to them, just means everything." [59]

[57] Conference in Morgenthau's home, June 5, 1940, *Ibid.,* Bk. 269, pp. 184–86. For Admiral Stark's actions in releasing the dive bombers, see also the conference of Treasury officials, June 7, 1940, *Ibid.,* Bk. 270, pp. 138–45.

[58] Conference re: Allied Purchases, June 7, 1940, 9:00 a.m., *Ibid.,* Bk. 270, pp. 2–34. For orders and correspondence concerning transfer of the A-17As, see Lyon Project Book 10F, "Chronological Summary of Foreign Release and Sale of Military Aircraft and Its Effect on Army Deliveries, June 1939–October 1940." See especially Tabs. 22–28.

[59] Telephone conversation between S/T and Purvis, June 9, 1940, Morgenthau Diary, Bk. 270, pp. 193–94.

When the Navy began to fly its 50 dive bombers into Buffalo, the press, as yet uninformed of Roosevelt's latest aid to the Allies, began to raise questions. On June 7 Roosevelt called a news conference. He denied that he had any plans for releasing "brand new" aircraft but said that military aircraft had a way of becoming obsolete very fast.[60]

Three days later at Charlottesville, Virginia, the President formalized his policy of aiding the Allies:

> We will extend to the opponents of force the material resources of this nation, and at the same time we will harness and speed up the use of those resources in order that we ourselves in the Americas may have equipment and training equal to the task of any emergency and every defense.
>
> All roads leading to the accomplishment of these objectives must be kept clear of obstructions. We will not slow down or detour. Signs and signals call for speed—full speed ahead.[61]

As the President delivered his address, Premier Reynaud, before evacuating Paris, again cabled across the Atlantic asking for "aid and material support by all means short of an expeditionary force." [62] This was the most recent in a series of what Secretary Hull was to label "extraordinary, almost hysterical appeals." [63] Reynaud

[60] *Press Conferences of Franklin D. Roosevelt,* 1940, vol. 15, microfilm roll 8, pp. 544–53. See also Hall, *North American Supply,* p. 137.

[61] *Public Papers and Addresses of Franklin D. Roosevelt,* compiled by Samuel I. Rosenman (New York, 1941), vol. 9, pp. 259–64.

[62] Reynaud, *France a sauvé l'Europe,* pp. 295–96; *FR, 1940,* vol I, pp. 245–46.

[63] Hull, *Memoirs,* vol. I, p. 767.

made it clear that further French resistance depended largely upon the policy of the United States.[64] Indeed, he held his cabinet together only until he heard President Roosevelt's reply. It arrived in France on June 14: "This Government is doing everything in its power to make available to the Allied Governments the material they so urgently required and our efforts to do still more are being redoubled." [65] But the President's message made little impact on the French Government.

The Premier made one last effort. On the night of June 13, he appealed by radio for "clouds of planes from across the Atlantic to crush the evil force that dominates Europe." [66] In the light of the obstruction which Reynaud, as Minister of Finance, had offered to the French purchase of American planes, and especially as he knew, at least since Monnet's memorandum of June 3, the exact number of planes held by the American Air Corps, his call for "clouds of planes" appears to have been aimed more at his French public than that of the United States as he sought to pass some of the burden for France's defeat onto American shoulders.

By June 16, when Reynaud resigned and turned the government over to Marshal Pétain, the Battle of France had been lost. As German tanks swept south of Paris during these last frantic days, the American bombers carried an increasingly heavy share of low-level attacks. On June 7 the largest number of Martins were used on a single day when 43 of them flew sorties with a loss of only one. Together with 8 Douglases, they outnumbered the 44 sorties flown by French-made bombers in the North East

[64] Langer and Gleason, *Challenge to Isolation,* p. 518.
[65] *FR, 1940,* vol. I, pp. 247–48.
[66] Reynaud, *La France a sauvé l'Europe,* pp. 329–31.

Zone. On the next day, 43 Martins flew. Four days later, 32 Martins were the only bombers in the French Air Force to launch strafing attacks, and on that day their losses rose to 4. Their last mission in the North East Zone came on June 14.[67]

Action in the Center Zone of the French air defenses began for 9 Douglases on June 10. Then, after a day of bad weather, 23 Martins, which had been shifted south from the North East Zone, went into action from airfields in the Center. On the following two days, both types of American bombers flew further missions. Then air action ceased on June 15 and all American bombers were ordered back to North Africa on the 16th.[68]

There was no question that the Martin and Douglas bombers, despite their lack of self-sealing gas tanks and armor for their crews, contributed to the Battle of France. Their daily sorties in the Zone of the North East appear small in number: available records show the Martins flew a total of 352 between May 22 and June 14, whereas the Douglases flew 61 between May 31 and the end of the aerial campaign. However their totals compared favorably with the French-made bombers. The Brequet 693s from May 22 to June 14 totaled 343 missions, whereas the Liore 45s flew only 196.[69]

The only other American planes that flew in the Battle of France were the 40 Chance Vought dive bombers. They were assigned to two naval squadrons and they failed to measure up. First one squadron lost all its 12 planes when

[67] "Missions de Bombardement de Jour," *Événements,* vol. II, pp. 349–50.

[68] Paquier, *L'Aviation de bombardement,* pp. 165–66, 176, 179, and 182.

[69] "Missions de Bombardement de Jour," *Événements,* vol. II, pp. 346–51.

on May 10 they were caught on the ground by the Luftwaffe. Then that same squadron lost 9 of its replacements to strafing attacks by Italian fighters later in June. The other squadron suffered equally. On May 20 it was sent to bomb a bridge over the Oise River. Of the 11 engaged, only 3 survived. Those 3, together with 2 replacements, continued to fly limited missions until the surrender when only 3 were left.[70] As one of the squadron leaders later reported in an understatement, these dive bombers "in 1940 were a very rudimentary form." While their failure stemmed in part from the inferiority of their equipment, their naval pilots also lacked training for ground warfare. In addition, these dive bombers were not given the fighter protection so necessary for their survival.[71]

American aid for France during the battle of May and June 1940 failed to halt Germany's armed might. Though most American planes on hand had performed successfully, there were too few and they were too ineffectively directed to do much good. The planes and arms released in June 1940 by the United States from its armed services, except those planes on board the *Bearn,* the French aircraft carrier which ended up in Martinique, were shipped too late to enter the battle and so were sent to Britain. The British also became beneficiaries of all outstanding French orders for American planes. Thanks to the courage of the French representatives on the Anglo-French Purchasing Commission in the United States, all French contracts for American planes and arms were signed over to the British

[70] For the combat record of the Chance Vought, see Fleury Marius Sieve, *L'Aviation d'assaut dans la Bataille en 1940: L'Aviation française au combat* (Paris, 1948), p. 155.

[71] See report of January 5, 1949, by Captain Mesny concerning his experiences as commander of the first Chance Vought squadron, *Événements, Rapport,* pp. 341–43.

on the night of June 17.[72] These contracts totaled $600 million, of which $425 million was for aircraft.

France fell before it could join Britain in further steps to harness American industry to their war machines. It was Jean Monnet who sparked the new effort when on May 19 he called upon Reynaud and then Churchill to initiate another joint drive to build American potential for arms production.[73] Though the plan stumbled as France fell, Monnet kept it moving and expanding. Ultimately it became the Victory Program which the United States adopted in the fall of 1941 to cover total needs for its as well as Britain's armies. That story remains to be told but, indubitably, U.S. aid to France laid a vital foundation for that later development of the American arsenal which finally brought overwhelming material superiority to bear upon Hitler's Germany and turned the tide of war.

[72] For a summary of this transaction, see Hall, *North American Supply*, pp. 146–52.

[73] Identical letters from Monnet to Reynaud, May 19, and from Monnet to Churchill, May 20, 1940, Monnet Papers, British Supply Council, Reynaud Correspondence. See also Hall, *North American Supply*, p. 159.

Bibliography

Primary Source Materials

MANUSCRIPT MATERIALS AND INTERVIEWS

French Material

Because of the fifty-year law which controls official French documents, the major sources of primary material were found in private collections of papers. Interviews provided supporting data.

LA CHAMBRE PAPERS These consist of the key documents on La Chambre's personal files and his Ministry's negotiations for American planes. Most important were the reports written by each of the air missions sent to the United States. These were supplemented by memoranda, letters, cables, and minutes of meetings. These papers were the most vital source for my study of French negotiations and provided significant new insights into American policy toward the sale of planes to France.

In the summers of 1961 and 1963 I interviewed M. La Chambre as well as M. Roger Hoppenot, who had been his *chef de cabinet civil.*

LA GRANGE PAPERS Baron Amaury de La Grange kept a record of his mission to the United States in the winter of 1938, and it offers the most complete source for the reconstruction of the air mission which initiated French purchases of American planes. Available are his handwritten notes of his talk with President Roosevelt on January 16, 1938, as well as additional reports on the American President's interest in helping France rebuild its air power. The Baron's manuscript, "Campaign Led in the Senate Between 1934 and 1940," covers his own efforts to help France as well as provides copies of letters and speeches the Senator made during those years. Baroness de La Grange holds the papers in Paris, and in the summer of 1961 she opened the pertinent papers to me.

MONNET PAPERS I studied those papers relative to Monnet's work in establishing and chairing the Anglo-French Economic Coordinating Commission. These papers begin with his suggestion on September 3, 1939, that such a joint economic commission be established, and terminate with the collapse of France. Until French and British documents for 1939 and 1940 are opened, M. Monnet's files provide the richest source for the study not only of the formation of the Economic Coordinating Commission but also of its role in directing France and Britain toward placing their large joint order for American aircraft in March 1940. M. Monnet left these files in London after the Fall of France. Thus, these papers were preserved, in contrast to his other files on his negotiations in the United States during the fall of 1938 and winter of 1939, which were destroyed during the German occupation of France.

THOUVENOT PAPERS These papers contained documents about the French efforts to assemble American planes after they arrived in Casablanca, as well as provided the major source of information about the problems that Thouvenot and his staff faced in assembling these planes for service in the French Air Force. M. Thouvenot also turned over to me a number of key charts relative to the Anglo-French purchases of March 1940.

My interview with M. Thouvenot about his joint air mission to the United States in the fall of 1939 offered important material about the preparation of that mission as well as its negotiations.

Further interviews were conducted with General Paul Jacquin, who came to the United States with three French air missions. Of particular interest was his account of the dramatic release by France of its aviation contracts to Britain during the night of June 16, 1940. In his interview, René Pleven, who led two missions to the United States which culminated in the Anglo-French order for 4,000 planes in March 1940, filled in significant gaps in the record. Paul Reynaud, whom I interviewed during the summer of 1963, dismissed the French negotiations for American planes as nothing but a commercial venture.

OFFICIAL FRENCH DOCUMENT COLLECTION The only pertinent collection of official French documents open for research is held by the Service Historique de l'Armée de l'Air at Versailles. The most important files were the minutes of the Air Ministry's Material Committee (Box B/104). They provide evidence of resistance within the French Air Force toward the purchase of American combat planes.

British Material

Britain's fifty-year law, recently reduced to thirty years, controls all official documents, and thus no official material is yet available relative to Britain joining France in the March 1940 order for 4,000 American planes. However, a supplement to British official histories is Jean Monnet's private papers which he collected as chairman of the Anglo-French Economic Coordinating Committee during the winter of 1940.

LORD ELIBANK PAPERS In the summer of 1961 Lord Elibank opened for me his correspondence with President Roosevelt from 1933 to 1940, as well as his notes on a visit with the President at Hyde Park in October 1938.

Two interviews, which were helpful in reconstructing negotiations in Britain, were conducted. The first was with Sir Henry Self, who led the British side of the Anglo-French negotiations for planes, and the second was with Air Vice Marshal George B. A. Baker, who accompanied Sir Henry Self to the United States to evaluate American combat planes.

American Material

FRANKLIN D. ROOSEVELT PAPERS The papers of President Roosevelt held in his Library at Hyde Park provide a disappointing record of his involvement in encouraging France to buy American aircraft. Since Roosevelt rarely kept records showing his personal thoughts and plans, there is scant evidence among his papers. Most important of the President's files for this study are the letters Ambassador William C. Bullitt sent to Roosevelt about the problems concerning French air power.

MORGENTHAU DIARIES Henry J. Morgenthau, while Secretary of the Treasury, kept a diary in the form of minutes of conferences, transcripts of telephone conversations, letters, cables, and reports. The many volumes of this diary are held by the Roosevelt

Library at Hyde Park. Although the diaries have been excerpted by John M. Blum in a three volume work, *From the Morgenthau Diaries* (Boston, 1959, 1965, 1967), much remains unpublished including Morgenthau's concern with France's efforts to rebuild its air power with American planes.

ARNOLD PAPERS (Manuscript Division, Library of Congress) General H. H. Arnold wanted to retain the latest American planes to build his Air Corps' strength, and his papers provide an important supplement to the Army Air Force Files. President Roosevelt's efforts to help France obtain planes is seen more clearly in both the Arnold Papers and the Air Force Files than in any other source except the Morgenthau Diaries.

ARMY AIR FORCE FILES (National Archives, Record Group 18) The Air Force Files, which contain material relative to French negotiations for planes, also contain the evidence of the Air Corps' opposition to the sale of latest American combat types. Further evidence is located in the Adjutant General Office Files (National Archives, Record Group 94), which conveniently place together the key documents concerning one topic. Important for this study, the Army Air Force Files contain the "Air Corps Project Records" collected by Major A. J. Lyon, which focus on specific problems and offer documentation concerning major Air Corps policy questions. See also *Army Air Force Historical Studies* (National Archives, Record Group 160).

No. 22, "Legislation Relating to the AAF Materiel Program, 1939–1945."

No. 40, "Expansion of Industrial Facilities under Army Air Force Auspices, 1940–1945."

No. 50, "Material Research and Development in the Army Air Arm, 1914–1945."

No. 106, "Distribution of Air Material to the Allies, 1939–1944."

STATE DEPARTMENT DOCUMENTS (National Archives, Record Group 19) Many documents on American aid for France, 1938–1940, appear in the multi-volumed *Foreign Relations of the United States*. However, numerous documents which are pertinent to a relatively narrow study such as this remain unpublished but available in the archives of the State Department.

"DIPLOMATIC JOURNALS OF JAY PIERREPONT MOFFAT, 1919–43" (Manuscript in the custody of the Houghton Library, Harvard University) Moffat was the head of the European section of the State Department during 1938–1940 and his daily journal contains helpful insights into the Department's attitude toward the sale of American planes to France.

PRESIDENT'S LIAISON COMMITTEE FILE (National Archives, Record Group 169) This Committee was set up in the fall of 1939 to deal with the prospective Anglo-French order for 10,000 planes. It kept extensive files which supplement the papers in the Morgenthau Diary.

NAVY DEPARTMENT FILES (National Archives, Record Group 72) While the Navy never became as involved as the Army Air Corps in the sale of planes to France, documents have been found in the Navy Files on President Roosevelt's efforts to gain the release of latest American war planes for France.

"DIARY OF WILLIAM D. LEAHY, 1938" (Manuscript Division, Library of Congress) Admiral Leahy was the Chief of Naval Operations from 1937 to 1939. He supported President Roosevelt's efforts to release American planes to France.

WAR DEPARTMENT FILES (National Archives, Record Group 165) Informative are the files dealing with the Chief of Staff's decision to release planes to France and Britain in 1939 and 1940.

GOVERNMENT PUBLICATIONS

French

Only one published source of primary materials has specific bearing upon French negotiations for American planes, 1938–1940, and the most important section is the testimony of Guy La Chambre: *Les Événements Survenus en France de 1933 à 1945, Témoignages et Documents Recueillis par la Commission d'Enquête Parlementaire,* 10 vols. (Paris, 1947). See especially vol. II.

Journal Officiel, Débat Parlementaire, Chambre des Députés, Comité Secret, Février 9, 1940 (Paris, 1940).

Journal Officiel, Débats Parlementaires, Chambre des Députés, 1938, 1939, 1940; Senat 1938, 1939, 1940.

American

Foreign Relations of the United States, 1938, 4 vols. (Washington, 1955); *1939,* 4 vols. (Washington, 1956); *1940,* 5 vols. (Washington, 1959).

Hearings Before the Committee on Military Affairs, United States Senate, 76th Congress, 1st session, on H.R. 3791, January 17–February 2, 1939 (Washington, 1939).

United States Congress, House of Representatives, Hearings on H.R. 9209, 76th Congress, 3rd session (Washington, 1940).

British

Documents on British Foreign Policy, 1919–1939, Third Series, 3 vols., eds. E. L. Woodward and R. Butler (London, 1950).

PUBLISHED COLLECTIONS OF LETTERS AND DOCUMENTS

Moffat Papers: Selections from the Diplomatic Journals of Jay Pierrepont Moffat, 1919–1943, ed. Nancy H. Hooker (Cambridge, Mass., 1956).

Roosevelt, Franklin D., *F.D.R.: His Personal Letters, 1928–1945,* ed. Elliott Roosevelt, vol. II (New York, 1950).

——, *Public Papers and Addresses,* 13 vols., ed. S. I. Rosenman (New York, 1938–1950).

Press Conferences of Franklin D. Roosevelt, 1938, microfilm vols. (Roosevelt Library, 1956).

AUTOBIOGRAPHIES, MEMOIRS, AND DIARIES

Armengaud, Gen. Paul F. M., *Batailles Politiques et Militaires sur l'Europ, Témoignages 1932–1940* (Paris, 1948).

Arnold, H. H., *Global Mission* (New York, 1949).

Baudouin, Paul, *The Private Diaries (March 1940–January 1941),* trans. Sir Charles Petrie (London, 1948).

Bonnet, Georges, *Defense de la Paix,* vol. I, *De Washington au Quai d'Orsay* (Geneva, 1946).

Bromberger, Merry and Serge, *Jean Monnet and the United States of Europe,* trans. E. P. Halperin (New York, 1969).

Churchill, Winston S., *The Second World War,* vol. II, *Their Finest Hour* (London, 1949).

Cot, Pierre, *L'Armée de l'Air 1936–1938* (Paris, 1939).

——, *Triumph of Treason* (New York, 1944).

Daladier, Edouard, *Les Grands Journees du Procès de Riom* (Paris, 1945).

De Gaulle, Charles, *War Memoirs*, vol. I, *The Call to Honour, 1940–1942*, trans. J. Griffin (London, 1955).

Dignac, Pierre, *Malfaiteurs Publics, Documents d'Histoire, 1924–1940* (Grenoble, 1944).

Eden, Anthony, *Memoirs of Anthony Eden, Earl of Avon*, vol. II, *The Reckoning* (Boston, 1965).

François-Poncet, André, *The Fateful Years* (New York, 1949).

Gamelin, Maurice, *Servir*, vol. II, *Le Prologue du Drama, 1930–Aout 1939* (Paris, 1946).

Hull, Cordell, *Memoirs of Cordell Hull*, 2 vols. (New York, 1948).

Ickes, Harold L., *Secret Diaries of Harold L. Ickes*, 3 vols. (New York, 1954).

Lyet, Pierre, *La Bataille de France, Mai-Juin, 1940* (Paris, 1940).

Maroselli, André, *Le Sabotage de Notre Aviation, Cause Principal de Notre Défaite* (Paris, 1941).

Morgenthau, Henry, "The Morgenthau Diaries, Part IV, The Story Behind Lend Lease," *Collier's*, October 18, 1947.

Perkins, Frances, *The Roosevelt I Knew* (New York, 1946).

Pertinax (pseud.), *Les Fossoyeurs*, 2 vols. (New York, 1943).

Reynaud, Paul, *Au Coeur de la Mélée 1936–45* (Paris, 1951).

——, *France a Sauve l'Europe*, 2 vols. (Paris, 1947).

Slessor, Sir John, *The Central Blue: Recollections and Reflections* (London, 1956).

Spears, Edward L., *Assignment to Catastrophe*, 2 vols. (London, 1954).

Stehlin, Paul, *Témoignage sur l'Histoire* (Paris, 1964).

CONTEMPORARY NEWSPAPERS AND JOURNALS

L'Action Française
L'Aeronautique
L'Air
L'Epoque
L'Europe Nouvelle
Le Figaro
L'Homme Libre
L'Humanité
L'Intransigeant

Le Jour-Echo de Paris
La Liberté
Le Matin
New York Times
L'Oeuvre
Paris-Soir
La Petit Parisien
Le Populaire
La République
Revues des Deux Mondes
Revue de Paris
Le Temps

BOOKS, ARTICLES, AND PAMPHLETS

Accart, Jean, *On s'est Battu dans le Ciel* (Grenoble, 1942).

Armengaud, Gen. Paul F. M., "Division Spirituelle des Français et Insuffisance de l'Aviation en France," *L'Europe Nouvelle,* May 21, 1938, pp. 537–8.

——, "L'Effort Exceptional du Reich dans le Domaine de l'Aviation Militaire," *Dépeche du Toulouse,* October 17, 1938.

——, "La Guerre d'Espagne: La Combinaison des Forces de l'Air avec les Forces Navales et avec l'Armée de Terre," *Revue Militaire Générale,* ser. 2, v. 2, March 1938, pp. 259–84.

——, "La Guerre d'Espagne: Technique et Tactique des Forces de l'Air," *Revue Militaire Générale,* ser. 2, v. 2, April 1938, pp. 413–49.

——, "Pour une Armée de l'Air Plus Forte," *Revue Militaire Générale,* ser. 2, v. 2, May 1938, pp. 531–8.

——, "Sécurité Aérienne et Offensive Aérienne," *Revue Militaire Générale,* ser. 2, v. 2, January 1938, pp. 43–58.

——, "Une Grand Armée, l'Arme de l'Air du Reich," *Revue Militaire Générale,* October 1938.

"Avions Américaines," *L'Air,* No. 444, May 1, 1938.

Bailby, Léon, "Avons-nous Besoin des Avions Américains?" *Le Jour-Echo de Paris,* February 2, 1939.

Bouché, Henry, "Pour une Armée de l'Air Plus Puissante," *L'Aéronautique,* May 1938, pp. 89–90.

"Commentaire de Presse," *L'Air,* May 20 and June 1, 1938.

Cot, Pierre, "La Lutte Aérien," *L'Oeuvre,* October 7, 1938.

"Curtiss Wright: Warrior," *Fortune,* XVIII, September 1938, p. 96.

Duval, Gen., "L'Aviation de Guerre," *Revue de Paris,* December 15, 1938, pp. 721–41.

Elibank, Lord, "Franklin D. Roosevelt: Friend of Britain," *Contemporary Review,* CLXXXVII, June 1955, pp. 364–7.

Faure, Pierre, "L'Aviation de Guerre," *Revue de Paris,* October 15, 1938, pp. 808–15.

Fleming, D. F., "Our Choice in Foreign Policy," *Events,* March 1939.

"The Great Problem of French Aviation," *L'Europe Nouvelle,* May 7, 1938, pp. 457–8.

Jayle, Christian, "La France Devrait-Elle Acheter des Avions Américains?" *L'Europe Nouvelle,* April 23, 1938, pp. 453–4.

Langeron, Lt. Col. André, *Misère et Grandeur de Notre Aviation* (Paris, 1941).

Laurent-Eynac, "Vers le Plan des 5,000," *L'Air,* November 1, 1938.

Maginel, Gen., "L'Intervention de l'Aviation dans la Lutte Terrestre," *Revue Militaire Générale,* ser. 2, v. 2, October, November, 1938, pp. 505–29 n, 675–84.

"Notre Aviation, Comment la Reconstruire," *Revue des Deux Mondes,* May 15, 1938, pp. 279–80.

Roland, Phillipe, *La Crise de Matériel de l'Aviation Militaire Française* (Paris, 1938).

Rose, Marc A., "Hitler's Aerial Triumph," *Forum,* vol. 101, March 1939, p. 126.

de Sales, Raoul de Roussy, "L'Amérique Incertaine," *Revue de Paris,* July 1, 1939, pp. 130–48.

de Torres, Peyronnet, "Nouvelles de l'Aviation," *L'Intransigeant,* a column which appeared frequently and sometimes daily from January 1938 to September 1939, when press censorship interfered.

——, "Des Avions, des Avions," *L'Intransigeant,* October 15–22, 1938.

——, "L'Achat d'Avions en Amérique," *L'Intransigeant,* May 1, 1938, p. 1.

——, "Demain dans le Ciel," 3ème Partie, *L'Intransigeant,* February 11, 1939, p. 1.

"United Aircraft," *Fortune,* XXIII, March 1941.

Secondary Source Materials

OFFICIAL GOVERNMENT HISTORIES

American

United States Army in World War II, War Department Series:

Smith, R. Elberton, *The Army and Economic Mobilization* (Washington, 1959).

Watson, Mark S., *Chief of Staff: Prewar Plans and Preparations* (Washington, 1950).

Army Air Forces in World War II Series:

Vol. I, *Plans and Early Operations, January 1939 to August 1942,* eds. W. F. Craven and J. L. Cate (Chicago, 1948).

Vol. VI, *Men and Planes,* eds. W. F. Craven and J. L. Cate (Chicago, 1955).

British

History of the Second World War, United Kingdom Civil Series:

Hall, H. Duncan, *North American Supply* (London, 1955).

Hall, H. Duncan, and C. C. Wrigley, *Studies of Overseas Supplies* (London, 1956).

Hancock, W. K., and M. M. Gowing, *British War Economy* (London, 1949).

Hurstfield, J., *The Control of Raw Materials* (London, 1953).

Medlicott, W. N., *Economic Blockade,* 2 vols. (London, 1952).

Postan, M. M., *British War Production* (London, 1952).

History of the Second World War, United Kingdom Military Series:

Ellis, L. F., *The War in France and Flanders* (London, 1953).

Richards, Denis, *Royal Air Force 1939–1945,* vol. I, *The Fight at Odds 1939–1941* (London, 1953).

Webster, C., and N. Frankland, *The Strategic Air Offensive Against Germany, 1939–1945,* vol. I, *Preparation* (London, 1961).

BOOKS AND ARTICLES

Alsop, Joseph, and Robert Kintner, *American White Paper* (New York, 1940).

Angot, E., and R. de Lavergne, *Le Général Vuillemin: Une Figure Légéndaire de L'Aviation Française de 1914 à 1940* (Paris, 1965).

D'Astier de la Vigerie, Françoise P. R., *Le Ciel n'etait pas Vide* (Paris, 1952).

Baumbach, W., "Les Armements Aériens de l'Allemagne Pendant la Deuxième Guerre Mondiale," *Forces Aériennes Françaises,* March and April 1954, pp. 384–401, 526–45.

Beaufre, André, *Le Drame de 1940* (Paris, 1965).

Benoist-Mechin, Jacques G. P. M., *60 Jours qui Ebranlèrent l'Occident,* 3 vols. (Paris, 1956).

Blum, John M., *From the Morgenthau Diaries,* vol. 1, *Years of Crisis, 1928–1938* (Boston, 1959); vol. 2, *Years of Urgency, 1938–1941* (Boston, 1965).

Bonnefous, Edouard, "Les Responsabilités Politiques et Militaires de la Défaite de 1940," *Revue Politique et Parlementaire,* May 1967, pp. 27–33.

Braddick, Henderson B., *Germany, Czechoslovakia, and the "Grand Alliance" in the May Crisis, 1938* (Denver, 1969).

Burns, James Macgregor, *Roosevelt: The Lion and the Fox* (New York, 1956).

Cairns, John C., "The Fall of France, 1940: Thoughts on a National Defeat," *Canadian Historical Association,* 1957, pp. 55–70.

——, "Great Britain and the Fall of France," *Journal of Modern History,* XXVII, December 1955, pp. 365–409.

Challener, Richard D., *The French Theory of the Nation in Arms, 1866–1939* (New York, 1955).

Chapman, Guy, *Why France Fell: The Defeat of the French Army in 1940* (New York, 1969).

Chilston, Viscount, "The Rearmament of Great Britain, France and Germany Down to the Munich Agreement," vol. III, *Survey of International Affairs, 1938,* ed. V. M. Toynbee (London, 1953).

Compton, James V., *The Swastika and the Eagle: Hitler, the United States and the Origins of World War II* (Boston, 1967).

Cort, Margaret L., *Mr. Baruch* (Boston, 1957).

Danee, R., "La Production Aéronautique Militaire Française Jusqu'en Juin 1940," *Revue d'Histoire de la Deuxième Guerre Mondiale,* No. 73, January 1969, pp. 75–110.

Davis, Forrest, and Ernest K. Lindley, *How War Came* (New York, 1942).

Divine, Robert A., *Illusion of Neutrality* (Chicago, 1962).

——, *The Reluctant Belligerent: American Entry into World War II* (New York, 1965).

——, *Roosevelt and World War II* (Baltimore, 1969).

Drummond, Donald, *The Passing of American Neutrality* (Ann Arbor, 1955).

Duroselle, J. B., *De Wilson á Roosevelt. Politique extérieure des États-Unis, 1913–1945* (Paris, 1960).

Eubank, Keith, *Munich* (Norman, Oklahoma, 1963).

Feiling, Keith G., *The Life of Neville Chamberlain* (London, 1946).

Friedlander, Saul, *Prelude to Downfall, Hitler and the United States, 1939–1941,* trans. from French by A. B. and Alexander Werth (London, 1967).

Frye, William, *Marshall, Citizen Soldier* (New York, 1947).

Furnia, Arthur H., *The Diplomacy of Appeasement: Anglo-French Relations and the Prelude to World War II, 1931–1938* (Washington, 1960).

Gardner, Lloyd C., *Economic Aspects of New Deal Diplomacy* (Madison, Wisc., 1964).

Gilbert, Martin, *The Roots of Appeasement* (London, 1966).

Gilbert, Martin, and Richard Gott, *The Appeasers* (Boston, 1963).

Goaster, Lt. Col., "L'Action des Forces Aériennes," *Revue d'Histoire Deuxième de la Guerre Mondiale,* June 1953, pp. 135–49.

Goodhart, Philip, *Fifty Ships That Saved the World* (London, 1965).

Goutard, Adolphe, *1940: La Guerre des Occasions Perdue* (Paris, 1956).

Haight, John McVickar, Jr., "France, the United States and the Munich Crisis," *Journal of Modern History,* XXXII, December, 1960, pp. 340–58.

——, "France's First War Mission to the United States," *Airpower Historian,* XI, January 1964, pp. 11–15.

——, "Franklin D. Roosevelt and a Naval Quarantine of Japan," *Pacific Historical Review,* forthcoming.

——, "Jean Monnet and the American Arsenal After the Beginning of the War," *French Society and Culture Since the Old Regime. The Eleutherian Mills Colloquium, 1964, of the Society for French Historical Studies and the Societé d'Histoire Moderne,* eds. E. M. Acomb and M. L. Brown, Jr. (New York, 1966), pp. 269–83.

——, "Les Négotiations Françaises pour la Fourniture d'Avions Américains, lère Partie, Avant Munich," *Forces Aériennes Françaises,* No. 198, December 1963, pp. 807–39.

——, "Les Négotiations Relatives aux Achats d'Avions Américains par la France Pendant le Période qui Précéde immediatement La Guerre," *Revue d'Histoire de la Duxième Guerre Mondiale,* No. 58, April, 1965, pp. 1–34.

——, "Reaction of the Paris Press to the Neutrality Policy of the United States, 1935–1939" (University Microfilms, 1953).

Hayez, Lt. Col., "Situation de l'Armée de l'Air en Avions Modernes aux Premiers Jours de la Guerre, 1939–1945," *Forces Aériennes Françaises,* December 1962, pp. 781–95.

Hebrard, J., *Vingt-cinq Années d'Aviation Militaire, 1920–1945,* vol. I, *La Genese du Drame Aérien de 1940* (Paris, 1946).

Hinton, Harold B., *Air Victory: The Men and the Machines* (New York, 1948).

Horne, Alistair, *To Lose a Battle: France, 1940* (Boston, 1969).

Janeway, Eliot, *The Struggle for Survival, A Chronicle of Economic Mobilization in World War II* (New Haven, 1951).

Jonas, Manfred, *Isolationism in America, 1935–1941* (Ithaca, N.Y., 1966).

Kaufmann, W. W., "Two American Ambassadors, Bullitt and Kennedy," *The Diplomats, 1919–1939* (Princeton, 1953), eds. G. A. Craig and Felix Gilbert.

Langer, William L., and S. Everett Gleason, *The Challenge to Isolation, 1937–1940* (New York, 1952).

de Lesquen, Col., "L'Armée de l'Air Française en 1940," *Revue de Defense National,* January 1952, pp. 74–84.

Loewenheim, Francis L., "An Illusion that Shaped History: New Light on the History and Historiography of American Peace Efforts Before Munich," *Some Pathways in Twentieth Century History, Essays in Honor of Richard Charles McGrane,* ed. D. R. Beaver (Detroit, 1969), pp. 177–221.

——, ed., *Peace or Appeasement? Hitler, Chamberlain, and the Munich Crisis* (Boston, 1965).

Lyet, Pierre, *La Bataille de France* (Paris, 1947).

Micaud, Charles A., *The French Right and Nazi Germany* (Durham, N.C., 1943).

Michel, Henri, *La Seconde Guerre Mondiale,* Vol. I, *Les Succés de l'Axe (1939–1943)* (Paris, 1968).

Noguéres, Henri, *Munich: ou, la Drôle de Paix* (London, 1965).

Paquier, Lt. Col. Pierre, *L'Aviation de Bombardment Française en 1939–1940: L'Aviation Française au Combat* (Paris, 1948).

——, *Les Forces Aériennes Françaises de 1939–1945* (Paris, 1949).

——, Pierre Lyet, Charles Cosse-Brissac, "Combien D'Avions Allemands Contre D'Avions Française le 10 Mai 1940," *Revue de Defense Nationale,* June 1948, pp. 741–59.

Pogue, Forrest C., *George C. Marshall,* vol. I, *Education of a General, 1880–1939* (New York, 1963); vol. II, *Ordeal and Hope, 1939–1942* (New York, 1966).

Ratliff, Ann, "Les Relations Diplomatiques Entre la France et les États-Unis (du Septembre 1938 au 16 Juin 1940)," *Revue de Historie de la Deuxième Guerre Mondiale,* vol. 75, Julliet 1939, pp. 1–41.

Rauch, Basil, *Roosevelt, from Munich to Pearl Harbor: A Study in the Creation of a Foreign Policy* (New York, 1950).

Rosenman, Samuel I., *Working with Roosevelt* (New York, 1952).

Rogé Lt. Col., "Les Aviations Allemands, Française et Anglaise du 10 Mai au 25 Juin 1940," *Revue Defense National,* 1951, pp. 162–76.

Salesse, Lt. Col., *L'Aviation de Chasse Française en 1939–1940: L'Aviation Française au Combat* (Paris, 1955).

Seive, Fleury Marius, *L'Aviation d'Assaut dans la Bataille en 1940: L'Aviation Française au Combat* (Paris, 1948).

Sherwood, Robert E., *Roosevelt and Hopkins, an Intimate History* (New York, 1948).

Tissier, Lt. Col. Pierre, *The Riom Trial* (London, 1942).

Weinberg, Gerald L., "The May Crisis, 1938," *Journal of Modern History,* XXIX, September 1957, pp. 213–25.

Werth, Alexander, *France and Munich, Before and After the Surrender* (New York, 1969).

——, *The Twilight of France, 1933–1940,* ed. D. W. Brogan (New York, 1966).

Wheeler-Bennett, John W., *Munich, Prologue to Tragedy* (New York, 1948).

Williams, John, *The Ides of May: The Defeat of France, May–June 1940* (New York, 1968).

Wood, Derek, and Derek Dempster, *The Narrow Margin* (New York, 1961).

Wright, Gordon, "Ambassador Bullitt and the Fall of France," *World Politics,* vol. X, No. 1, October 1957.

——, *France in Modern Times* (Chicago, 1960).

——, *Ordeal of Total War 1939–1945* (New York, 1968).

Zay, Jean, *Carnets secrets de Jean Zay (de Munich á la Guerre)* (Paris, 1942).

Index